Fringe Benefits and
Their Federal Tax Treatment

Number 600

COLUMBIA STUDIES IN THE SOCIAL SCIENCES

EDITED BY THE FACULTY OF POLITICAL SCIENCE

OF COLUMBIA UNIVERSITY

Fringe Benefits and

Their Federal Tax

Treatment

Hugh Holleman Macaulay, Jr.

COLUMBIA UNIVERSITY PRESS

New York   1959

The Columbia Studies in the Social Sciences (formerly the Studies in History, Economics, and Public Law) is a series edited by the Faculty of Political Science of Columbia University and published by Columbia University Press for the purpose of making available scholarly studies produced within the Faculty.

TO MY WIFE, MARY FRANCES

Preface

THE federal income tax is the principal single source of revenue for the federal government and therefore its continued functioning is of the greatest importance. As a consequence, sources of weakness in its operation have attracted considerable attention and discussion, principally under the heading of "erosion of the tax base." Several chips off the tax base, such as capital gains, depletion allowances, and tax-free interest on municipal bonds, have long histories and have been widely discussed. Others, like medical expense deductions, split income computation of tax liability, and retirement income credits, have arrived more recently but have been sufficiently important to lead to study. Fringe benefits, however, have been a recent arrival, have been of such a complex nature as to defy clear, concise definition, and have often been pictured as going to persons in the lowest tax brackets; for these reasons consideration of these benefits has been piecemeal, with little realization of their size, importance, and tax treatment. This study is a modest attempt to focus attention on this feature of our economic life and to offer suggestions for tax treatment.

Many persons have contributed greatly towards making this study a more enjoyable project and have improved its quality. By giving freely of their time in listening to the ideas set down here and offering suggestions for improving them, my colleagues at Columbia University and Clemson College have led to the elimination of several errors. My greatest debt in this respect, however, is to Professor Carl S. Shoup, who has been very patient and helpful in pointing out errors and weaknesses.

Since not all the advice of these friends was accepted, responsibility for errors lies where it properly should—with the writer.

Throughout the period of research and writing my wife has been a constant source of encouragement while at the same time running our family and typing and correcting the manuscript.   No greater sacrifice could have been asked; no greater help could have been received.

HUGH HOLLEMAN MACAULAY, JR.

Clemson College
Clemson, South Carolina

Contents

Preface   vii

PART ONE. THE OVER-ALL PROBLEM

I. HISTORICAL GROWTH AND QUANTITATIVE IMPORTANCE
OF FRINGE BENEFITS   3
    A. Definition of Fringe Benefits   3
    B. Past Growth in Both Form and Size   8
    C. Reasons for Birth and Growth of Fringe Benefits   11
    D. Prospects for Future Growth   15
II. PROBLEMS CREATED IN PUBLIC FINANCE   19
    A. Problems in Defining Taxable Income   19
    B. Historical Development of the Treatment of
        Fringe Benefits under the Federal Income Tax   23
    C. Present Treatment of Fringe Benefits under the
        Federal Income Tax   25
    D. Problems Arising from Taxation of Fringe
        Benefits   34
    E. Problems Arising from Tax Preference
        Accorded Fringe Benefits   39
III. ECONOMIC EFFECTS OF PRESENT TAX TREATMENT   54
    A. Goal of a Lack of Effect   54
    B. Effects on Allocation of Resources   54
    C. Effects on the Mobility of Labor   73
    D. Effects on Cyclical Stability   78

PART TWO. TAX TREATMENT OF SPECIFIC BENEFITS

IV. THE TREATMENT OF RETIREMENT BENEFITS   89
    A. Pension Plans   90
    B. Profit-sharing Plans   117
V. LIFE INSURANCE AND DEATH BENEFITS   125
    A. Life Insurance   125
    B. Social Security   131
    C. Widow's Benefits   138
    D. Miscellaneous Death and Retirement Benefits   143
VI. UNEMPLOYMENT AND HEALTH INSURANCE   146
    A. Unemployment Insurance   146
    B. Hospitalization and Surgical Insurance   151
VII. FRINGE BENEFITS IN KIND   158
    A. Introduction   158
    B. Meals   159
    C. Housing   167
    D. Medical Care for Employees   171
    E. Other Fringe Benefits in Kind   173
VIII. Summary and Conclusions   179

APPENDIX

I. Enumeration of Wage Supplements   185
II. Fringe Benefits in a Survey by the Associated
    Industries of Cleveland   187
III. Fringe Benefits by Type of Payment, 1953 and 1957   189
IV. Total Qualified Pension, Profit-sharing, and Stock
    Bonus Plans in Operation, 1930–1958   191
V. General Requirements for Qualification of a Pension
    or Profit-sharing Plan   192

Notes   193
Bibliography   233
Index   243

Part One

The Over-all Problem

• I •

Historical Growth and Quantitative Importance of Fringe Benefits

THE federal income tax was designed to be a tax on the income of the spending unit: the individual or the family. Professor Haig in 1921 expressed his approval of the concept of income to be taxed, as contained in the Revenue Act of 1918, because of its breadth of coverage,[1] and a broad concept of gross income continues to exist in the Internal Revenue Code.[2] Economists have attempted to purify the concept and have observed that many forms of income currently excluded should be included in the tax base to give a more consistent treatment. Items such as voluntary leisure,[3] as distinct from that imposed by involuntary partial or total unemployment, and imputed income from consumer durables[4] have been mentioned as theoretically proper components of income, but the possibility that both lawmakers and taxpayers would have difficulty in conceiving of these items as taxable income, consequently giving rise to administrative difficulties, has so far kept them from being seriously proposed for inclusion in the code definition of income. Other items, however, like imputed income to homeowners, tax-free interest on municipal bonds, and the full amount of capital gains, seem to most economists familiar with income taxation to be logical components of taxable income, conceptually understandable by the public, and administratively feasible, and so their inclusion in income has been actively urged.[5] But inertia and the development of institutions based on their exemption from tax have prevented this correction. As a result, sources of revenue seem to have been lost while sources of inequity seem to have been gained.

The latest candidate for admission to this select fraternity is the newborn but rapidly growing group of fringe benefits. If past experience is any guide as to future growth and treatment, an attempt should be made to see if these benefits can be detected, evaluated, and integrated into the present income tax system before, unnoticed, they reach maturity with the protection similar to that accorded infant industries long after their infancy exists only in memory.

What, then, are fringe benefits? They are of recent origin and so interest has only lately begun to focus on them. Perhaps because of their newness many who write about them do not define them; [6] practically all others arrive at differing definitions. These definitions may be both very broad and very narrow; they are sometimes very broad in including income that is usually recognized as wages and regularly taxable, such as overtime payments, and they are at other times very narrow in excluding payments that seem designed to benefit the employee and might properly be taxable, such as board and lodging, health services, and perquisites of office. An examination of the term seems, then, to be in order.

For purposes of the present study a fringe benefit may be defined as a payment for something which furnishes utility to the employee, paid by the employer to or on behalf of the employee, over and above straight-time and overtime wages or regular piece rate wages. Some of the other, different definitions might be repeated and briefly discussed. Landman, for example, says, "Fringe benefits are goods and services in addition to wage payments as conditions of employment, as incentives for greater effort, as conveniences for the employer, and/ or as promoters of employee health, good will and efficiency." [7] Each of the qualifying phrases in this definition has at one time or another been cited as a reason for granting a fringe benefit and as a reason for not taxing it. The National Industrial Conference Board points out that definitions range between two extremes. "Any expenditure on labor other than straight-time wages"[8] is the broadest definition, which could include items such as water coolers, which are usually considered as "conditions of work," overtime pay, and even the wages of the personnel department. The narrower definition classifies as a fringe benefit "any company expenditure, above straight-time pay, that has cash value to the individual employee."[9] The "cash value" aspect of this definition refers to the ability of the employee to convert the benefit into cash and would eliminate employee meals, recreation, most life insurance, and most pension plans.

The National Industrial Conference Board agrees that definition is difficult but that fringe benefits have these characteristics:

1. They all cost the employer money. . . .
2. They all either add to the employee's pay or are of some benefit or service to him. . . .
3. They are available to all or most of the employees.
4. Their cost goes up or down as the size of the work force changes.[10]

Yet even these characteristics are subject to dispute; recent discussions about executives' fringe benefits would seem to rule out characteristics 3 and 4 above.

Perhaps as a result of the disagreement over definition, fringe benefits are more often listed than defined. Thus writers will list "the following fringe benefits," but the precise confines of the term are abandoned to individual judgment, imagination, or estimation. There are some extensive listings, such as the one by Professor C. W. Sargent, of the Amos Tuck School, who has itemized nearly sixty individual wage supplements.[11] (See Appendix I.) The Associated Industries of Cleveland has also presented a list of fringe benefits. It listed twenty fringe benefits in its 1953 survey and asked the companies surveyed to list any other fringe benefits they granted; as a result, thirty-eight additional benefits were listed.[12] (See Appendix II.)

The National Industrial Conference Board also puts forth a

list of thirty-five candidates for the name "fringe benefits" and then presents the views of nine companies on each candidate. This list and the opinions reveal the following:

1. All nine companies agreed that the following were fringe benefits: paid holidays, vacations, summer military leave and jury duty, pensions, group life insurance, hospitalization, group health and accident insurance, medical-surgical insurance, federal old-age benefits (employer's contribution), unemployment insurance, workmen's compensation, and state disability insurance.

2. All of the companies that had the following benefits would include them as fringe benefits: paid sick leave, paid excused absence as for death in the family, profit sharing, paid wash-up time, and paid lunch periods.

3. Most of the companies would include: premium pay for Saturday, Sunday, sixth or seventh day or holiday work, paid rest periods, severance pay, losses on cafeteria, recreation plans, and Christmas bonus.

4. The companies were about evenly split over inclusion of the following: overtime pay (premium only), shift differentials, call-in pay, length-of-service bonus, and education subsidies.

5. Most of the companies would exclude: pay for grievance and negotiation time, credit union, length-of-service gifts, medical services, safety clothing, and suggestion awards.[13]

These different groups indicate that fringe benefits mean different things to different people. And, too, time works to alter ideas. For example, in 1950 the Quaker Oats Company, one of the nine companies surveyed, reclassified some of its fringe benefits, removing from its fringe benefit classification health and accident insurance because the "average" employee did not use it, and paid military time off because it affected so few employees. It also deleted paid rest periods, because this would be "stretching" the point, and medical service because it was required for on-the-job accidents and it helped prevent absenteeism.[14]

Items which were not considered as fringe benefits might have been classified either as wages, which would be taxable, or as conditions of employment, which would not be taxable. For example, in group three above, the companies that felt that premium pay for Saturday and Sunday work was not a fringe benefit probably considered it as a part of regular wages, since they felt that the "employee must be paid a premium in return for giving up his normal days off." [15] But those companies excluding losses on cafeterias and expenses for recreation plans doubtless leaned more toward considering these as conditions of employment rather than taxable wages. These companies noted that not all employees used the facilities and that the recreation plans had no cash value to the employees.[16]

Rewards for labor seem, therefore, to fall into three categories: wages, fringe benefits, and conditions of work, and these three shade one into the other; indeed, they overlap as we have just observed. The term "conditions of work" probably at first referred to utilities which flow naturally from a particular type of employment; examples might be fresh air and sunshine for farmers, regular hours for shopkeepers, longer vacations for schoolteachers, etc. As employers began to pay to provide goods and services which would make the employee's time spent at work more pleasant, these, too, were included in the term. And as these expenditures have broadened in scope to where they make more pleasant the employee's time spent away from work and in some cases replace his private expenditures, they, also, have been included by some in the term conditions of work. Thus, conditions of work have also become important in compensating employees.

This threefold classification of employer expenditures is important in (1) determining whether or not employers must bargain over the particular expenditure under terms set forth in the National Labor Relations Act, and (2) determining what is the tax status of the expenditure. In the first of these cases employers are required to bargain with representatives of workers "in respect to rates of pay, wages, hours of employment or other conditions of employment." [17] The distinction between wages and conditions of employment is not so important in this case, since both may be subjects of bargaining.

But whether a particular expenditure is to be classified as one of these or neither is important, for, if it is neither, bargaining is not required.

When, however, the question of taxation arises, the distinction between conditions of employment and wages takes on even greater significance. Discussion of this distinction, revolves around attributes affecting taxability and will be considered in Chapter II, where the tax treatment of fringe benefits is discussed. Before turning to this, the development, size, and future of fringe benefits will be examined to get a clearer picture of the magnitude of the problem involved.

B. PAST GROWTH IN BOTH FORM AND SIZE

Before the 1930s fringe benefits were of minor consequence and "were confined largely to executives, supervisors and white-collar workers." [18]   In view of the fact that executives were, because of their tax rates, in a position to take advantage of the tax favor granted stock-bonus, profit-sharing, and pension plans, it would be logical that they should be the principal beneficiaries of these fringe benefits. Since high personal exemption allowances kept most workers off the tax rolls, fringe benefits held no tax favor for them. Paid vacations probably account for the inclusion of white-collar workers in this group.

The National Income Division of the Department of Commerce estimates that "supplements to wages and salaries" in 1929 were $662 million, while "wages and salaries" were estimated at $50,423 million.[19]   Of the $662 million in wage supplements, about five sixths represented payments into retirement, pension, and welfare funds and payments as compensation for injuries, and so were not taxable. These untaxed wage supplements were about 1.1 percent of total wages and salaries.

The 1930s witnessed the inauguration of social legislation and produced a fifteenfold increase in tax-preferred employer contributions for social insurance from 1929 to 1939.[20]   Thus, by 1939 wage supplements listed in national income had increased over threefold to $2,167 million, while wages and salaries had actually declined from their 1929 level to $46 billion.[21]   Only about $120 million of these wage supplements were treated as regular taxable income, so that the listed tax-preferred wage supplements were about 4.4 percent of wages and salaries.

The decade of the 1940s saw another shift in fringe benefits. With social insurance legislation already in force and wage controls in effect during the first half of the decade, the emphasis shifted to other labor income such as pensions, health and accident insurance, group life insurance, and paid vacations and holidays.   Consequently, by 1949 wage supplements had again tripled but the components had increased at different rates.   "Employer contributions for social insurance" increased from $1.5 billion to $3.5 billion, while "other labor income," primarily pension and welfare contributions, increased from $627 million to $3.0 billion.   Total wage supplements of $6.5 billion contained only $.3 billion of fully taxable income, the balance receiving tax-preferred treatment. This $6.2 billion was about 4.6 percent of wages and salaries for 1949.[22]

This percentage is smaller than that of the Chamber of Commerce estimate made in 1949, which placed fringe benefits at 15.4 percent of payroll costs.   Of this Chamber of Commerce figure, about 6.6 percent of payroll costs represented pay for time not worked, which is not included among the national income wage supplements.[23]   The remaining 8.8 percent of payroll costs, composed largely of tax-preferred fringe benefits, differs from the 4.6 percent national income figure for at least two reasons.   The National Income Division figures covered all employees drawing wages or salaries, which would include executives of corporations.   It should be expected that a smaller percentage of the salaries of these executives would go to old-age and survivors insurance, unemployment insurance, and health insurance.   Also, they could be expected to receive tax-preferred fringe benefits in the form of expense accounts and perquisites of office, which would not be reflected in the National Income Division figures.   The second cause of discrepancy stems from the Chamber of Commerce's using a somewhat broader list of fringe benefits. Thus, they include discounts on goods and services, free meals, tuition refunds, paid sick leave, death benefits, etc., that the national income figures do not include. National income figures, although not strictly in accord with the usual figures representing fringe benefits, nevertheless are valuable in showing the historical growth of fringe benefits both in quantity and in form.

The Inland Steel decision by the courts in 1948 added pensions to the list of items about which management had to bargain [24] and so made possible an expansion of this benefit. National income figures show that employer contributions to private pension and welfare funds more than doubled between 1949 and 1952, reaching $4.2 billion in 1952,[25] and rose to $5.7 billion in 1956.[26] Along with this, the growth in other fringe benefits has continued.

The Chamber of Commerce reports that 102 companies submitted reports in each of its first six biennial surveys on fringe benefits. These companies indicate that from 1947 to 1957 fringe benefits have risen steadily from 15.0 percent to 23.7 percent of the payroll so that, while payrolls have increased, fringe benefits have increased even more. Just under half of these benefits are in the form of pay for time not worked or, in other words, a granting of more leisure (nontaxable) with the same pay. The other half is composed of goods and services that are almost without exception not subject to current income taxation.[27]

In the 1950s national income figures continued to show growth in fringe benefits. In 1949 total wage supplements were 4.85 percent of wages and salaries and it is estimated that most of this amount, 4.6 percent of wages and salaries, was not subject to current income taxation. By 1956 wage supplements were 6.2 percent of wages and salaries and again most of this, 5.9 percent of wages and salaries, was estimated to have escaped current income taxation. While an advance from 4.6 percent to 5.9 percent is considerable, it should be noted that these are average figures. If calculation is made at the margin, as economists are wont to emphasize, the figures show that wage increases from 1949 to 1956 were matched by increases in currently untaxed wage supplements equal to 7.8 percent of the wage and salary increases.[28]

Other indications of fringe benefit growth may be gathered from the following surveys. The Bureau of Labor Statistics, in studying health, insurance, and pension plans negotiated by unions under collective bargaining, found that the number of union workers covered by one or more of the plans increased from .5 million in 1945 to 7.7 million in 1950 and to 11.3 million in 1954. At the same time the proportion of employees covered by plans under which only the employer contributed rose from 55 percent to 62 percent for health and insurance plans and from 74 percent to 85 percent for pension plans.[29] Fisher and Chapman found that fringe benefits over the five-year period 1948-1952 increased 61.6 percent per payroll hour. However, while benefits which are largely taxable (premiums for time worked) and admittedly nontaxable (increased leisure with no reduction in pay) increased only 50 percent during this period, those benefits which are largely tax-preferred increased just under 80 percent.[30] In the field of hospitalization and surgical insurance there has been a remarkable increase in coverage. In the decade from 1941 to 1951 group hospitalization insurance brought an additional 56 million people under its wing, while group surgical insurance increased its coverage by about 47 million.[31] Blue Cross plans alone served 345,000 companies in 1955 by providing hospitalization insurance to 46 million employees of these companies.[32] The growth of other individual fringe benefits is described below as they are separately discussed.

C. REASONS FOR BIRTH AND GROWTH OF FRINGE BENEFITS

Some scattered measures of the size and growth of fringe benefits have been noted, but what reasons can be offered for their development? Several factors, such as a rising social consciousness, the advent of wage controls, competition among employers for workers, and increased tax rates seem primarily responsible.

Aroused social responsibility was one cause of legislative action in the 1930s establishing the social security system, which required the employer and employee to set aside certain funds for the employees' security against financial difficulties resulting from unemployment, death, and old age. The idea that minimum protection in old age and unemployment is the responsibility of a larger group than the individual and his family has been adopted by other groups beside the legislators. Unions, too, voiced this idea. The United Automobile, Aircraft and Agricultural Implement Workers (UAW-CIO) has stated that the cost of social security cannot be met by a slice taken from wages. Rather, "industry's social responsibility requires that it assume financial responsibility for Workers Security Programs established through collective bargaining." [33] Management has voiced related feelings in commenting on in-plant medical care for employees by saying that it was "the right thing to do" to maintain and improve the health of the employees in the most economical way.[34] The Steel Industry Board, composed of "three public members" [35] selected to investigate the 1949 dispute in the steel industry, recommended that the steel industry provide social insurance and pensions because of "the social obligation which the Board finds rests upon industry to provide insurance against the economic hazards of modern industrial life, including retirement allowances, in an adequate amount . . . ." [36] Because of such feelings, fringe benefits which offer security against these events have usually been considered as prima facie desirable; consequences other than increased individual security have received less attention.

, Wage controls during the Second World War also increased the use of certain fringe benefits. While cash wages were subject to rather strict regulation, the Treasury held that increases in compensation in the form of insurance and pension benefits, to the extent that they were reasonable in amount, would not be considered as salary increases subject to wage controls.[37] In addition the War Labor Board allowed additional fringe benefits which fitted the Board's conception of reasonableness.[38]

Thus, in the years of wage controls, 1942-1945, total wages and salaries rose by 50 percent, but employer contributions to private pension and welfare funds rose by slightly less than 200 percent.[39]

The wage stabilization program of the Korean period, after recognizing that wage rates *plus* fringe benefits should be regulated, proceeded to give preferential treatment to fringe benefits. Thus, increases in fringe benefits made before January 25, 1951, did not count toward the permissible 10 percent increase over January, 1950, wages; increases in certain fringe benefits classified as "minor fringe benefits" were automatically allowed; increases in all fringe benefits were allowed if it was shown that such increases would bring the firm up to the level prevailing in the area or industry.[40] The results can be seen in the fact that while wages rose during this period, fringe benefits rose to a larger percentage of the increased wages. While the freezing of wages during the two wars brought a burgeoning of benefits, the end of the freeze did not witness the passing of these hardy perennials. Rather they have remained and have drawn sustenance from other sources.

One of these other sources is the continued competition among employers for workers. Although cash wages are the traditional weapon used in this battle, fringe benefits have become more important as a supplementary artillery piece. It is argued that these benefits not only attract new workers to the firm but that they also help the firm to hold on to its workers and to improve the productivity of these workers. As a result, practically all firms have been forced to adopt the fringe benefits that were originally offered by only a few competitors. The widespread emphasis given fringe benefits in hiring practices may be seen in the advertisements for engineers carried in the Sunday New York *Times* and in the job literature given college students by campus representatives. The situation has shifted from the case where the firm offering fringe benefits had a great attraction for new workers to the case where the firm not offering fringe benefits fails to attract workers. Although some few critics have voiced doubt over the efficacy of fringe benefits in attracting and holding workers,[41] management has continued to use them for this purpose. When all firms, or at least competing firms, offer the same benefits, their power of attracting new workers supposedly ceases; however, their power of holding workers still lives, as will be seen later.[42]

Perhaps the most important single cause of the growth of fringe benefits has been their tax treatment. This influence of taxes has brought about pressure from two directions: (1) certain of these fringe benefits are tax-preferred and so are desired by employees, especially employees in the higher income brackets, and (2) high corporate tax rates and excess profits tax rates have lowered the resistance of business to additional fringe benefits. This latter consideration would have been just as valid in the granting of higher wages, but, generally speaking, excess profits taxes have been accompanied by wage controls; thus, fringe benefits emerged dominant. The tax preference granted to certain benefits, although a cause of their growth, is seldom mentioned in arguments for these benefits, except in the case of executives. A single sentence in a UAW-CIO handbook, for example, deals with this feature by pointing out that "expenditures made by employers, through the Workers Security Trust Fund, will buy 20 percent *more* benefits than the same amount will buy when paid to the workers as wages and then deducted from take home pay." [43] In actuality, if the worker is in the 20 percent marginal tax bracket, the expenditure by the employer will buy *25 percent more* than the cash wage would buy. The wartime and postwar increases in personal income tax rates, which initiated millions of Americans into the fraternity of income tax payers, would seem to argue that this cause of growth has not declined in importance.

To these major causes of fringe benefit growth might be added a list of lesser influences. For example, the sales efforts of banks, trust companies, and insurance agents, following the issuance of Treasury Decision 5186 removing insurance and pension contributions from wage controls, have been cited by

Dearing.[44] Court interpretations of the Taft-Hartley Act have broadened the area of collective bargaining to include, under certain conditions, individual fringe benefits like pensions,[45] group insurance,[46] stock bonuses,[47] houses,[48] and meals [49] furnished by the employers. In periods of economic recession, such as 1949 and 1954, unions have concentrated on securing increased fringe benefits rather than cash wage increases.[50]

The fact that all the above factors except wage controls and excess profits taxes are either presently or potentially operative presages the continued growth of fringe benefits.

D. PROSPECTS FOR FUTURE GROWTH

The future total amount of fringe benefits will depend on the introduction of new fringe benefits, changes in the quality or form of existing fringe benefits, and changes in the number of workers and dependents covered by fringe benefits. A consideration peculiar to the tax aspect is the change in the percentage of cost of these fringe benefits borne by the employer; generally contributions by employers are not taxed while contributions from employee wages are considered as coming from taxable income. There are indications that all these components are increasing fringe benefit expenditures.

The list of fringe benefits seems ever to grow so that any list of "new" fringe benefits compiled at any one time would soon be out of date. However, among those making their debut in the 1950s and achieving limited adoption have been Salk vaccine shots, influenza shots, legal advice and representation, company-financed vacation trips for all employees, a full year's vacation with pay for 10 years' service, medical diagnostic service, a car for every employee (including floorsweepers), eyeglasses, false teeth, meals for retired employees, and speed reading courses.[51]

To this list of benefits that have been introduced but have not grown significantly might be added a few that have experienced a large growth in percentage terms but still are small in total quantity. The guaranteed annual wage became known as supplemental unemployment benefits and spread from a few

firms to a few industries.   Still, coverage is presumably confined to very few workers.   Another such benefit is major medical insurance, which is being offered in addition to hospitalization and surgical insurance.   A 1953 American Management
Association survey of companies known to have liberal executive benefit programs showed that over 10 percent of those
companies had such insurance for their executives.[52]   Another
report shows that coverage by major medical insurance has increased almost fiftyfold between 1951 and 1955 with about 5¼
million people covered in 1955—over 90 percent of these
covered by group major medical insurance.   During 1955 alone,
coverage increased 152 percent in group plans.   Comparison of
the approximately 4¾ million people covered by group major
medical insurance with the approximately 90 million people
covered by group hospitalization insurance indicates its growth
possibilities.[53]

A second source of fringe benefit growth deals with the increase in the quality and cost of existing fringe benefits.   Major
medical insurance might be considered an example of improvement in the quality of health insurance rather than a new
fringe benefit as it has been classified in the preceding paragraph.   Less controversial examples, however, might include
the shift toward the "vesting" of pension rights and the liberali-
zation of benefits under old-age and survivors insurance.   Vesting gives the worker a stronger claim on money contributed to
the pension plan and therefore increases the cost of the plan.
The pension plans of 1949 and 1950 largely neglected the vesting provisions in order to secure benefits for workers nearing
retirement, but pension plans adopted and renegotiated since
then have been subject to pressures for increased vesting, as is
evidenced by the vesting provisions of the United Automobile
Workers contract with Ford and General Motors in 1955.[54]   As
for old-age and survivors insurance, in the three years 1956
through 1958, changes in the laws have included the addition
of disability insurance, the early retirement of women, and increased monetary payments at retirement.   Improvement in
the quality of fringe benefits given is also evident in health in-

surance, unemployment insurance, meals, retirement plans, recreation facilities, and many others.

Besides the introduction of new benefits and the improvement in quality of existing benefits, there may also be a wider use of benefits already enjoying rather widespread acceptance. An indication is Dearing's estimate that while there were about 11.2 million workers covered by industrial pensions in 1951, there should be about 22 million covered by 1960.[55] Another example is the Keogh Bill, the "Individual Retirement Act of 1955," a proposed bill that could allow over 43 million self-employed and non-covered employees to pay themselves a tax-preferred fringe benefit like that received by workers under existing pension plans.[56] This bill did not pass, but similar bills have been introduced in succeeding sessions of Congress. The bill introduced in 1957 was passed by the House in 1958 but was not passed by the Senate. In subsequent discussion reference will be made to the 1955 bill, since extensive hearings were held on it, but the discussion applies equally to subsequent similar bills.

While fringe benefits are being extended to more workers, a parallel movement is taking place with respect to their dependents. This is particularly true with respect to insurance benefits, and it is also worthy of note in the case of other fringe benefits. With regard to insurance, coverage under group life insurance has been extended to dependents of employees and in 1953 included in its coverage over 700,000 employee dependents; this was a sixfold increase from 1948. Group medical insurance for dependents may be broken down into hospital, surgical, and medical insurance. In 1953 in these fields of insurance, private insurance companies insured, respectively, 19 million, 19 million, and 7 million dependents; these figures represented increases since 1945 of 460 percent, 1,100 percent, and 7,000 percent respectively.[57] In the case of benefits other than insurance the employee's family is also being considered. Recreation facilities and medical care are being made available to workers' families under collective bargaining contracts,[58] while participation in country club memberships, trips abroad, and trips to combination resort-health clinics is being broadened to include wives and families.[59]

Together, new benefits, higher quality, and increased coverage could lead to a sizable increase in fringe benefits. Dearing estimates that contributions to pension funds will rise from the $2.4 billion annually of 1951 to $6.6 billion annually in 1960.[60] Fisher and Chapman estimate that fringe benefits should continue to grow at 12 percent a year, the rate of growth, according to their findings, for the five years ending in 1953. They add, "The imposition of another $20 billion to $25 billion on the American industrial community in order to produce a better way of life for the millions of workers involved is not in itself a startling prospective burden." [61] While such benefits may not be a burden, the form and taxability of such benefits are definitely of interest.

Walter Reuther has indicated that there should be little straying from the fringe benefit path. Shortly after the United Automobile Workers signed its 1955 contract with Ford and General Motors, Mr. Reuther, in speaking to local union leaders, pointed out that the union had scored big improvements in pension plans over the past six years since the principle had been established. Then he said, "You'll see what we can do in a like six year period in raising the benefits now that we have the guaranteed annual wage." [62]

Past growth of fringe benefits has been noted; future growth has been predicted. The ease with which a pattern of tax treatment which has little or no economic support can become firmly established can be noted from the consistent growth of depletion allowances. Tax preference for fringe benefits should enlist even more support since fringe benefits directly affect more people and since many of these benefits are justified by supporters on grounds of social responsibility. Therefore, the effects of such tax preference are worthy of examination, and the sooner attention is focused on these effects, the better is the chance that necessary correction might be made.

· II ·

Problems Created in
Public Finance

A. PROBLEMS IN DEFINING TAXABLE INCOME

SOME fringe benefits have been called tax preferred, but this implies some concept of income which would include them as taxable income. To arrive at a proper concept, consideration should be given to the economic, legislative, and judicial definitions of income.

In the United States economists have centered their interest on the "net cash yield" or "spendings" concept of income as advocated by Irving Fisher [1] and on the "accretion" concept of income as advocated by R. M. Haig [2] and Henry Simons.[3] Under Fisher's definition fringe benefits would be taxable at the time they were consumed. Thus, fringe benefits received and consumed within the taxable year would constitute taxable income, although Fisher felt these would seldom be important.[4] Those fringe benefits received in one year but not consumed until later years, e.g., pension plans, would not be taxable until the later years of consumption, and in the event that the employee's heirs held the benefit payment as savings, as is possible in the case of a widow's benefit, the fringe benefit might never be taxed.

Haig observed that the theoretically correct measure of income was utility or satisfaction received but that the satisfactions or "usances" were economically significant only when they could be evaluated in money terms. From these considerations he derived his definition that "income is the money value of the net accretion to one's economic power between two points of time." [5] This definition would seem to include both fringe benefits in an immediately consumable form and fringe benefits which promised future payment, a result which differs from Fisher's. Haig emphasized the necessity of evaluation in money terms, and this requirement seems admirably met by fringe benefits, which are customarily presented as being equivalent to "x¢ per hour." Haig realized that his definition was subject to administrative difficulties in that certain forms of income might be difficult to tax, e.g., imputed rent of home owners and increases in the value of property held. In such cases allowances should be made in the tax treatment, but the items should still be understood as constituting income.[6] Some fringe benefits, it will be found, might fall in this classification.

The economic definition of income most closely corresponding to currently accepted income tax policy is Haig's definition, and it includes the general class of fringe benefits in taxable income. However, taxation depends on legislative enactments with administrative regulation and court interpretation.

The legislative definition of gross income subject to tax as contained in the federal Income Tax Act of 1913 states, "The net income of a taxable person shall include gains, profits, and income derived from salaries, wages, or compensation for personal service of whatever kind and in whatever form paid," [7] and this phraseology continued through the 1939 Internal Revenue Code. This would appear to include fringe benefits in taxable income because of their falling under "compensation for personal service . . . in whatever form paid . . .";[8] some fringe benefits might better be excluded, however, as noted above in the discussion of economic definitions of income, for administrative reasons.

However, the inclusiveness of this definition of income has been diminished by specific exemptions; sections 101 through 121 of the 1954 Internal Revenue Code, which come after the definition of taxable income and items which are specifically included in gross income, proceed to list the items which are specifically excluded from gross income, and almost half of these apply to fringe benefits. As a result the requirements seem ever to increase for income received by a taxpayer to be considered unequivocally taxable. For example, the income recipient must be still living (capital gains, returns from life insurance in excess of premiums paid, and payments up to $5,000 by an employer to an employee's widow are all not taxable income if realized after death); he must be employed (unemployment compensation is not subject to tax, and supplemental unemployment benefits, although subject to income taxation, may not be subjected to withholding, taxed under the social security acts, nor considered as wages within the meaning of the Fair Labor Standards Act); he must be at work (if he is ill, money to pay medical and hospital bills and money to replace wages are not taxable income); he must be paid in cash (meals served on the employer's premises may fall outside gross income); and the cash payment must not be designated as a subsistence payment (this would not be taxable income to military officers). Should any one of these conditions not be met, the payment may or may not be considered as taxable income; the Code and regulations must be consulted to find out. It is only when all the above conditions are met that a payment by an employer, benefiting an employee, is unequivocally taxable income. It is, of course, within the power of Congress to make exceptions for income which is administratively difficult to tax and in those cases where it wishes to bring about social reform, but once a general rule for taxation has been laid down, the cost of the various departures from this rule should be considered.

Concerning his definition of income, Haig noted that "so long as taxable income differs appreciably from this definition, there will be anomalies and injustices in income taxation, and every step marking a clearer approximation of this definition will result in the elimination of irregular and eccentric results." [9] The closeness of the Internal Revenue Code concept of gross income to Haig's concept of administratively taxable income makes his warning equally applicable to those attempts to mark a departure from the Code concept of income. Recent expressions of concern over the erosion of the tax base show that fringe benefits are only one of the forms of erosion,[10] but they merit attention because they are one of the fastest growing forms.

An example of Treasury thinking on the subject at the time of formulation of the Internal Revenue Code of 1954 can be obtained from Dan Throop Smith's discussion of fringe benefit taxation under the Code. He notes that although many people favored an all-inclusive definition of taxable income, "it appeared that the common-sense approach was more useful than an attempt to develop a theoretically perfect law which did not correspond to popular ideas of what is and what is not income." [11]   For example, to tax "an imputed value of a sick benefit or a death benefit coverage which he did not desire would be repugnant not only to those immediately affected but to the general public conscience." [12]

If the decision on whether or not to tax fringe benefits is to derive from "common-sense," the treatment would depend on whose common sense was utilized. If we resort to the common sense of the person receiving the fringe benefit, the opinion concerning the tax treatment is quite likely to be biased. And if we extend the inquiry to the general public, most of whom also have a vested interest in the subject of fringe benefits, the answer is likely to remain unchanged. As manufacturers of bicycles are reluctant to criticize the tariff on felt hats, so might employers exercise discretion in passing judgment on the taxability of, say, contributions to pension or retirement funds. Resort to some other bench mark is needed and the one laid down in section 22(a) of the 1939 Internal Revenue Code appears satisfactory.

The courts, it would seem, have been even less successful in arriving at a single, logical concept of income subject to taxation. In the case of Commissioner v. Wilcox (1946) Mr. Justice Murphy of the Supreme Court stated:

Not every benefit received by a taxpayer from his labor or investment necessarily renders him taxable. Nor is mere dominion over money or property decisive in all cases. In fact, no single, conclusive criterion has yet been found to determine in all situations what is a sufficient gain to support the imposition of an income tax. No more can be said in general than that all relevant facts and circumstances must be considered.[13]

Mr. Justice Holmes was of a similar opinion in stating:

But it is not necessarily true that income means the same thing in the Constitution and the Act [1913]. A word is not a crystal, transparent and unchanged, it is the skin of a living thought and may vary greatly in color and content according to the circumstances and the time in which it is used.[14]

With a legislative definition of taxable income subject to many exceptions and with court precedent in the form of opinion such as above, the courts have ruled on fringe benefits in such a way that, from a layman's viewpoint, the results appear to be inconsistent. The courts have, for example, granted varying treatment to Jones, an army officer, and Van Rosen, a master of a merchant ship, both of whom normally received tax-free quarters. When Major Jones went to Washington for temporary duty and was given a subsistence allowance, this was held nontaxable; [15] when Captain Van Rosen's ship was in port for repairs and he was given a subsistence allowance, this was held taxable.[16]

The tax treatment of fringe benefits is based fundamentally on the laws of Congress, the regulations and rulings of the Treasury, and the decisions of the courts. These three bodies have decided on the taxation of individual fringe benefits as they arose, and these decisions, collectively, form the foundation for present day fringe benefit tax treatment.

B. HISTORICAL DEVELOPMENT OF THE TREATMENT OF FRINGE BENEFITS UNDER THE FEDERAL INCOME TAX

As has been noted, the definition of taxable gross income has traditionally been quite inclusive. Landman observes that the definition has undergone little change since the 1862 income tax, through the sixteenth amendment to the Constitution, the 1913 Revenue Act and over thirty subsequent revenue acts.[17] But the broad confines of the concept, which included, among other things, receipts for services "of whatever kind and in whatever form paid," [18] began early to be less inclusive than the above statement implies. Favorable treatment for certain goods and services furnished to employees was established in a 1919 Treasury ruling which stated that board and lodging so furnished would not be taxable income to the employee if it were furnished "for the convenience of the employer." [19] Another Treasury ruling the following year granted tax exemption to premiums paid by an employer for group life insurance.[20] The 1921 Revenue Act declared employers' contributions to trusts set up as a part of a stock-bonus or profit-sharing plan not to be income to the employee until the benefits were distributed to him; [21] in 1926 Congress extended this treatment to pension plans.[22]

The Social Security Act of 1935 made provision for non-wage benefits to flow to employees from funds created by contributions from employers, and later rulings by the Bureau of Internal Revenue held that neither payments into the funds by employers on behalf of employees nor payments of benefits from the funds to employees would be considered as income subject to tax.[23]

Favorable treatment for employer contributions to pension, stock-bonus, or profit-sharing trusts for "some or all employees" had existed since 1921 and 1926, but these devices were used largely for the benefit of "some" rather than "all" employees.[24] Therefore the Revenue Act of 1942 introduced the requirement that such plans must cover a certain minimum number of employees to be qualified for favorable tax treatment.[25] A ruling in 1943 brought exemption from taxation for hospitalization insurance premiums.[26]

In 1950, however, the Treasury undertook to tighten up on the taxability of certain benefits, and this shift in policy is doubtless responsible for some of the increased interest in fringe benefits. In Mimeograph 6472 the Treasury stated that "the 'convenience of the employer' rule is simply an administrative test to be applied only in cases in which the compensatory character of such benefits is not otherwise determinable." [27] Thus, if room or board furnished were considered as compensation, it would be taxable whether or not it was furnished for the employer's convenience. The Treasury also reversed its policy of allowing death benefits paid to an employee's widow to be considered as nontaxable income; it ruled that such payments would be taxable to the widow if they were made in consideration of services rendered by the employee.[28]

The year 1954 saw a shift back toward pre-1950 concepts. This was the year of the adoption of the new Internal Revenue Code and some of the thinking that went into the development of the Code has been cited. This called for a more "common sense" and less inclusive concept of income. The Senate more specifically felt that a return was necessary, pointing out what change had been wrought by the 1950 ruling and recommending that no tax be levied on meals and lodging so long as they were given primarily for the convenience of the employer— whether or not they were also given as compensation.[29] This philosophy evidenced itself in the 1954 Code in more liberal treatment of employee death benefits, payments for injury and sickness, subsistence payments to police officers, and certain other fringe benefits, as well as for meals and lodging.

The 1954 Code has thus taken a step in one direction, but it is a step that has been subject to criticism. If these criticisms of present fringe benefit tax treatment are valid, it is important that changes be made before this treatment becomes intrenched. The amount of fringe benefits being offered has been estimated and their growth predicted, but, using the above inclusive Code concept of income, what amount of tax preference is involved?

C. PRESENT TREATMENT OF FRINGE BENEFITS UNDER THE FEDERAL INCOME TAX

Business Week implies tax favor by stating that "wage fringes . . . are pretty largely tax exempt," [30] but it offers no supporting evidence. Guttentag, Leonard, and Rodewald are more conservative in their statement that "to a large extent non-cash compensation has escaped federal income taxation," [31] but their "non-cash compensation" classification probably excludes pay for time not worked and premium pay, often a large component under some definitions of fringe benefits.

Examining fringe benefits, we find that tax favor generally emerges in one of three forms: (1) when tax is deferred, as on employer payments into employee pension funds which will be distributed to the employee at some future date and taxed at that time, (2) when tax is not levied at all on (a) certain payments made in kind to employees (such as free meals, medical care, group life insurance, hospital and surgical insurance, clothing, recreation facilities, tuition, etc.), (b) certain payments into funds from which tax-free payments will be made to the employee upon certain contingencies (such as employer's contributions to old-age and survivors insurance, unemployment compensation, and workmen's compensation), and (c) certain payments to the employee while he is ill (a 1954 addition), and (3) when tax is levied at the capital gains rate (as on lump-sum benefits received from qualified deferred profit-sharing plans).

Fisher and Chapman, investigating the cost of fringe benefits in 1953, found from a survey of 162 companies that the average cost of fringe payments was about 41¢ per productive hour per employee.[32]   Of this total almost 7¢ per productive hour per employee went as employer contributions to pension plans. The tax on this would be deferred until the employee's retirement.   An average of about 11¢ per productive hour per employee went for fringe benefits which are generally tax-free.[33] Thus about 18¢ per productive hour per employee, or 44 percent of total fringe benefits, was tax preferred, and the authors noted that this was the fastest growing group of fringe benefits.[34]

The Chamber of Commerce, in the same year, found that fringe benefits averaged about 19.2 percent of the payroll for 940 companies surveyed; this amounted to an average figure of 34.6¢ per payroll hour per employee.[35] (See Appendix III.) Of the benefits listed, pension plan premiums were 3.8 percent of payroll costs or 6.8¢ per payroll hour.   Other fringes that are generally tax-free averaged about 5.2 percent of the payroll, or about 9.4¢ per payroll hour.[36] Employer contributions to profit-sharing plans equalled .6 percent of payroll costs but not all of this was tax preferred. It would seem safe to consider at least two thirds of this amount as tax preferred through postponed taxation and possible capital gains treatment, since a 1954 survey of 320 companies showed that there were four times as many employees under deferred payment profit-sharing plans as there were under cash payment plans.[37] This conservative estimate would give us a figure of about .7¢ per payroll hour as tax preferred. Summing up these tax-preferred fringe benefits, we get 9.4 percent of payroll costs or 16.9¢ per payroll hour per employee, which is close to the figure derived from the Fisher and Chapman study.[38] Of the remaining 17.7¢ per payroll hour of fringe benefits about 14.8¢ was in the form of pay for time not worked, which represents an increase in nontaxable leisure with the same pay, and about 2.9¢ per payroll hour was for fringes which were presumably taxed, such as Christmas bonuses, suggestion awards, and similar payments.[39]

These figures of the Chamber of Commerce and Fisher and Chapman apply only to hourly rated employees and salaried employees whose pay varies with time worked.[40] Besides these groups, executive and supervisory groups also receive tax-preferred benefits. Although fringes for this group have not been subjected to the total cost study that fringes for hourly workers have received, individual forms of benefits such as expense accounts, use of company property, and restricted stock options have received attention. Thus, while it is more difficult to determine the total value of these, many individual instances of the first two items listed have been publicized,[41] which indicates their use is continuing undiminished, if not increasing. The importance of deferred compensation for executives may be inferred from the fact that of the 1,087 companies listed on the New York Stock Exchange in 1954, over 900 had in operation some form of deferred compensation for company executives.[42]

The Chamber of Commerce in 1953 found that the 19.2 percent of payroll costs for fringe benefits equalled $720 per year per employee.[43] This would indicate an annual salary of $3,750, which may be compared with the national income figure of $3,643 average annual earnings per full-time employee in private industry for 1953. The total figure for these earnings is $164.5 billion.[44] If, as we have found above, about 9.4 percent of payroll costs comes in as a tax-preferred fringe benefit, this would indicate a total of about $15.5 billion. This figure would not include tax-preferred fringe benefits received by government employees nor perquisites of office received by executives. Thus there is a sizable amount of potentially taxable income at stake.

While the 1953 figures of Fisher and Chapman and the Chamber of Commerce support each other, the subsequent reports in 1955 and 1957 by the Chamber of Commerce, which are without comparison, report even higher fringe benefits. If the methods of calculation used in the preceding paragraph are applied to the 1957 data, the results are as follows. The Chamber of Commerce in 1957 found that 21.8 percent of payroll costs was paid for fringe benefits and this equalled 47.4¢ per payroll hour per employee or $981 per year per employee —$162 higher than two years before and $261 higher than four years before. The indicated annual salary of $4,500 may be compared with national income figures which show an average salary of approximately $4,310 per employee in private industry, excepting agriculture.[45] Examination of fringe benefits receiving tax favor shows them to be about 11.5 percent of payroll or about 25¢ per payroll hour per employee. Total private payrolls outside agriculture were $195 billion in 1957 and 11.5 percent would give over $22 billion of tax-preferred fringe benefits. And again this does not include fringe benefits received by workers in agriculture or government, where payrolls were $43 billion.

One of the principal reasons advanced for the exclusion of fringe benefits from income taxation is the contention that they are conditions of employment rather than compensation for employment. Conditions of employment seem to include expenditures by the employer designed primarily to benefit

himself, usually by increasing production. Compensation, on
the other hand, is paid to yield benefit to the employee. Consequently, public opinion calls for personal income taxation to
apply to compensation but not to conditions of work. But
obviously the line between the two is a hazy one—if there is a
line.

Note, for example, that employers traditionally spend money
as long as the marginal revenue from the particular expenditure exceeds the marginal cost. This may call for the purchase
of raw materials, tools, buildings, and labor. The expenditure
on labor, wages, should also benefit the employee since the
worker can use the wage as he sees fit. Other employer expenditures may not be so clear cut. The employer expenditure
on tools, for example, may help the employee by making his
work easier, but basically tools are not an economic good or
service that the employee would voluntarily buy for consumption. Employer expenditures for goods such as water
fountains, rest rooms, and pleasant surroundings are also for
the purpose of increasing profit, but this time the goods also
furnish utility to the employee and may replace money he
might have expended.[46] Employer expenditures for employee
meals, recreation plans, life insurance, pension plans, and
other similar goods move even closer to the wages concept.
Thus the benefit accruing from employer expenditures is not
confined to the employer alone. The employer is not expected
to pay out any money, even wages, unless he anticipates that it
will increase his profit, and many of his expenditures will, like
wages, provide "usances" or utility to employees.

Many writers have recognized this inherent difficulty in
classifying as income outlays by the employer in forms other
than cash wages. Pigou, while not mentioning the difference
between conditions of employment and compensation, notes
that the tax gatherer will have to be content with assessing only
money income because of administrative costs of taxing other
forms of income.[47] Vickrey notes that trying to tax medical
and recreational facilities furnished by employers gets "fairly
close to attempting to evaluate working conditions as such, an

undertaking that would encounter almost insurmountable difficulties." [48]   Simons in discussing taxation of compensation in
kind, is no more optimistic:

There is here an essential and insuperable difficulty, even in principle. The problem of Kleinwachter's *Flugeladjutant* is insoluable
and certainly is not amenable to reasonable solution on the basis of
simple rules which could be administered by revenue agents.[49]

And the critic of these views is invited by Simons to present
constructive proposals.[50]

The problem is just as difficult of solution today as it was
when the statements by Pigou, Vickrey, and Simons were made.
An example of the difficulty, as it applies to the classification
of fringe benefits, may be found in employer expenditures for
employee health.   An employer may maintain in his place of
business a first aid stand to help employees when injured or ill
at work.   Or he may establish, instead, more elaborate facilities which call for the presence, either part time or full time,
of a physician to care for both minor and more complicated
disorders.   Again, he may provide, in addition to this service,
medical, surgical, and hospitalization insurance to see that the
workers are cared for in more serious cases of illness, and these
benefits may further be extended to dependents of workers.
In addition, the form of medical care may be extended from
the curing of illness and injury to their prevention.   Thus the
employer may purchase safety clothing and safety glasses, or
he may purchase the diagnostic services of physicians to give his
employees health examinations.   The examination of higher
paid employees is sometimes held at resort areas like Palm
Springs, Florida, or White Sulphur Springs, West Virginia.

In all the above cases the employer is spending money to
care for the health of his employees.   The cases cited, although
they may appear discrete, can be made to shade smoothly one
into the other.   While many observers would call the provision
of a first aid stand to care for injuries received at work a condition of employment, the provision of medical care for dependents or of medical checkups for employees, especially when

conducted at a place like the Greenbrier Hotel or at some similar fashionable resort, would appear to many as a form of wage payment. Where, between these two extremes, has the fringe benefit changed from its status as a nontaxable condition of employment to that of a taxable wage?

In an attempt to answer this general question Arthur Goldberg, general counsel for the Congress of Industrial Organizations, has argued that fringe benefits are conditions of employment and should not be subject to personal income taxation. He argues that conditions of work are those benefits, other than cash, which people consider it the duty of the employer to provide and/or those benefits which are usually provided by employers. Such expenditures by the employer, even if they replace expenditures which would have been made by the employee, are not income to the employee.[51] On the positive side, compensation, in Goldberg's view, is given in proportion to services rendered and is available to be spent by the employee at his discretion.[52] Guttentag *et al.* criticize Goldberg's position, but they note "there is some validity in the argument, however, in that there is no clear line of demarcation between compensation and conditions of employment although there is certainly an intuitive difference." [53] Thus it appears to all concerned that income paid in kind, or at least not in cash wages, is quite difficult to tax because it silently merges into conditions of employment.

In reality the benefits from an appeal to the distinction between conditions of employment and compensation for work are more apparent than real. Although such a term as conditions of employment exists in our everyday vocabulary and is used in books dealing with labor economics and wage theory, the term, like fringe benefits, has no commonly accepted bounds, and, more important, it seems nowhere to be defined in relation to wages.[54] In fact, until the quite recent advent of fringe benefits, little importance was attached to the term. So long as most firms maintained similar conditions of employment, the importance of considering definition was evidently minor, and while tax treatment of additional employee benefits was questionable and tax rates low, at least one pressure encouraging extended adoption of fringe benefits was absent. When, subsequently, conditions arose favoring non-wage expenditures to benefit employees, the distinction became significant, but so far this significance appears to have been largely confined to the field of taxation. The appeal, therefore, to the term "conditions of employment" for guidance in tax policy is likely to add little light; rather, it is more likely that the concept of conditions of employment can gain in precision through reference to considerations of tax treatment of individual employer expenditures.

A logical, consistent definition of income would appear to be the starting point in a search for tax treatment of fringe benefits; this would also furnish a standard, to which comparison could be made as problems and variations in treatment increased. The discussion of income above has indicated that the accretion definition proposed by Haig and Simons comes closest to the concept in the Internal Revenue Code, is a logical and consistent definition of income, and so constitutes a favorable point of departure. Under this definition any utility, satisfaction, or "usance" which the employee enjoys because of expenditures of the employer would constitute consumption by the employee and so income to him. Administrative difficulties with this definition, foreseen by Haig, make room for nontaxation of certain services such as heat, light, air conditioning, water coolers, sanitation facilities, and the like. But if the group of fringe benefits not subject to regular income taxation is greatly increased, a tax saving becomes possible.

The presence of a potential tax saving has been an important factor leading to the adoption of fringe benefits. This tax saving, in turn, has been closely connected with the implicit classification of the fringe benefit as a condition of employment or something approaching that so that the tax might be postponed, reduced, or forgiven. Thus the terms wages, conditions of employment, and fringe benefits are closely related to taxation of income. They may be tentatively defined so that wages are considered as straight-time and overtime or premium pay plus taxable fringe benefits; fringe benefits, as above, a payment for something which furnishes utility to the employee, paid by the employer to or on behalf of the employee, over and above straight-time and overtime wages and regular piece-rate wages; conditions of employment as those natural benefits connected with an employment plus employer-purchased fringe benefits that are not considered as taxable income. Fringe benefits, it will be observed, are the overlapping element in these definitions; the individual benefits may qualify as wages or conditions of employment. Since the importance of the distinction between wages and conditions of employment hinges to a great extent on taxability, stress will later be placed on those factors important in determining the taxability and nontaxability of these benefits.

The tax treatment of fringe benefits entails one set of difficulties if the benefits are taxed and a different set of difficulties if they are not taxed. Therefore, in discussing the tax treatment of any particular fringe benefit, consideration should be given to these two groups of difficulties, and an attempt should be made to choose that course of action which would entail minimum aggregate difficulty. The term "difficulty" as used here implies more than mere difficulty in administration. It embraces problems in equity, tax rates, incentives, resource allocation, business fluctuations, and many other fields as well as administration. Since these fields of difficulty have no common unit of measurement, the minimization of these difficulties or problems will largely rest on the relative values assigned to them by each individual. What should be attempted, then, is a discussion or description of the difficulties likely to be encountered in each of these areas, first, under the assumption that fringe benefits are not taxed and, second, under the assumption that fringe benefits are taxed. The individual, having the sum of these difficulties laid before him, is then in a better position to decide on their tax treatment.

In the past the difficulties from taxing certain fringe benefits have evidently been held to be greater than the difficulties which would arise from giving these fringe benefits tax preference. Thus we find that lawmakers, after defining income to be taxed, have itemized fringe benefits which they feel deserve tax preference. The Treasury has exercised its administrative powers in decreeing nontaxability for other fringe benefits. The courts have done the same in attempting to fathom the meaning of the Internal Revenue Code and the regulations. Not every candidate for admission to the ranks of tax-preferred fringe benefits has been so honored by these groups, but many have been.

D. PROBLEMS ARISING PROM TAXATION OF FRINGE BENEFITS

1. Administrative Difficulties

Because of administrative difficulties the cost of collecting the tax on a fringe benefit might exceed the amount of tax collected, which, considering revenue only, would argue for nonimposition of the tax. There are at least two factors which might contribute to this type of difficulty: first, the value of the fringe benefit may be small or, second, the cost of administering the tax on the fringe benefit may be high.

The statement that the value of the fringe benefit may be small must be made more precise in order to have operational meaning. For example, "small" is a relative term and so needs to be set in its proper context. To lend some substance to the term it might be suggested that fringe benefits amounting to less than $15.00 or $25.00 a year per employee be considered too "small" to include in taxable income. This would result in a change in tax of only $3.00 to $5.00 for the lowest bracket taxpayer; and the smaller the amount of tax involved, the more likely it becomes that collection costs might exceed the tax collected. Such a procedure would give rise to a notch problem in that fringe benefits just exceeding the minimum amount would be taxed fully while those just below the minimum would escape taxation, but the jump in tax for the taxpayer in the lowest tax bracket would be only about $3.00 to $5.00 per year and so should not prove troublesome. Although figures are not involved, the concept is, in the regulations governing the tax on wages under the Federal Insurance Contributions Act and the Federal Unemployment Tax Act. Here certain facilities or privileges, when furnished by an employer to his employees, are not considered as taxable wages if they "are of relatively small value" and are furnished "as means of promoting the health, good will, contentment, or efficiency of his employees." [55]

A second point to be made concerning the "smallness" of value of a particular fringe benefit concerns the imprecision that exists in determining the boundary to be used in defining a fringe benefit. In this case the fringe benefit should be defined as broadly as possible; otherwise, a narrowly defined fringe benefit will nearly always qualify as "small." To illustrate, a company may offer its employees a fringe benefit in "recreation and entertainment" which might amount to $50.00 a year per employee. Yet, if this fringe benefit expenditure should be listed under five separate fringe benefit headings such as "bowling league," "company picnic," "swimming pool," "music and dancing lessons," "company club house," each benefit might be considered "small" and so "thrown back in." Collectively, however, they might constitute a sizable amount. The definition used for fringe benefit should, therefore, be as broad as possible.

The second factor contributing to administrative difficulties is the possibility of a high cost of administering and collecting a tax on fringe benefits. These collection difficulties might exist where the benefit is offered to only a few scattered workers or where records are not generally kept, as in the many small businesses in France or in United States agriculture. In those cases where the cost of administering and collecting the tax exceeds the amount of tax collected, this would be a strong argument against levying the tax. However, this should not be a sufficient condition for abandoning the tax; the cost of administering and collecting the tax on a fringe benefit like stock options might exceed the amount of tax collected, but abandonment of the tax would lead to considerable inequity in present and future tax treatment.

2. Uncertainty of Value

Evaluation of the fringe benefit may be difficult or impossible. This is probably the most serious hurdle to overcome. It, too, may arise for different reasons.

First, the benefit may be valued by the recipient at less than cost or market value. Under the accretion definition of income, if it could be applied with theoretical perfection, only the value to the recipient-consumer should be taxable, and evaluation of the benefit to each individual recipient would be difficult. Kleinwachter's *Flugeladjutant* again illustrates this point, although the modern day traveling salesman is also a good example.

Second, the benefit may be one which has neither market value nor cost of production, and so valuation for tax purposes presents a difficult problem. Leisure is a good, if not the only, example of this. It may be felt that no tax problem is created here, since the money received for a week's vacation with pay is taxed along with other income,[56] but note that it is taxed at the same rate as the money received for a week of work which yields no additional leisure income.

Third, the benefit may be contingent on certain happenings and so, although a payment is made by the employer today, there is no assurance that the employee will ever receive the benefit. Employer contributions to non-vested pension plans, unemployment insurance, and workmen's compensation are examples.

3. Public Antipathy

Public antipathy may constitute a hurdle to the taxation of certain fringe benefits. Some expenditures by the employer for his employees' welfare are considered by the public as "rights" of the workers and not as income to them. Cooperation of taxpayers in the collection of a mass income tax is a necessity for its successful functioning. If an attempt is made to tax items which are widely and strongly considered as something other than income, resistance on the part of taxpayers might necessitate checking over 60 million individual income tax returns. Under such circumstances the result could be either abandonment of the tax, drastic reduction in number of taxpayers, or multiplied costs of collection.

4. Social Goals

Social goals might call for favorable treatment of some fringe benefits. Such an argument may be based either on a desire to promote the consumption of certain goods or services or on the desire to promote the welfare of some group of income recipients. Several specific fringe benefits, such as pension plans, old-age and survivors insurance, unemployment compensation, health and accident insurance, and hospitalization and surgical insurance, have been encouraged on the grounds that they are desirable goods and services, and surveys show they have grown at a more rapid rate than cash wages.

The related goal of helping some particular group through special tax treatment of fringe benefits can be used on behalf of any group of taxpayers, and use has been made on behalf of widely separated groups. It has been argued that income in kind should not be taxable to the "marginal taxpayer, i.e., the one who just manages to struggle along . . . because a disproportionate increase in the taxes of low income groups, which would result, is socially undesirable." [57] At the other extreme it is argued that high tax rates on the upper income brackets call for deferred compensation, stock option plans, and use of company property if the taxpayer is to benefit to more than a minor extent from salary increases.

The argument of promoting social welfare is often cited as a reason for freeing certain fringe benefits from taxation, but it should be remembered that this argument is subject to special considerations. Since social welfare rests on value judgments which are on a lower level of precision than measuring administrative costs, there is likely to be a wider area of disagreement. Evaluation of such arguments might better be left in Congressional hands; as elected representatives of the people, the members of Congress have been chosen to reflect the value judgments of their constituents. Yet it is sometimes the most vociferous, rather than the most numerous or most learned, that attract the ear and gain the favor of Congress. Finally, as it has been almost universally held that a traiff is inferior to an outright subsidy as a means for promoting the production of some goods, so it may be argued that tax favor given some form of income may be inferior to an outright subsidy as a means of promoting the consumption of some goods or of helping some particular group.

One or more of the above difficulties could be cited as applying to every non-cash wage benefitting the employee. When these difficulties, then, are coupled to the political popularity which springs from a failure to tax (or, conversely, to the political unpopularity that arises when new items are subjected to tax), the result is a strong predisposition toward tax preference for fringe benefits. The general acceptance of the term, "fringe benefits," implies that a benefit or income accrues to the recipient and so argues for taxation; the fact that fringe benefits are almost universally presented as having a certain value reinforces the argument for their inclusion as income subject to tax. But the finding that out of 47.4¢ per hour in fringe benefits paid, about 25¢ per hour is given tax preference testifies to the effectiveness of the above arguments. This figure is elevated in importance when it is noted that beside the 25¢ per hour receiving tax preferences, about 19¢ per hour is for paid vacations and holidays, additional leisure with pay at the stated wage rate. This paid time-off, if extensive, may be looked at as a fringe benefit in the form of additional tax-free leisure income. If the paid time off is considered as the normal amount of leisure that any job allows, the payment would be considered part of the wage and not a fringe benefit at all. The net result is that only about 3¢ per hour comes in as fringe benefits fully subject to the income tax.[58]

E. PROBLEMS ARISING FROM TAX PREFERENCE ACCORDED FRINGE BENEFITS

The difficulties which might arise from an attempt to tax fringe benefits have been noted. Possibly as a result of these arguments, fringe benefits have largely escaped taxation. But what picture appears on the reverse side of the coin; what are the difficulties which might arise from excluding these payments from taxable income? The difficulties might be divided into two groups: Those which are peculiar to the field of public finance and those which extend to the functioning of the economic system. The remainder of this chapter will be devoted to the difficulties in public finance; Chapter III will be devoted to factors which affect the functioning of the economy.

1. Problems of Equity

Equity in taxation is recognized as one of the necessary attributes of a tax or tax system. This is generally interpreted to mean equal treatment of equals, or a Pigou puts it, "Different persons should be treated similarly unless they are dissimilar in some *relevant* respect." [59] For the income tax this would mean that similarly situated people with equal incomes would pay the same tax. Fringe benefits, however, introduce a new dimension and a departure from this principle, since taxation then depends on the *form* in which income is received as well as the amount received.

Examples arise whenever a good, the expense of obtaining which does not constitute a personal income tax deduction, is purchased by some taxpayers from taxable income while other taxpayers receive the good as a tax-free fringe benefit. Numerous examples could be cited ranging from expenditures on necessities such as food to items exemplifying the luxury, or marginal expenditure, category such as yachts.

The extent to which the taxpayer who receives a tax-free fringe benefit is favored varies directly with the taxpayer's income tax bracket and is easily determinable as long as the in-

clusion of the fringe benefit in taxable income leaves the taxpayer in the same tax bracket, as may be the usual case for a
particular fringe benefit. To illustrate this, let y be an addition
to taxable income, this addition not being great enough to
move the taxpayer out of his present marginal tax bracket; let
t be the marginal tax rate which will apply to additional income, $y;$ and let n be the increase in income after tax. It can
be seen that the increment to income after tax is equal to the
increase in taxable income less the tax on this addition to taxable income. This can be stated in simple algebraic terms as
$n = y - ty$ or $n = y\,(1 - t)$. If a worker receives a tax-free fringe
benefit in the amount of \$$x$, his after-tax income has been in-
creased by this amount, but what amount of taxable income is
equivalent to this? In this case the value sought is the amount
of taxable income equivalent to \$$x$ of after-tax income. The
above equation may be easily transposed into an equation
where the addition to income after tax and the marginal tax
rate are known and the equivalent amount of additional taxable income is unknown: $y = \dfrac{n}{1 - t}$. From this equation the
amount of additional taxable income equivalent to a certain
amount of additional, nontaxable, fringe-benefit income can
be found.

If an employee is offered the choice between receiving a
wage increase of a certain amount in the form of taxable income or in the form of a tax-free fringe benefit, he will be able,
by accepting the latter, to effect a tax saving. This tax saving,
$s, = n\,\dfrac{t}{1 - t}$ and it becomes equal to n when t reaches 50 percent.
At rates above 50 percent, s exceeds n, which means that if a
worker in this tax bracket receives a tax-free fringe benefit
rather than an increase of the same amount in taxable wages,
he will be left with more than twice as much income after tax
by accepting the fringe benefit rather than the wage increase.

The formula given above to show the amount of taxable income equivalent to a given amount of after-tax income may be
changed slightly from $y = \dfrac{n}{1 - t}$ to $y = n\,\dfrac{1}{1 - t}$ to show this equiva-

lent amount of taxable income expressed as a multiple or percentage of the tax-free income. The latter formula shows that the amount of taxable income that must be received to be equal in value to a tax-free fringe benefit ranges from 125 percent of the benefit received for the taxpayer in the 20 percent marginal tax bracket to 1,111 percent of the benefit received for the taxpayer in the 91 percent marginal tax bracket.

From these formulas it can be seen that a tax-free fringe benefit of a certain size is equivalent, in after-tax income, to a much larger amount of taxable income. Consequently, even if the fringe benefit were subjected to tax, it might be felt that the fringe benefit recipient would still be favored, but to a lesser extent than before, since his tax base would be smaller than that of the taxpayer who received the equivalent, but larger, amount of taxable income. This, however, is not correct. Assume, for example, that a $1,000 tax-free fringe benefit is given to a taxpayer, A, in the 60 percent marginal tax bracket, so that $y = \$2,500$. If this fringe benefit were made taxable, the recipient would seem to pay tax on only $1,000 income rather than on the $2,500 equivalent income his similarly situated neighbor, B, would have to receive in cash in order to purchase on the market the same good that A received tax-free. But note that the $600 tax which A must now pay is to be paid from his income after taxes. In order for A to have the $600 to pay his tax, he would have to earn $1,500 more, of which $900 would go as the tax on the extra $1,500 cash income and the remaining $600 would become tax revenue because of taxation of the $1,000 fringe benefit.

The unequal treatment of equals which results from tax-free fringe benefits is thus seen to exist at all levels of taxable income, but it has attracted the most attention in those cases where n is large relative to the balance of the income of the recipient and where t is near its upper limits. Two examples that have attracted much attention are (1) the expense account salesman compared with his middle-income neighbor who cannot travel, eat, and entertain in expensive circles, and (2) tax-preferred, deferred compensation and pensions for employees compared with the absence of such deferred income for self-employed people. Dearing has noted the favor accorded one group over another in stating, "It appears that industrial pensions must be viewed as a device by which a limited number of specially situated workers may, through group action, supplement their private savings or government-provided retirement benefits." [60]   Realization of unequal treatment has evidenced itself in the Individual Retirement Act of 1955 which proposes to allow self-employed persons and non-covered employees to set aside certain amounts annually for retirement, these amounts to be free from tax until received during retirement. It should be noted here that the proposed remedy for the existing inequality follows what Heller has called the "most-favored-taxpayer principle." [61]

Beside the above-mentioned cases where fringe benefits might alter the relationship between income before and after tax, there is a less obvious situation which might easily escape detection. In the calculation of the personal income tax, the law allows the taxpayer to subtract from his adjusted gross income amounts spent for certain purposes which Congress has considered worthy of deduction. If the taxpayer does not choose to itemize these deductions, or if they total less than 10 percent of his adjusted gross income, he may, in lieu of taking these itemized deductions, subtract 10 percent of his adjusted gross income as an optional standard deduction. There is a restriction on the optional standard deduction stating that it may not exceed $1,000 and this tends to limit its use by taxpayers reporting over $10,000 adjusted gross income. The result of this provision is that taxpayers spending money on items allowed as deductions may or may not get tax relief because of such expenditures, depending on the total amount of all deductions and the total income for each taxpayer.

Some of the fringe benefits granted workers are of a type which will replace expenditures which might otherwise have been considered as deductions from income. And since some of the workers would have used the standard deduction, while others would not have done so, substitution of a nontaxable fringe benefit for a taxable wage plus personal expenditures for deductible items will create differences in the amount of income tax paid by these workers. An example will perhaps further clarify the problem and demonstrate how benefits will go to the taxpayer using the optional standard deduction.

Assume that there are two similarly situated [62] taxpayers, A and B, but that A itemizes his deductions, which exceed 10 percent of his adjusted gross income, while B takes the optional standard deduction because his deductions do not exceed 10 percent of his adjusted gross income. If both taxpayers are now granted a fringe benefit, it might be felt that both have benefited to the same extent, and, if both are in the same marginal tax bracket, each one has experienced the same amount of tax savings. However, if this fringe benefit is one which replaces an expenditure which would otherwise have been allowed as a personal deduction, one of the taxpayers will be benefited more than the other. An example of such a fringe benefit would be an interest-free loan from the company, group hospitalization or surgical insurance provided by the company, or the furnishing of medical examinations to employees or dependents.

To see how both A and B fare when the fringe benefit has replaced a deductible expense, assume that each has received in lieu of present cash wages a fringe benefit valued at $x. With this change in the form of compensation, A's adjusted gross income and deductions are both reduced by $x, leaving his taxable income unchanged. On the other hand, B's adjusted gross income has been reduced by $x, but his optional standard deduction has been reduced by only one-tenth $x, thus leaving his taxable income nine-tenth $x lower than before.

If a slightly different assumption is used, an odd result may be observed. If the fringe benefit, of a deductible expense nature and equivalent to $x, is given as a form of wage increase *in addition* to existing wages, then for both A and B adjusted gross income is unchanged. But A, who has been itemizing his deductions, now finds that certain of these deductible expenses have been replaced by employer fringe benefit expenditures so that his itemized deductions are reduced, and his taxable income raised, by the $x of fringe benefits. Here the employee being given, say, hospitalization insurance worth $100 a year, which would normally be deductible from income, finds his taxable income raised by the same amount. B, however, finds his adjusted gross income, standard deduction, and taxable income all unchanged.[63] Whether or not these cases create an inequity is a value judgment, resting in part on how one views the optional standard deduction as a substitute for itemized deductions. What can be said is that the tax burden has shifted from the distribution which prevailed before the fringe benefit was granted, even though everyone might have received the fringe benefit.

A second meaning attached to the concept of equity calls for an equitable distribution of the burden of taxes among different income groups. Adam Smith, in calling for equality in taxation, proposed that people should contribute to the government approximately "in proportion to the revenue which they respectively enjoy under the protection of the state." [64] Just what is meant by "in proportion" has been interpreted differently by various writers and governments. In the United States, Congress, in setting the tax rates, determines what proportion of the tax burden should be borne by each income group, and in this particular case it has determined that the rates should be progressive. However, when fringe benefits appear in differing amounts for different income groups, this distorts the stated Congressional allocation of the tax budren. Furthermore, not all individuals within any income group receive any one fringe benefit or even the same total amount of fringe benefits, and so the allocation of the tax burden is changed even more.

Not only does this distort inter-group and intra-group equity but it may also be used to support arguments for further tax preference. It is not surprising, therefore, that Solomon Barkin of the Textile Workers Union of America (CIO) has called attention to the fact that "management of course receives its compensation in the form of salaries, bonuses, stock options, and a miscellaneous list of other awards in the form of expense allowances, life insurance, medical benefits, home facilities, discount privileges, educational advantages and delayed compensation." [65]   Meanwhile, corporate executives are arguing that they need benefits from employers to equalize their position with that "of small businessmen, of investors, and of inventors—who pay at only a 25 percent tax rate on their gains, with no income tax at all if they refrain from selling during their lives." [66] An additional twist to the same argument is the reluctance of one group of fringe receivers to object when another group presses for tax-preferred benefits.[67]

It was mentioned above that taxpayers may resist taxation when they feel that they are being taxed on fringe benefits which they strongly consider not to be income.   These same taxpayers again resist taxation just as actively, if not more actively, if they feel that they are being treated unfairly relative either to others in their own income class or to others in different income classes.   Such a feeling could arise if some are given tax-preferred fringe benefits while others are denied receipt of tax favor; the agitation for individual retirement plans is an example.   Practically all writers in public finance emphasize the importance of the taxpayer's feeling that he is being treated equitably, but perhaps Haig's comment is best.   "Certainly such changes in the abstract definition of income as are necessary to make the statute practical and workable must be accepted, provided the cost in terms of equity is not so great as to make some available alternative tax a more attractive method of raising revenue." [68]   Fringe benefits by themselves at present are hardly in danger of upsetting the income tax, but coupled with other chips off the tax base, the shift to other sources of revenue is not out of the realm of possibility.[69]

2. *Problems of Revenue, Tax Base, and Tax Rates*

The effect on the tax base of an exemption from that tax base has long been recognized although not usually publicized. When Gladstone was arguing against the continuance of exemption of Ireland from the income tax, he said,

Let me remind the committee what exemption means; it does not mean that we have got a bottomless purse, that we can dispense exemptions to one man without injuring another. No, sir. The exemption of one man means the extra taxation of another. . . .[70]

To the extent that fringe benefits constitute income and are exempt from taxation, the same warning would be applicable. Whenever there is a given amount of revenue to be raised, the elimination of some item or items from the tax base results in higher rates of taxation on the narrower tax base, and this can be the source of additional problems.

One of these problems concerns the height of the tax rate. The distinction between the marginal and average rates of tax is not often appreciated by the taxpayer. For example, while the marginal tax rate on $100,000 of taxable income was, under the laws applicable to the calendar year 1954, 87 percent, the effective, or average rate of tax, on the same amount going to an unmarried taxpayer was 67 percent.[71] In addition, the distinction between marginal rates and average rates as made in the Statistics of Income [72] is also often overlooked. In the above example, the $100,000 of reported income might have been composed of $60,000 wages and $40,000 capital gains. Here the $60,000 in wages would be subject to a maximum marginal tax rate of 75 percent; but in the computing the average tax rate, only one half the capital gains would be considered as income and taxed at the maximum tax rate of 50 percent, so that the tax of $44,320 on the $80,000 of income would give an average tax rate of only 55 percent.[73] Noted even less often is the distinction between marginal tax rate and the average rate of tax on total net income as described by Butters, Thompson, and Bollinger.[74] In the example just cited the marginal rate would remain unchanged, but the average rate on total income would be computed by dividing the actual tax by total dollar income, including full capital gains in this income. The average rate of tax in this case would be 44 percent.

Thus, if the same amount of tax revenue is raised before and after the advent of fringe benefits, and if the nontaxable fringe benefits are accompanied by a corresponding reduction in cash wages, both marginal and average rates on *taxable* income will be raised while the actual average rate of tax on *total* income will remain unchanged. However, fringe benefits are usually given as a form of salary increase rather than merely as a change in the form of salary paid. Consequently, tax rates are not usually raised when fringe benefits are granted, and so the higher tax rates predicted are not observed. Assuming unchanged revenue requirements, if wage increases were in the form of taxable income, tax rates could be lowered. It is relative to this situation that tax rates are high.

A second problem arises in connection with the inequities mentioned above. As tax rates either rise or remain higher than they otherwise would be, the unequal treatment of equals becomes more pronounced; the higher value of t increases values of y and makes tax-preferred benefits worth even more under the higher tax rates. In other words, as the marginal tax rates rise due to a narrowing of the tax base, each fringe benefit takes on a greater value when expressed as before-tax income. If everyone received fringe benefits so that his actual tax burden in dollars remained unchanged from what it would be if he had been given only cash income, this gain of a smaller tax base would be only apparent and not real, in view of the offsetting higher tax rates. But, more realistically, those receiving proportionally more fringe benefits than others would experience real gains while those receiving proportionally less would have real losses.

A third problem concerns the increased attempts at tax avoidance due to higher marginal rates. With a greater spread between y and n due to a higher t, there should be greater pressure on the part of employees to get any specific fringe benefit. Virtually all writers on the subject mention the disparity between tax rates on income and on fringe benefits as one of the causes of the growth of fringe benefits for highly paid employees. Tax shelter in the form of fringe benefits is only one of many possible avenues of avoidance which might be sought, but as searchers are successful, this will only accentuate the problem. As marginal tax rates rise, the efforts at tax avoidance are increased; as these efforts are successful, marginal tax rates must rise in order to yield a constant revenue. There is a tendency here toward an undesirable form of perpetual motion. In addition to encouraging attempts at tax avoidance, high tax rates might also be expected to promote tax evasion. Such an argument is frequently used with respect to the United States tax on spirits, and Adam Smith pointed out that injudicious taxes promote smuggling, so that penalties must rise proportionately with taxation.

A fourth effect of higher tax rates concerns net social surplus (consumers' surplus plus producers' surplus). To the extent that there is a shift toward new excise taxes and increases in existing excise taxes because of a narrowing of the income tax base, the loss in net social surplus will vary approximately with the square of the tax rate while revenue raised will vary slightly less than in proportion to the tax rate.[75]

A fifth effect which should be considered deals with the effect on incentives to work; this is sometimes referred to as the transformation effect. With regard to incentives to work, most taxes have two countervailing effects. When it is introduced, the tax will have the effect of reducing the taxpayer's disposable income, thus increasing the marginal utility of the remaining dollars. This is the income effect. It will tend to make the taxpayer increase his labor offered on the market, since the marginal utility of money to him has risen while the marginal disutility of work has presumably remained unchanged. At the same time most taxes will also have a marginal effect of reducing the proportion of the last dollar earned from which the taxpayer may benefit. This reduction in the utility he may command with the earnings of his marginal hour of work will tend to make him equate it with his marginal disutility from work at a lower number of hours where the marginal utility from the pay received would be higher and the marginal disutility from work would be lower. Thus, if the substitution of fringe benefits for money wages equally among all taxpayers resulted in higher tax rates on a narrower tax base, there would be an unchanged income effect, since total tax revenue is considered unchanged, but higher marginal rates and a stronger marginal effect; the result would presumably be a substitution of leisure for work. However, since it is not certain whether the income tax has led to an increase or a decline in leisure, compared with the effect of no income tax at all, this effect cannot be compared to the pre-income-tax situation but only to the pre-fringe-benefit situation.

If tax-free fringe benefits are offered not as a substitute for existing taxable wages, but as a form of increase in the rate of pay, then, assuming unchanged total tax revenue, the effect is the reverse of that described above. When, for example, pay increases are given in the form of tax-free fringe benefits, the marginal rate of taxation drops to zero while the income effect remains unchanged. The effect should be to promote more work and less leisure. For individuals in the higher tax brackets conditions appear to be particularly favorable for this effect. These taxpayers are subject to both high income effects and high marginal effects. But when the reward for greater effort or productivity is held out in the form of fringe benefits such as the use of company property, deferred compensation, stock options, widow's benefits, and the like, the marginal rate drops quite far: from a high marginal rate to a maximum 25 percent capital gains rate or to zero. What is left, then, is a relatively high income effect with a relatively, or even absolutely, low marginal rate. It is possible that this combination of high rates on much of the taxpayer's income, giving a high income effect, when coupled with greatly reduced marginal rates on additional increments of income has resulted in more work than would have occurred in the absence of an income tax.[76] Instead of justifying the usual conception that the income tax discourages incentive, the tax with fringe benefits may be partly responsible for overwork leading to the prevalence of ulcers and heart trouble among business executives.

An additional incentive effect has been pointed out by George Break.[77] When a deduction from the tax base is allowed for expenditures on goods that are essentially for personal consumption and are of a non-luxury nature, the incentive effect of the tax is reduced. For example, the employee must work to provide food and lodging and other necessities for himself and his family, but if these are provided tax free, the income effect of the tax is reduced. This indicates that under certain conditions particular fringe benefits may reduce incentives to work.

There will presumably be an increase in tax rates due to the need to maintain revenue while some income is exempt from tax; for those taxpayers who receive no fringe benefits or whose fringe benefits are an unchanging part of their income, marginal rates are raised. For those whose increases or decreases in income are partly or fully in the form of fringe benefits, marginal rates are lowered. The former case has some applicability to all taxpayers, while the latter takes on greater importance where fringe benefits vary greatly and tax brackets are high. Presumably the former would apply more to self-employed persons and wage and salaried workers, while the latter would have a greater effect on highly paid corporation officers.

3. Problems from the Use of Different Definitions

The above discussion has dealt with the federal taxation of income, but income also serves as the tax base for other taxes, such as those imposed by the Federal Insurance Contributions Act, Railroad Retirement Tax Act, Federal Unemployment Tax Act, numerous state and municipal income tax acts, and, for a few taxpayers, foreign income tax acts. Wage income is also important for the Fair Labor Standards Act. Since these taxes are levied under different laws, and since the role of fringe benefits as a constituent of wage income is subject to wide variations of opinion, the amount of wages subject to tax varies among taxing units. This leads to difficulties for both the taxpayer and the tax collector.

The taxpayer may encounter difficulty in having to compute two or more wage incomes subject to different taxes, although this burden will more than likely fall on his employer. An example may be taken from Mimeograph 5657 which notes that although the "convenience of the employer" test is used when determining whether meals and quarters are wages for income tax purposes, it is not relevant when computing income for Federal Insurance Contributions Act (OASI) and Federal Unemployment Tax Act (UI) purposes.[78] Even with meals and quarters included in wages, their valuation for unemployment insurance may vary from state to state. Thus in 1949 the California Employment Commission regulations called for housing to be valued at two thirds the market rental value and food at $1.15 per day with a provision for gearing the latter valuation to changes of 10 percent or more in the Consumers Price Index. At this same time New York had a minimum rate for room and board which was $7.75 a week, unchanged since 1941.[79]

The initial tax treatment of supplemental unemployment benefits, a form of guaranteed annual wage, illustrates the independent action that various taxing bodies may take. Soon after this fringe benefit was introduced, and before the federal government passed judgment on its taxability, the city attorney of Columbus, Ohio, ruled that supplemental unemployment benefit payments would be subject to the City's $\frac{1}{2}$ percent income tax. This ruling was made even though pensions, disability benefits, annuities, and gratuities were exempt from the Columbus tax.[80] The Internal Revenue Service reached the same conclusion for certain types of supplemental unemployment benefit plans, so that citizens of Columbus are relieved of considering this fringe benefit two different ways. But the same Internal Revenue Service ruling held that benefit payments under these plans were not wages under old-age and survivors insurance, unemployment insurance, or withholding provisions.[81]

Besides creating confusion and extra work on the part of the taxpayer, differences in treatment should promote pressure for a most-favorable-tax-collector principle, whereby the taxpayer would urge different collection units to bestow upon his income the treatment accorded it by the tax collection unit giving it the most favorable tax treatment. In the operation of this principle it is probable that the federal government would exercise more influence over state governments than vice versa.[82]   If the federal government bestows favorable tax treatment on a fringe benefit, the entire body of taxpayers in a state will become aware of this and doubtless will press for similar treatment by the state.   If, however, a state gives the more favorable treatment, only a fraction of the national population may be aware of it and so pressure should be less.   But governmental units which are adjacent to one another or which have similar patterns of income receipts should be influenced by each other in their tax treatment of fringe benefits.

The fact that the treatment of meals and lodging under the tax giving them the most favorable treatment, the federal income tax, has not spread to other tax collecting bodies, such as old-age and survivors insurance and unemployment insurance, is possibly explained by the fact that benefits under these two laws are tied directly to wages earned and taxes paid, while benefits from the federal income tax are not.   Thus, where there is a benefit tied to taxes paid, this pressure for the same treatment as given by the most favorable tax collection unit does not seem to be so strong.   A different situation might exist under the Fair Labor Standards Act where, for those receiving less than the minimum wage in cash, if fringe benefits are not counted as wages, the cash wage must be raised to reach the minimum wage.   Here exclusion of fringe benefits from income would benefit these workers, but this exclusion would hurt those workers who are paid for overtime on the basis of some multiple of their regular wage rate.[83]

Not only domestic but also international dissimilarities in the definition of income due to fringe benefits can cause taxpayers trouble.   Citizens of the United States living in Japan have encountered this problem because many fringe benefits, including the services of geisha girls, are supplied by Japanese employers and these are not considered as income.   Consequently, some Japanese executives pay less income tax than some non-Japanese clerical workers.[84]

While differences in the treatment of fringe benefits probably put the heaviest burden on taxpayers and their employers, they also impose a burden on the tax collecting agencies. These differences in treatment mean that tax collecting agencies cannot readily compare their figures with those of other collecting agencies. Conformity in definitions and procedure would also encourage the existing tendency toward increasing use of machines for administrative and statistical work. Mechanization here can release resources to handle problems where conformity is not so easily established.

The above problems arising from different definitions of wages used by different taxing bodies call for a common definition of wages but plead for no particular definition. However, in choosing a definition, consideration should be given to the problems in the field of public finance which are discussed in this chapter. Other considerations should deal with how fringe benefits affect the functioning of the present-day economy and these will be discussed in the next chapter.

· III ·

Economic Effects of
Present Tax Treatment

A. GOAL OF A LACK OF EFFECT

WHEN a tax or tax system is instituted to raise revenue, one of the attributes commonly sought is a lack of interference with the normal functioning of the economic system. Yet this goal is seldom, if ever, achieved, and so the discussion of almost any tax must include as one of its facets the economic effects of the tax. Economic effects will follow not only from the imposition of a tax but also from any exemption from the tax, which is an indirect or hidden subsidy in the same sense that exemption of domestic products from the burden of a tariff constitutes a subsidy to the exempt producer. To the extent that fringe benefits are considered as income and their exemption from taxation is allowed, they are proper matter for examination in this light.

Such an examination could extend to many phases of the operation of the economy, but it seems desirable to limit the investigation to those fields where the effect on economic activity seems to be greatest. The list of effects to be investigated would probably vary with each writer, but the following list includes some phases of the operation of the economy which have been or might be greatly affected by the tax preference granted to fringe benefits: allocation of resources, mobility of labor, and cyclical stability.

B. EFFECTS ON ALLOCATION OF RESOURCES

1. Cause of a Change in Allocation: Presence of Tax Saving

An employee who has performed his duties may be paid for his labor either in money or in goods and services. If there is no tax benefit attached to payment in goods and services, or if there are no economies from the employer's purchasing them in large quantities and undertaking distribution himself, the employee would be expected to ask for payment in money or perhaps in those goods which he was planning to purchase with his money wage. Should the employee be offered a good which cost the same as one of the goods that he was planning to buy, but which had a lower marginal utility, he would refuse this substitute good and hold out for either the money or the good to which he attached a higher value. Under these conditions the same goods would be consumed whether the employee were paid in cash or in goods and services; the allocation of resources would be unaffected by payment in goods and services.

However, in some cases when payment is made in goods and services a tax saving is possible. This tax saving, being predicated upon payment in these goods rather than in money, encourages the consumption of these goods so long as the reduction in utility from consuming these rather than other goods does not exceed the increase in utility available from using the tax saving to purchase additional quantities of these or other goods and services. Under these circumstances it is easy to see that economic goods with a marginal utility per dollar spent lower than that being obtained from other goods being bought voluntarily in the market may nevertheless be consumed because they are accompanied by a tax saving which reduces the cost per unit of product consumed. The size of the tax saving will influence the willingness to accept for use goods which would not otherwise have been consumed or consumed in such quantities, and the size of this saving is primarily dependent on the tax bracket of the recipient of the fringe benefit. Under the present federal income tax this saving ranges in value from 25 percent of the tax-free fringe benefit for taxpayers in the lowest income tax bracket to just over 1,000 percent for taxpayers in the highest tax bracket. From this it can be seen that the effect on the allocation of resources is potentially large, and the larger the saving achieved by the use of a fringe benefit, the larger the total effect of allocation.

2. *Distribution of the Gain*

Although it can be established that there is a tax saving to be had, the effect on the allocation of resources will depend to some extent on who gets this gain.   To illustrate the problem, assume that an employee spends $1.00 a day for lunch for 20 days during the month or $20.00 in a month.   Assume also that this employee is in the 20 percent marginal bracket, the lowest tax bracket, so that in order to have $20.00 after tax, he would have to have income of $25.00.   If the employer subsequently is considering a raise of $25.00 per month per worker, he may realize that benefits equivalent to the $25.00 income can be had for $20.00 if they are tax free and so he might offer free lunches on the premises rather than the money wage increase.   Since these two alternatives lie on the same indifference curve for the worker, they would be equally desirable to him.   In this way the employer could pay for the presumed increase in marginal productivity of $25.00 with an outlay of $20.00 on food rather than by an additional $25.00 outlay in cash; in this case the gain would accrue to the employer.   On the other hand, the worker might realize that the employer would be willing to pay more than the cost of the free lunches and so might secure an additional $5.00 wage increase.

The size of the gain above is determinable, although it will differ for workers in different marginal tax brackets, but the distribution of the gain is much less certain.   The level of wage rates under collective bargaining is theoretically indeterminate, and the introduction of tax-preferred fringe benefits merely adds an additional element of uncertainty to this area of bargaining.   Analyzing the case by considering it an example of bilateral monopoly is another way of trying to reach a conclusion about the division of the spoils, but this also gives a solution of indeterminacy.

In attempting to determine the distribution of the gain from tax saving, there is one factor that appears to be of particular importance in the case of fringe benefits.   This is the tendency for fringe benefits to be granted where pressure is greatest and then to spread to areas where pressure is less. The pressure is greatest where the tax saving is greatest, and this is where fringe benefits have been more readily granted.[1] But the granting of fringe benefits to one group of employees makes it difficult for employers to refuse fringe benefits to other employees. And if the employees in the higher marginal tax brackets secure most of the tax saving for themselves, then the recipients of fringe benefits in lower tax brackets will be in a stronger bargaining position to receive the gain.

3. Effects If the Gain Goes to the Employee

So far the attempt has been made to show that compensation through tax-preferred fringe benefits gives rise to a tax saving, that this gain will go to employees and/or employers, and that the proportion going to each is indeterminate. Assuming, however, that some portion or all of the gain does go to employees, how will this affect the allocation of resources?

The first result will be that more of the good offered as a fringe benefit will be produced and consumed. This will stem from two causes. First, employees may have been consuming certain amounts of the good before its being granted as a fringe benefit. Human beings differing as they do, it is likely that the amounts consumed would vary among these employees. With the granting of the fringe benefit some will likely receive more than they purchased before and some less. For those who receive less, there is no particular problem; they reduce their private purchases by the amount of the fringe benefit and continue to purchase enough to leave their consumption unchanged.[2] Those who are given more may completely abandon private purchases of the good and still be left with an increased amount of the good. Under these conditions, if the fringe benefit given to each employee is greater in quantity or quality than the smallest amount consumed by any employee, the consumption of the good will have increased.

The assumption that the gain goes to the employee furnishes a second, but less important, reason for increased consumption of the fringe benefit good. As the tax saving makes it possible for the employee to consume more goods, one of the goods he may choose may be the fringe benefit good.   These two forces, then, encourage a changed allocation of resources.

The increase in consumption referred to could be an increase in either the quantity or the quality of the product consumed. Both increases seem to be taking place.   The extent to which increased consumption of a good is due to its being granted as a fringe benefit is difficult to measure.   Rough indications may be gathered from the growth of pension and health insurance plans since the early 1940s, when wage controls and favorable tax rulings encouraged their increased use as fringe benefits. A more recent example of limited size is the growth of major medical insurance; during 1955 group coverage increased by 152 percent while individual policy coverage increased by only 58 percent.[3]   Part of the group increase could be due to group rates being lower.

Indications that consumption is being upgraded in quality may be gathered from an estimate published in *Life* that in large cities like New York, Chicago, and Washington, at any moment over one half the people in the best hotels, night clubs, and restaurants are paying for the services they receive via the expense account.[4]   This is reinforced by an interview with a Seattle restaurateur, Peter Canlis, who stated that he opened an expensive restaurant since there was so much expense account money not being spent "because there was no place fancy enough to gobble it up—and I was happy to fill the gap."[5]   A comparison of the employee's spending habits when using his income with his spending habits when using the company's expense account also shows increased consumption through quality upgrading.   A further evidence of increased consumption may be taken from the fringe benefits offered by the Prudential Life Insurance Company's Houston, Texas, office.   *Life* reports that "the company piled on 'fringe' benefits—not only the usual life insurance and medical checkups, but such unprecedented luxuries as a free swimming pool, free books, free lunches, free tennis courts—in surroundings suggestive of spacious and graceful living."[6]   The reference here to "luxuries"

indicates that these are goods which would not have been consumed had they not been given as fringe benefits.

A second effect on the allocation of resources would be that
employees would tend to go into those industries granting tax-
preferred fringe benefits. Rather than wages being equated
for similar workers, after-tax wages would be equated; and
since cash wages would be subject to tax, while wages in the
form of fringe benefits would not, the marginal productivity of
workers in industries or firms paying cash wages would necessarily be higher. This new equating of after-tax wages would
result in a shift of workers relative to the situation where
pre-tax wages and marginal productivities were equal.

One of the reasons cited for not taxing fringe benefits is that
rather than being wages they are "a means of promoting the
health, good will, contentment, or efficiency of . . . employees." [7]
Wages, too, however, are meant to perform some of these func-
tions. To what extent fringe benefits have actually led to a
shift of workers is difficult to measure. However, there are
some interesting cases concerning the relationship between
fringe benefits and employment. The National Industrial
Conference Board, in discussing cooperative medical programs
as a form of fringe benefit, points out that "nurses are often
more interested in industrial employment than in hospital
nursing, because they have better and more regular hours and
are eligible for the fringe benefits granted other workers." [8]
And the Prudential Insurance Company's Houston office, after
instituting new fringe benefits, reported that no positions were
open; this despite the fact that one of their employees, Oveta
Smith, supposedly typical, had turned down a job with another
insurance company at $180 a month to take a job with Pruden-
tial at $140 a month.[9] Another story, which does not claim to
be typical, tells of a young deputy sheriff who enjoyed his work
enough to work long hours for rather low pay, but when tax
exemption of his $5.00 a day subsistence allowance was taken
away, in effect reducing his salary by about $30.00 a month, he
quit.[10] Against these examples may be cited Reynolds' survey
of workers in a New England town, where he found that work-

ers did not mention fringe benefits as one of the factors attracting them to new jobs and holding them there.[11] These examples will neither substantiate nor refute the hypothesis without more information,[12] but a worker who is aware of the alternatives might be expected to choose the job which would offer him more after-tax income.

4. Effects If the Gain Goes to the Employer

The effects just discussed are those which presumably will follow if some or all of the tax saving is passed on to the employee. To the extent that the employer is the beneficiary, slightly different effects may be expected. First, it is probable that more of the goods and services being given as fringe benefits will be produced than would have been produced without the giving of fringe benefits, but the increase should be smaller than when the gain went to the employee. When the gain went to the employee, the employer not only replaced a part of the employee's after-tax wage with the fringe benefit but also passed on the gain to the employee, possibly in the form of an increased purchase of the fringe benefit. Under the assumption that the employer retains the gain, only an amount equal to the given portion of the employee's after-tax wage is put into the fringe benefit. However, even this, it has been pointed out, will lead to increased employee consumption of the fringe benefit good if any employee had not been consuming as much of the good as was given him as a fringe benefit.

If the gain accrues to the employer, there are two additional possibilities of altering the allocation of resources. If entry into the industry is difficult, then the gain will remain with the employer and will evidence itself in increased consumption of goods of his choosing, presumably those with a relatively high income elasticity of demand. If, on the other hand, entry into the industry is not difficult, the presence of increased economic profits should attract other entrepreneurs. This rightward-shifted supply curve will give an equilibrium at a larger output and a lower price. In this case some of the gain will be passed on to consumers of the product of the industry giving fringe benefits.

Besides the tax saving from nontaxation of fringe benefits there is another source of saving that is usually considered as going to the employer. This arises from the fact that if fringe benefits are not income to the employee for federal income tax purposes, neither, usually, are they income subject to old-age and survivors insurance tax, unemployment insurance tax, workmen's compensation tax, or similar taxes based on wage income. Similarly, in the case of overtime work, fringe benefits may remain a constant amount per hour or, in some cases, may be reduced to zero. Pension plans may be used to illustrate this point. Some plans call for a contribution of a certain percent of total wages by the employer; here the fringe benefit would be one and one-half times as great for overtime. Some plans call for a contribution of so much per hour worked; here the fringe benefit would be unchanged for overtime. Some plans call for a fixed amount of payment and some for a fixed percentage of the weekly straight-time payroll; here the fringe benefit drops to zero for overtime.[13] These savings are, however, like those from preferred income tax treatment and may or may not, through the workings of competition, accrue to the employer. Other possible eventual recipients are employees of the firm giving fringe benefits and consumers of the firm's output.

5. Loss in Utility from Use of Fringe Benefits

It has been pointed out that the presence of tax-free fringe benefits is likely to lead to a changed pattern of production and consumption from that which would exist if workers were paid only in taxable cash. This alteration stems from two causes: (1) some workers will probably be given more of the fringe benefit than they would voluntarily have purchased, and (2) a net tax saving may accrue to employer, employee, or certain consumers.

This changed allocation has been viewed in different lights.

Some observers of the scene conclude that this shift is on balance desirable. The Associated Industries of Massachusetts expresses pride that Massachusetts industry is a leader in the granting of liberal fringe benefits. "While this [liberality] may cost several hundreds of millions of dollars, it brings with it worker satisfaction and employment stabilization that are well nigh invaluable." [14] Or again, "The conclusion is ineluctable that whatever may have been or may be the means, the ends obtained [from getting management to give and workers to accept fringe benefits] have been most desirable." [15] But some others, notably economists, have arrived at different conclusions. They have implicitly recognized a shift in resources by proposing that wage payments in kind be taxed at less than full market value because often these goods are not what the employee would voluntarily have chosen.[16]

If there is this change in the allocation of resources, is there any criterion of resource allocation which may be used for comparison? If competitive conditions are assumed, the price of a good will equal its marginal cost of production or the sum of marginal returns to factors of production just sufficient to overcome their marginal disutilities or opportunity costs in producing this unit of output. At the same time this price will represent the marginal worth of the good to the purchaser, or its ability to create additional utility when used by the purchaser. In money terms, then, the disutility due to production and the utility stemming from consumption of the marginal unit of the good are equal.[17] Any time, then, that the recipient of a good values the good at less than its market price, the equality between marginal utility and disutility in money terms is violated.

The above discussion deals with the allocation problem for society as a whole; but each individual is also faced with an allocation problem in the maximization of his individual welfare. Since in this case there is not the problem of interpersonal comparisons, the conclusions reached are on a higher level of precision. In this case the individual's welfare will be maximized if the ratio of the marginal utility from each different item purchased to the price of the item is the same. In the case of an individual's being given a fringe benefit where this ratio of the marginal utility he received from the additional units of the fringe benefit to the cost of the good to the employer is below the constant established by his free market purchases, his welfare is less than the maximum which could be obtained by paying him in cash and allowing him to allocate his income among purchases of his own choosing.[18]

It is desirable next to determine in what ways this constant ratio is altered when the employee receives fringe benefits. Although the implication so far has been that the ratio is lowered, it is possible that the fringe benefit might bring more utility per dollar spent than would a good which was freely purchased from money income. This occurs in cases where there are economies to be achieved from mass purchases, as seems to be true in the case of group insurance. Here more product can be bought with a given dollar outlay if it is purchased in group form; and if the product is one that employees would have purchased anyway, then total utility will be increased.[19] Another source of increased utility could arise if the fringe benefit were a good that was produced under conditions of decreasing costs and the rate of this decrease in costs was more rapid than the rate of decline in the marginal utility of the good to the employee; but these conditions appear too restrictive to be of any practical importance.

Consequently, it is possible that the granting of fringe benefits can result in a higher marginal utility per dollar spent and so an increase in total utility, but this is not to be expected as a general rule. The more normal relationship would be the case where the fringe benefit has a smaller value to the recipient than the amount of money representing the cost. Barring the above case of more efficient purchases by the employer, the employee will follow the principle stated above of increasing his purchases of a good so long as the marginal utility per dollar spent is greater from this good than from other goods. If the employer now provides the employee with some of this good, these additional units will bring a smaller marginal utility per dollar spent on them unless the worker can reduce his purchases to the point where his total consumption of the good is unchanged in quantity and quality. If either the quantity or the quality of the fringe benefit is above that which the employee would have selected, there is necessarily a violation of the principle leading to maximization of individual utility. Under these assumptions, then, it becomes impossible for the use of fringe benefits to improve on the allocation of resources by increasing the welfare of the individual from given resources, but there is a distinct possibility of a reduction in his welfare. Note that this statement does not mean that employees cannot gain from the introduction of tax-preferred fringe benefits; that they can gain has been indicated by pointing out the tax saving available, the possibility of its accruing to the employee, and the possibility that offsetting tax increases may fall on someone else. The statement says, rather, that, lacking economies of mass purchasing and a shifting of the tax burden, dollars spent on fringe benefits cannot bring more utility to workers than dollars freely spent from money wages, but they can bring less utility.[20]

The above results are derived from a priori reasoning and not from employee expressions on the subject. In fact, statements on the value of fringe benefits to employees run the entire range from "invaluable" to words meaning that they are not appreciated. While there are a few scattered statements of employee opinion and a few opinions expressed by observers of the scene, there seems to have been no systematic investigation of the relationship between the cost of fringe benefits and their worth to the worker.

The National Industrial Conference Board reports that occasionally when employers have informed employees of fringe benefits in terms of additional earnings, employees have stated that they prefer the money to the fringe benefit.[21] Even among unions there seems to be a difference of opinion as to the desirability of fringe benefits versus cash wages. Dearing has observed that "in contrast to the CIO most AFL affiliates have chosen to use their bargaining power to obtain direct pay increases rather than pensions and other fringe benefits." [22] This difference may be noted by comparing the handbooks on pension plans published by two different labor organizations. One, published by the United Automobile Workers (UAW-CIO), to inform members of the union program, emphasizes that it is the responsibility of management to provide workers' security programs. It is nowhere mentioned that the plan is an alternative to a wage increase.[23] The other booklet, published by the American Federation of Labor, stresses that the choice is between cash wages and pensions and that the latter should be chosen only after existing wage levels and the need for pensions have been considered.[24]

One investigation, confined to the Greater Boston area, concluded that, although worker ideas on fringe benefits vary with age, sex, neighborhood, and other factors, in general wage earners would take a wage increase over fringe benefits. However, labor leaders have decided for rank and file workers in the choice of fringe benefits and have encouraged their acceptance by offering negotiated contracts including fringe benefits for worker approval. Thus workers are usually confronted with a choice not between fringe benefits and cash but between approval and disapproval of the contract.[25]

The disparity between the cost of a fringe benefit and its worth to the employee leads to the problem of what value to assign to the fringe benefit if and when it is included in the tax base. When the disparity has been noted, it has universally been in the case where the fringe benefit had a value to the recipient lower than cost.

Due argues that in taxing income in kind, the worth of the good to the income recipient should be considered, because to the recipient the good may be worth less than its cost. He cites the *Flugeladjutant* as an example.[26] Vickrey takes cognizance of this argument and comments that "lack of free choice may be a reason for valuing the services or commodity at something less than what the ordinary consumer would have to pay for the item in a market where he would have the advantage of free choice, but hardly for excluding the item altogether." [27] Guttentag *et al.* choose a discounted market value for inclusion because cost is not a good measure of the value of the benefit to the employee.[28]

The court has at times adopted the same philosophy but to a more extreme degree. When the court held that housing furnished a Major Jones and money given to him for housing during an assignment in Washington did not constitute income, it cited the British case of Tennant v. Smith, where a bank clerk who lived in the bank building as an employee of the bank was held to have received no income in kind in the form of housing. It was pointed out that "it is not . . . what is paid out but what comes in that constitutes income." [29]

This treatment of fringe benefits appears from the above statements to rest primarily on the desire to treat the fringe benefit recipient in a fair and just manner. If he places little value on the benefit, then it follows that little tax should be imposed. But this treatment creates other difficulties which may more than offset this particular advantage.

The use of fringe benefits is encouraged by giving them tax preference in taxing them at some value lower than cost or market value. The increased use of fringe benefits, in turn, gives rise to the change in the allocation of resources described above. There are, however, additional shifts in the allocation of resources due to the increased use of fringe benefits. One allocational effect frequently overlooked is that besides the out-of-pocket cost of fringe benefits, there are often additional costs in calculating costs, planning coverage, collecting contributions of employees, bookkeeping, rent of space furnished, review of programs, and related matters. Such cost increases may escape notice, while disputes arising over coverage may decrease the eventual utility derived.[30] A third change in the allocation of resources stems from the effect of fringe benefits on the relationship between tax collectors, taxpayers, and tax pleaders. Blum points out that special provisions complicate the job of the tax collector and encourage the use of more tax advisers who may become special pleaders for taxpayers and thereby lose sight of the system as an entity.[31]

The above-mentioned tax preference proposed for fringe benefits can be traced to earlier discussions of the concept of income. Haig raises the question in the case of a man who receives a dollar and spends it on a dinner. "Is his income the dollar, or is it the dinner which he buys with the dollar, or is it, at bottom, the satisfaction of his wants which he derives from eating the dinner . . .?" [32] In the subsequent discussion he concludes that although it is the satisfactions or "usances" which are income in the economic sense, for the purpose of taxation they are significant only when they can be evaluated in money and that goods received should be evaluated in money terms and included in income—presumably at market value.[33] Professor Hewett poses the same question in attempting to arrive at a definition of income [34] and concludes that "real income must be expressed in money according to market prices." [35]

These statements of Haig and Hewett seem to argue that a tax on income should be levied on the money value of the good received even though the recipient or user of the good in question may get more or less benefit from the good than might be expected from considering only its market price. The application of this principle to the taxation of fringe benefits would call for taxation of these benefits at their market value or cost. Such a policy would remove one of the principal causes of fringe benefits' being given when the employee does not value the benefits as highly as the market, and a reduction in this class of fringe benefits should reduce the misallocation of resources as described above. The effect of taxation at market value on the expenses connected with assessing and accounting for fringe benefits is indeterminate; they might be reduced if the number or extent of coverage of fringe benefits is reduced as a result of taxation, but they might be increased from the necessity of keeping records of the receipts of fringe benefits by individual workers. At any rate these administrative costs should not be an important fraction of total costs. As for eliminating disputes between taxpayers and tax collectors, the removal of fringe benefits from a tax-preferred status is not likely to prove effective.   What is more likely to occur is that the battle will continue to be waged along battlelines drawn in a different location.   The distinction between conditions of work as non-income, business expenses, and rewards for work as taxable income would still be a no man's land, but in a different locality.   Although one side might have taken over certain territory, the battle would doubtless continue.

It is probable that the principal argument to be raised against such treatment would be that the employee was being over-taxed on a good which had little value to him.   If, however, the employer is furnishing this good for the purpose of promoting the health, good will, and efficiency of his employees or to better their lot in some other way, then an alternative to the fringe benefit should be available to the employee in the form of cash equivalent to the cost of the fringe benefit to the employer.   If employees felt that taxation based on the market value of the fringe benefit was unjust because the fringe benefit had little value to them, they could exert pressure for payment in cash instead.   It is possible that the employee might complain that he is worse off receiving fully taxable cash than he was when receiving a tax-preferred fringe benefit, but this would merely indicate that he was previously enjoying a tax saving either through undervaluation or through lower tax rates, presumably at the expense of some other taxpayer.   A system of taxation at full valuation would put him on the same basis of taxation as other taxpayers.

The effect of taxation based on cost or market value should be to give the employee a greater awareness of expenditures made by the employer to increase his welfare, and it should give him more incentive to express himself in the choice of fringe benefits.   Both of these features should bring the employee closer to achieving maximum welfare from given resources by encouraging the equating of the marginal utility derived, measured in money terms, to the price of the goods, thus bettering the allocation of resources.

The preceding discussion of the effect of fringe benefits on the allocation of resources has sought an optimal allocation under the income tax and has not considered how the tax itself may have altered the allocation of resources. Ideally, the tax should not affect this allocation; the goal, then, should be to see that the use of no single resource or method of production is favored over another. Thus production would continue after the tax as before. Vickrey, however, indicates that all is not well. He points out that one of the reasons usually offered for excluding payment in kind from the income tax base is that it is sometimes special compensation for unusually arduous or distasteful working conditions, and he comments that this reason is valid.[36]

If wages received by an employee represented only a net increase in utility for him, the money received could correctly be called his income, and a tax on all such incomes would not cause a shift in the use of labor. But wages are not given only as a net addition to utility; they are also given to overcome the disutilities associated with work. Thus we may say that the supply curve of labor for a particular industry and the size of an employee's wage are influenced by two factors: the disutility connected with a particular job and the net utility available in other jobs held by workers of similar ability. Under these assumptions, workers would try to maximize their net utilities (the wage minus the amount necessary to offset the disutility connected with a particular job) rather than their total wage. And under competitive conditions, workers with similar abilities and likes and dislikes would find themselves not drawing equal wages but receiving wages which give equal net utilities. In this way the employee engaged in a particularly unpleasant job would draw a higher wage than a similar worker engaged in a less distasteful occupation.

Under the income tax it is the total revenue which is taxed, and, in view of the situation just described, the tax on total revenue can lead to a shift in the use of resources. To illustrate the point, assume two occupations, A and B. Occupation A is highly unpleasant, so that the weekly pay for this job is $80.00 of which $30.00 is required to offset the unpleasant conditions of work. Occupation B, on the other hand, takes place in what society and employees consider pleasant working conditions, and so only a $50.00 wage is required to attract and hold workers in this field.   In both occupations the price of the product is such as to overcome particular unpleasant conditions associated with the production of the good and still give a net return equivalent to that in other fields; thus the wages in the two occupations will differ, but the net utilities accruing to the similar workers in both occupations will be the same. The marginal utilities and disutilities associated with each occupation will be measured in money terms.   Net utility for each worker will be maximized, and for similar workers it will be equal.   This is a component part of the system which, abstracting from the problem of interpersonal comparisons, gives the optimal utilization of resources.

The above assumption will give a certain pattern of production and consumption if there is no income tax.   However, when the income tax is introduced, there will be a shift in this pattern.   Since the total income of the individual is taxed, the tax will fall on monies given to overcome disutilities as well as to provide net utilities.

If the figures above are used and coupled with an average rate of tax of 40 percent, the results can be observed.   The worker in occupation A with $80.00 income will pay a tax of $32.00, which will leave him $48.00.   The disutility connected with this particular type of work he values at $30.00, so that his net gain in utility is only $18.00.   His companion of similar nature who works in business B is drawing only $50.00 and so pays $20.00 tax, leaving him $30.00 against which no disutility is set, and so this figure represents a net gain in utility to him.   It is now possible for workers in occupation A to obtain an increase in welfare after tax by shifting to occupation B until once again the two occupations offer similar net utilities to similar workers.   The situation is similar to that which would exist if the income taxes on business were levied on gross income rather than net income.

The income tax can thus be seen as causing a shift in resources away from those occupations where higher wages are offered to offset unpleasant attributes of the particular job. In this case tax-preferred fringe benefits offer a potential remedy. If certain fringe benefits are offered to overcome or offset particular difficulties or unpleasant conditions inherent in a particular type of work and if they are given tax-free treatment, the overtaxation of earnings in that occupation would be mitigated or offset. Some examples might be: frequent medical examinations given employees working where there is a danger from lead poisoning, radiation, silicosis, or other occupational diseases; housing provided employees who are required to work where rental housing is economically unrealistic, as in logging camps and on merchant ships; free meals given where the employee is subject to call to duty at any moment and is frequently called for this duty, as in the case of hospital interns.

The lack of reliable forms of measurement and units of measurement makes this principle difficult to apply. Presumably there are jobs with all degrees of unpleasantness available for workers with given abilities and these could be arranged in a continuous scale from unpleasant to pleasant. To arrange for tax-preferred fringe benefits to differ in quantity or quality with each job would be an impossibility. Consequently, the application of this principle should be confined to those cases where disutilities connected with the work are universally agreed on as being greater than normal and where this opinion is supported by wage payments which are noticeably higher than payments to workers with similar abilities in other jobs.

If all workers were alike and there were no fringe benefits offsetting the more unpleasant conditions in certain occupations, then the wages in those occupations would be higher than wages in more pleasant jobs. But if workers, rather than having similar likes, are different in their likes and dislikes, then some workers will find not so distasteful the jobs which others consider unpleasant and so will accept employment there at a lower wage. This would tend to work toward an equalization of the money value of disutilities connected with each occupation and therefore an equalization of wages; in such a case the income tax would not operate to alter the allocation of labor among occupations. The utilization, then, of fringe benefits to offset certain unpleasant working conditions would lead to a different use of labor from that which would have resulted under no income tax in that the conditions which are considered unpleasant to some are not classified as unpleasant by other workers.

If there is a possibility of conditions associated with certain occupations being considered by some as unpleasant but by others as neutral or even pleasant, then, as far as allocation of resources goes, fringe benefits designed to offset these conditions should not be granted tax-preferred status. But where conditions are considered by all as being unpleasant, fringe benefits designed to offset these could be allowed a tax-preferred status without working against the optimal allocation of resources assumed under a competitive system.

It is from these considerations that the term "conditions of work" should take on added clarity. Those conditions of pleasantness or lack of unpleasantness which are expected by all workers could be classified as conditions of work, so that in any business where they are absent fringe benefits designed to offset their absence could be tax preferred. Workers today expect, among other things, conditions of adequate heat, light, water, and rest room facilities. In addition to being rather universally desired, these goods seem to be desired in about the same quantity and quality by all workers. They are consumed collectively, consumed on the premises of the employer, and have a low marginal cost for additional workers. The list of conditions of work is flexible, and doubtless the attributes of a condition of work will change, too. But for the present the above considerations may be used as guideposts.

6. Effect on a Money Economy vs. a Barter Economy

One last factor worthy of consideration is that the granting of fringe benefits to employees constitutes a movement toward a barter economy. The disadvantages of a barter type of organization with its narrowing of the market are well known. When services are purchased with goods and other services, as is done when workers are paid in fringe benefits, rather than with money, this is a form of barter. The Japanese, who have a custom of including many fringe benefits in their wages, have sought to discourage payment in the form of fringe benefits through article 24 of their 1947 labor standards law which states that "wages must be paid in cash and in full [except where] otherwise provided for by law or order or labor agreement." [37] Yane notes that non-cash income has undergone a sharp drop since this law was passed in 1947, although these payments are still considered significant.[38]

Professor Ratchford has commented that the trend toward the use of fringe benefits as a form of compensation is the reverse of that which took place after the feudal period. Increasing amounts of tax-preferred fringe benefits and concomitant higher tax rates on money income have led him to comment, "Perhaps the time will come when the individual unfortunate enough to receive all his wages in money will have an impossible tax burden." [39]

C. EFFECTS ON THE MOBILITY OF LABOR

One of the assumptions usually made in economic analysis is that labor is completely mobile and is therefore free and willing to move to a new job whenever rewards will be greater. When this assumption is fulfilled, along with the other assumptions of the competitive system, output will be maximized. Whenever mobility of labor is less than perfect, the net product is reduced and output is not maximized. Consequently, factors which restrict the mobility of labor are, from the standpoint of output maximization, not desirable. That fringe benefits have affected the mobility of labor has been noted by several writers; in what way and to what extent should be examined.

Ordinarily it might be expected that most fringe benefits would not exercise a great influence on the mobility of labor. If there are several industries competing for workers and offering equal wages and one industry then offers, in addition to its regular wages, fringe benefits, this industry can be expected to attract workers. If other industries meet this competition for workers and offer similar fringe benefits, then the competitive advantage of the first industry disappears. The effect is no different from that which would follow from competition for workers by means of higher wages.

But not all fringe benefits are as neutral as this. Some benefits are "earned" over a period of time and then paid at the end of that period; furthermore, unless certain conditions are met, one of which may be continued employment with the firm, a reduction may be made in the amount to be paid. This reduction may be so great as to eliminate entirely the prospective payment. There are several fringe benefits which have this deferred, contingent compensation aspect; these are fringe benefits which reduce the mobility of labor. Examples would include non-vested pension plans, annuities, life insurance, widow's benefits, deferred compensation, profit-sharing plans, and stock options.

Most of the other fringe benefits are neutral in their effect on mobility of labor, provided they are offered by all firms and provided receipt is not contingent on continued employment in the future. But there is at least one tax-preferred fringe benefit which encourages, or reduces the cost of, mobility. This is the moving allowance or the actual moving of the new employee's family and belongings to the new place of employment.

In a competitive economy without the income tax a worker would change his job if the new wage gave a net utility at least as great as his former job plus a surplus, the present value of which was sufficient to overcome the costs of moving himself, his family, and his belongings to the new place of work. If, now, the income tax is added to the picture and these moving expenses are considered to be personal expenses and therefore not deductible, which corresponds to their present tax treatment,[40] the difference between the old and new wage must be sufficient to pay not only the moving expense but also the income tax on the money for moving.

If, instead of attracting employees to new jobs with higher wages which are subject to tax, the appeal were made in the form of slightly higher wages plus paid moving expenses which were exempt from tax, mobility could be expected to return to its pre-tax higher level. A given amount of money expended in this particular way would exert a greater influence in attracting workers than when given as taxable cash wages.[41] This is actually a more specific example of the general case concerning disutilities connected with different jobs as discussed above. One of the disutilities which may be encountered by workers seeking work is the necessity of moving. If this meets with the criterion set forth, that it is regarded by practically all workers as being a disutility, then allowing it to be offset by a tax-free fringe benefit will improve the allocation of resources—in this case, the allocation of labor.

The discussion of moving expenses has dealt with the horizontal mobility of workers, but a discussion of mobility should also include vertical mobility or the ability of a worker to advance to jobs with higher productivity and higher rewards. This advancement depends on several factors, not the least important of which is education. Education granted as a tax-preferred fringe benefit will operate as a stimulus to vertical mobility. With that tax preference education would be encouraged relative to its present status under the income tax where it is considered as a personal expense and is not deductible. Whether it would be encouraged relative to its pre-income-tax status depends on the attitude of the taxpayer toward his education. If he sees it as a consumption good designed to increase his happiness, the present income tax treatment is correct and tax-preference would encourage the use of this consumption good relative to other consumption goods. If, on the other hand, the education is considered a business expense of time and money which will produce increased future earnings whose discounted present value exceeds present costs, then the income tax has hindered this expenditure and a tax-free fringe benefit in the form of education would help offset this hindrance. Actually, most education is undertaken for both the reasons cited above, and this is probably true even for that offered as a fringe benefit. What can be said, however, is, that with the granting of education as a fringe benefit, vertical mobility is not reduced and is more than likely encouraged relative to the pre-income-tax situation, and it is certainly encouraged relative to the present-income-tax situation. This again is a special case of the general rule above that the income tax has discouraged entry into fields with attributes considered undesirable. To the extent that some people do not consider education as a disutility, it has not been discriminated against any more than any other consumption good.

An evaluation of the effect of fringe benefits on mobility can better be made by dividing the fringe benefits into the three groups mentioned, those which restrict, those which are neutral, and those which encourage, and evaluating the effect of each group. The group of fringe benefits which is neutral in effect by definition need not be considered. The two fringe benefits encouraging mobility have been mentioned, but the value to be assigned them is low. Under law both of these benefits—company-furnished transportation in the case of a new job and company education scholarships—appear to be taxable; but the former have been received tax free and it is possible that the latter can be made nontaxable.[42] At the present time, however, both amounts involved appear to be small. In a story dealing with company expenses associated with transferring current employees, *Business Week* emphasizes the expense involved but notes that "new employees usually pay their own moving expenses." [43] Expenditures for company-financed education also appear to be small. The National Industrial Conference Board, in a study of education as a fringe benefit, found that 131 companies out of 166 reporting this benefit reported the amount offered as tuition aid; of these 131 companies 40 percent spent less than $1,000 a year on the program and an additional 20 percent spent less than $2,000 a year; 55 percent of the programs showed that only between 1 percent and 5 percent of eligible employees participated and that the median of the company average benefits per participant was $48.00.[44]

The retarding influence of fringe benefits on the mobility of labor appears to be of considerably greater importance. Indicative of this is the tendency of pension plans to be of a non-vested type, which means that, although the employer contributes periodically to the employee's pension, the employee does not become entitled to it unless he remains with the firm a certain length of time, in some cases until retirement. Should he leave the firm at any earlier date, he receives nothing from his pension plan fringe benefit. The employee's departure reduces the liability of the employer and brings to the employee's attention the fact that the value of this particular fringe benefit is contingent on one condition—continued employment by the same employer.[45] When the employee first goes to work, there is no money in this "reserve" and no deterrent to his changing jobs. But after he has been employed ten, fifteen, twenty, or more years, the fund takes on greater size and is potentially his —if he does not change his job. The larger the fund and the closer he comes to having an undisputed claim on it, the stronger should be his desire to remain in his present employment.

In an attempt to determine the effect of pension plans on labor mobility, the Bureau of Labor Statistics in late 1952 made a study of vesting provisions of pension plans. In this study of 300 pension plans covering 4.9 million workers the Bureau found that only 25 percent of the plans covering only 16.5 percent of the workers had vesting provisions, and that not one provided for immediate full vesting. The length of employment required for full vesting ranged from five to thirty years with a median of thirteen years.[46]

Another study of the effect of pension plans on labor mobility tried two approaches to the problem. Statistics on labor turnover were examined and it was noted that turnover has diminished since the advent of pension plans, but it was realistically noted also that there were so many other factors affecting the turnover that the part attributable to pension plans was highly uncertain. The second attack was to question management personnel and labor relations men about the effect. With about 54 usable answers to 93 letters of inquiry, "the preponderant opinion" of both company and union respondents was that pensions had immobilizing effects, although there were qualifications about their importance.[47]

The evaluation so far has been confined to pension plans; but there are other fringe benefits of similar nature, such as stock options, deferred compensation, widow's benefits, and others mentioned above. Most of these plans have been instituted with the avowed purpose of keeping employees, usually executives, with the firm. One observer has commented on the scene in this way. "In every company I know there are dozens of people who should have left the company—or should have been fired—but who stay on because the penalty of leaving is simply too great." [48] He adds that the plans for rewarding executives have become schemes to tie them to the company and so "attempt to establish a monopoly on talent." [49]

From the above considerations the net effect of fringe benefits on the mobility of labor appears decidedly restrictive due to the prevalence of restrictive provisions in retirement and pension type fringe benefits. The effect of these is difficult to quantify, but is doubtless a direct function of the amount of payment deferred, the length of employment required for vesting rights, and the saving involved in the plan expressed as a percentage of income. It is an inverse function of the prevalence of early and full vesting provisions and of the coverage under multi-employer pension plans. To the extent that a flexible economy is considered a favorable characteristic, the above limitations on mobility will be undesirable.

D. EFFECTS ON CYCLICAL STABILITY

The economic effects which have been discussed so far have been those which deal with the allocational problems. But in addition to this modern economics requires consideration of the effects of any action on the maintenance of cyclical stability at full employment. Fiscal policy is one of the means used in achieving this end, and tax policy is an important tool in the fiscal policy kit. Therefore, the question to be examined here is to what extent, if any, do fringe benefits alter the effectiveness of this tool?

The elementary theory of income determination revolves around the presence on the market of the quantity of goods produced by "full employment" and the effective demand materializing, which may be too little, too much, or just sufficient to absorb this quantity of goods at existing prices. Since the supply of goods is relatively fixed by "full employment," the problem of maintaining stability at this level of employment becomes a problem of affecting demand. This takes the form of trying to alter the components of effective demand—generally classified as consumption, investment, and government expenditures. Actually, there are two problems here. The first is that of determining just how much effective demand is likely to materialize under given conditions and whether or not this will be sufficient to achieve full employment; the second is, if this level of employment is less or greater than full employment, to what degree the components of demand can be altered.

Fringe benefits as defined above are given to employees as consumers and so they affect consumption—but they affect it in two opposing ways. Some fringe benefits when given to employees increase present consumption by the employee; meals, lodging, medical care, education, and other consumption goods are examples. Other fringe benefits given to employees decrease consumption and increase saving; pension plans, deferred compensation, old-age and survivors insurance, stock options, widow's benefits, and other similar deferred payment plans are examples.

If full employment has depended on a certain level of consumption before the granting of fringe benefits, it is difficult to say whether this level of consumption has been increased or decreased after fringe benefits have been granted. The final answer will depend on how much of the fringe benefits is devoted to consumption type goods and how much is devoted to savings type benefits and the extent to which these fringe benefits, which are considered as replacing wages, are replacing consumption or saving. The figures compiled by the Chamber of Commerce indicate that most of the money spent on fringe benefits for employees whose wages and salaries vary with time worked goes for benefits which are a form of saving for the employee receiving the benefit.[50]

Some fringe benefits, such as hospitalization and surgical insurance, involve only temporary saving; practically all that is paid for this benefit is spent for the particular service before the accounting period, usually one year, expires. Still other fringe benefits, such as pension and deferred payment profit-sharing plans and old-age and survivors insurance, involve saving over a longer period of time. Actually, although this latter class of fringe benefits may involve definite savings for the individual employee, nevertheless, there is a savings for the economy as a whole only if payments into the fund exceed payments from the fund. In the early days of these fringe benefits a large part of the contributions is devoted to building up the fund for future payments. Most fringe benefits of this character are still in this stage of development; in 1957 federal old-age and survivors insurance benefit payments exceeded contributions for the first time, but this was expected to be only temporary.

Since the income group covered by the Chamber of Commerce survey is usually considered to have a relatively high marginal propensity to consume, the net effect on this income group is probably a shift away from consumption.[51] For the higher income groups there are no large group surveys, and so the results rest more on conjecture. However, it has been noted that these groups value both consumption and saving fringe benefits highly, so that probably a higher percentage of their fringe benefits is in consumption goods. Also this group, when paid in cash wages, normally has a higher marginal propensity to save. From these observations it can be said that, when payment is made in fringe benefits, the shift toward savings is not so great for the higher income groups, and it is even possible that the result is a net shift toward greater consumption.

During the Second World War inflationary pressures abounded and efforts were made to keep wages from rising and accentuating the trend. Nevertheless, while wages were supposed to remain largely unchanged, it was held that compensation could include insurance and pension benefits and, to the extent that these benefits were reasonable in amount, they were not considered as part of a salary subject to wage controls.[52] The War Labor Board also ruled on "fringe issues," which they listed as vacations, insurance plans, paid meal periods, weekly and daily overtime, holiday pay, penalty rates of pay for unpleasant or dirty work, sick leave, and several others, and in general they allowed such benefits to be adopted by industries within certain prescribed limits. It was evidently felt that in these cases the spreading of these fringe benefits would not seriously affect the attempt to attain cyclical stability.[53]

If fringe benefits have shifted the disposition of the employee's wages toward an increased volume of saving, then, given certain levels of investment and government expenditures, this would mean a smaller effective demand. During a period of depression this influence would be undesirable.[54] But since fringe benefits have spent most of their years of maturity in times when inflationary pressures were predominant, they may be considered to have been a blessing. In any particular case the desirability of this attribute of fringe benefits will depend on the existing state of effective demand.

The above considerations have dealt with the effect of fringe benefits on the level of economic activity. Besides this they also exert an effect on attempts to stabilize this activity when it reaches the full employment level. Classical economists held that price flexibility would stabilize economic activity at full employment, and although complete price flexibility is not a characteristic of the present economy, whenever it can be achieved, it will exert a favorable influence on stability. The effect of fringe benefits on price flexibility is twofold and may be discussed under the headings of "active" and "passive."

"Active" price flexibility refers to the response of prices to overt actions on the part of one or more parties to change them. The relevant question with regard to fringe benefits in this case would be whether they are more or less flexible than cash wages. That both have flexibility in an upward direction is easily established. Neither, however, appears, in the present setting, to be greatly flexible in a downward direction. In recent years there has been very little pressure on wages to move downward. Thus, while figures on the relative flexibility of wages and fringe benefits are not at present obtainable,[55] should the situation ever arise where one or the other would have to be altered, the results would be important in evaluating the effect on wage flexibility and economic stability.

"Passive" price flexibility refers to the tendency of prices, in this case wages, to change without any overt action on the part of the parties involved. If wages are paid to some extent in the form of consumption goods fringe benefits and there were to be a general decline in the price level, then presumably the cost of these goods furnished as fringe benefits would also decline and, as a consequence, so would the money value of these wages, although, it might be noted, real wages would remain unchanged. Savings type fringe benefits promising a fixed number of dollars would, of course, not produce this effect; but those fringe benefits which promise future payment in services, such as hospitalization, surgical, and catastrophe medical insurance, would have the same effect as consumption goods. Since savings type fringe benefits are no more passively inflexible than cash wages, the net effect here is toward a somewhat greater price flexibility for fringe benefits.

Although fringe benefits may encourage economic stability through their influence on price flexibility, attention is frequently centered on the effect of tax rates as a component of fiscal policy. There is a degree of automaticity in the stabilizing effect of the income tax. As incomes rise, so will revenue, and usually, although not necessarily, even more in percentage terms because of the progressivity of the rates. With the advent of fringe benefits these tax rates will necessarily be higher in order to raise a given amount of revenue from a smaller tax base. As rising incomes are subjected to these higher tax rates, this would seem to increase the stabilizing effect. But would the increase in income in all likelihood be similar to existing income, that is, composed of tax-preferred fringe benefits in the same proportion? Calculations made at page 10 above indicate that the proportion of fringe benefits in wage increases is greater than that in existing wages. In such a case a given tax rate would be less stabilizing in a time of income change than would be the case in the absence of fringe benefits, or if fringe benefits were the same proportion of income changes as of existing income, or if fringe benefits were a smaller proportion. However, wage changes will be composed of different proportions of fringe benefits, depending on whether the change is a wage decrease, a small increase, or a large increase.

Besides the automatic changes in tax revenue, there may also be changes in tax rates brought about by legislative bodies. Here the results are more clear cut. If a given amount of revenue is sought for reasons of stabilization, then tax rates will necessarily be changed to a greater extent when part of a person's income is in tax-preferred fringe benefits than when all his income is taxable. Although in the two cases the amount taken in tax would be the same, nevertheless, the tax rates would differ and the effects of higher tax rates on incentive, equity, and evasion discussed above would follow. In light of this, there would be a greater reluctance to rely on changing tax rates as a tool of fiscal policy.

A related problem in stability concerns state and local governments, but here the problem is stability of yield rather than stability of economic activity. To achieve that end one of the taxes proposed has been an income tax with no exemptions and no deductions,[56] and such a tax is a part of the tax system of some municipalities.[57] The introduction of personal exemptions or any other exemption, such as the homestead exemption, operates to increase the progressivity of the average rate of tax and the variability of the yield, given a certain change in income. Thus exemptions from tax are undesirable on the grounds of stability of yield, and fringe benefits might be construed as fitting this classification. However, fringe benefits differ in an important respect from these other exemptions:

fringe benefits affect not only present taxable income but also marginal increments of income if, as is usually the case, increases in income are composed of both cash and fringe benefits. If the ratio of fringe benefits to cash income is the same in a salary increase as it was in the previous salary, then a given percentage increase in income, although partially in tax-preferred fringe benefits, will result in the same percentage increase in tax abstracting from progressivity. If the percentage of fringe benefits in the salary change were greater than the percentage in the total salary, that is, if the marginal ratio of fringe benefits to salary were greater than the average ratio, then a given change in salary would result in a smaller increase or decrease in tax revenue—an even closer approach to stability.

While it is probable that fringe benefits would not seriously interfere with stability of revenue at this level of government, this particular type of income tax would create new problems in carrying out the principle of equal treatment of people with equal incomes. Some outcry would doubtless be raised regarding the failure to exempt even a minimum of income while exempting certain fringe benefits like country club dues. In addition, a new source of unequal treatment would arise under this type of tax. Under the federal income tax a person who does not receive a fringe benefit in the form of hospitalization insurance but purchases it himself may, under certain conditions, take part of this as a deduction; thus it is possible that neither the fringe benefit recipient nor the cash wage recipient will pay tax on the amount of the money for this service. But under the no-deduction municipal income tax, such funds would be taxable in full if received in cash, but probably not taxable if received in the form of a fringe benefit. Other fringe benefits to which the same treatment would apply would be surgical and catastrophe medical insurance, accident insurance, and interest-free loans. These fringe benefits are in addition to those involving goods on which private purchasers usually get no deduction and inequality of treatment is more obvious; examples would be meals, lodging, clothing, recreation, and savings under a pension plan.

In summary, it appears that the introduction of fringe benefits into the economic system will lead to a lower level of consumption from given expenditures made on behalf of lower income employees; will not make it any easier to change wages as economic conditions change but will introduce an element of automatic wage flexibility since wages are paid to some extent in kind; will make it necessary to have larger changes in tax rates to achieve a given effect on economic stabilization; will lead to a changed allocation of resources resulting in a lower level of consumer satisfaction from given expenditures on employees; has been designed to and has reduced the mobility of labor in many cases; and will probably aid state and local governments using an income tax to achieve a more stable revenue, but at a cost in terms of equity.

Part Two

Tax Treatment of
Specific Benefits

· IV ·

The Treatment of
Retirement Benefits

FRINGE benefits have been considered above largely as though they were a homogeneous mass producing the effects on public finance and economic activity described. But fringe benefits vary widely and are given in many different forms; some of these may produce certain of the effects listed while other fringe benefits will perhaps produce exactly the opposite effect —the effects of non-vested pensions and moving allowances on labor mobility have been cited. Thus, although a verdict on the tax treatment of fringe benefits as a whole might be rendered, this would be placing an inordinate value on uniformity of treatment. It is safer to subject the individual fringe benefits to examination one at a time and then to try to reach a decision on each one of these as to effects of the present tax treatment and possible alternative forms of tax treatment.

The examination of fringe benefits has been only in the light of their effects on public finance and economic activity while there are, of course, many other effects which flow from them. One of the frequently cited reasons for the growth of pension plans, for example, is that they are a result of an increasing social consciousness on the part of employers. Where these reasons have been given for the adoption of favorable tax treatment of fringe benefits, they will be cited, but largely the analysis of the individual fringe benefits will turn on how they affect the factors which have been discussed in the last two chapters.

By far the largest group of fringe benefits in terms of dollars spent is that group which provides for payments at or after retirement. The variety of these benefits appears almost infinite, with several major classes composed of more numerous sub-classes and an even greater number of classifications of lower order. This variety of different forms of retirement fringe benefits has made systematic analysis and evaluation as a unit quite difficult. Even for major units, like industrial pension plans, accurate current figures are hard to obtain; those which are available are estimates made by individuals and organizations and are often not kept current.[1] Nevertheless, the figures which are available should be considered along with the present tax treatment of the fringe benefits involved in order to evaluate this treatment and recommend alternative policies if needed. In this chapter two fringe benefits, pension plans and profit-sharing plans, offering assistance at the time of retirement, will be examined.

A. PENSION PLANS

Private industrial plans are, very generally, plans providing for employers to pay employees certain sums of money upon the employee's leaving the firm under certain conditions. This definition may appear obvious, but almost any other definition would seem to exclude certain groups of pension plans because they were qualified or unqualified, insured or non-insured, non-vested, partially vested, or fully vested, forfeitable or nonforfeitable, contributory or noncontributory, or contained some other restricting provision. It is these different features of pension plans and the variations in tax treatment due to these features which make pensions difficult to classify and treat as a unit.[2] Nevertheless, certain conclusions applicable to pensions as a whole may be drawn and then refinements may be made for special features of some pension plans.

1. Growth of Pension Plans

Private industrial pension plans have existed in the United States since at least 1875, the year in which a plan was founded by the American Express Company,[3] but their growth in quantity and quality has been largely confined to the last fifteen years. A 1925 study of pension plans showed 245 plans in operation, with 215 of these plans reporting 2.8 million employees,[4] but the coverage offered was of uncertain quality. It was reported that "a large majority of plans expressly reject the contractual theory" and "insist on the voluntary character of all awards and the provisional quality of the rules themselves."[5] Financing, for example, rested largely on hand-to-mouth appropriations to meet current demands,[6] while a majority of the plans contained a clause similar to the following: "It is also expressly understood that every pension hereunder will be granted only in the discretion of the Company, will be continued only at its pleasure, and may be revoked by it at any time."[7] A 1952 study showed 720 plans in operation in 1930 with 2.4 million workers covered, while by 1940 the number had grown to 1,965 plans covering 3.7 million workers.[8] Since 1942 both the number of plans and the number of workers covered have increased rapidly to over 23,000 plans at the end of 1956[9] with approximately 14 million workers covered.[10]

Although the number of plans and the number of covered workers are two measures of the importance of pension plans, a measure of monetary importance is also desirable. In December, 1953, the Federal Reserve Bank of New York estimated that the total amount of money held by pension funds was about $17 billion and growing at a rate of about $2 to $2¼ billion a year, and that this rate of growth had been accelerating by about $300 to $350 million a year since 1949.[11] An indication of annual employer contributions to pension funds may also be obtained by determining the amounts that corporations have taken as deductions under the Internal Revenue Code of 1954, section 404 (section 23(p) in the 1939 Code), which deals with contributions to qualified pension, profit-sharing, and stock bonus funds. The figures in the following table represent these annual contributions by corporations only.[12]

Two other studies also indicate the annual contribution to pension funds. The Securities and Exchange Commission, in a study of non-insured corporate pension funds, found em-

TABLE I.   DEDUCTIONS TAKEN BY CORPORATIONS UNDER SECTIONS 23 (P),
1939 INTERNAL REVENUE CODE AND 404, 1954 INTERNAL
REVENUE CODE (all figures in millions)

Year	Amount	Year	Amount
1945	$ 766	1951	$2,327
1946	835	1952	2,552
1947	1,038	1953	2,936
1948	1,153	1954	2,840
1949	1,216	1955	3,296
1950	1,661		

ployer contributions in 1954 to be $1.6 billion.[13] For the same year the Institute of Life Insurance found employer contributions to insured pension funds to be over $1 billion.[14] Thus total contributions by employers exceeded $2.6 billion, and since the Securities and Exchange Commission study did not include banks, railroads, and investment companies nor non-incorporated businesses, the total was doubtless larger. The income of pension funds was even larger because of earnings of pension funds.

From these funds benefits are being paid to retired workers, but these are not yet large relative to the payments into the funds because (1) the newness of most of the plans has led to a low ratio of retired workers to covered workers, (2) furthermore, those who are retired generally receive smaller-than-normal pensions because of the brief period of contributions in their names, and (3) employers' contributions are larger than normal in order to make up for past service of employees. In 1954 benefit payments from non-insured pension plans were $363 million; this was 23 percent of employer contributions to these plans and only 17 percent of total receipts of these pension funds.[15] Eventually benefit payments may equal or exceed contributions to pension plans, but if pension plans continue to grow, this day may be postponed for many years.[16]

2. Tax Treatment

The tax treatment of funds passing through pension plans involves the tax treatment of the employer-contributor, the pension fund, and the employee-recipient. The deductibility of the contribution of the employer to employee pensions was implied early under the income tax with a Treasury ruling that "amounts paid for pensions to retired employees or to their families or dependents on account of injury received are proper deductions as ordinary and necessary expenses." [17] Later Treasury regulations made their deductibility more explicit, while implying the deductibility of contributions to a pension trust fund if the fund were not held by the employer.[18]

In 1942 amendments to the Revenue Code were made which increased the requirements for a qualified pension trust; unless the pension trust met these requirements, employer contributions might not be deductible. The most important alteration was that instead of the trust being "for the exclusive benefit of *some or all* of his employees" [19] it now had to be for the benefit of either (1) at least 70 percent of all employees, or (2) at least 80 percent of the eligible employees if 70 percent or more were eligible.[20]

If the employer contributes to a pension fund which does not qualify for the above treatment by meeting all the conditions, then the contribution is a deductible expense only if the employee's interest in the fund is nonforfeitable.[21] These laws and regulations would tend to encourage qualified pension plans or nonforfeitable non-qualified plans as far as employers are concerned.

Pension trusts set up under qualified pension plans have received favorable tax treatment since the legislative enactments in 1921 and 1926, and this treatment has continued to the present in section 501(a) of the Internal Revenue Code of 1954. This favorable tax treatment is in the form of exempting from current income taxation amounts earned by the pension trust. Were this trust treated like a corporation, the earnings would be subject to the corporate income tax at the end of the year when earned and the remainder would then be taxed as personal income if and when distributed to stockholders; if the pension trust were treated as a proprietorship or partnership, the earnings would be taxable to the owners at the end of the current taxable year, whether or not distributed.   The pension trust combines the most favorable features to the taxpayer of both the above forms of tax treatment: no current business income taxation and no personal income taxation until distribution occurs.

Tax treatment of the employee's contributions to and benefits from pension plans depends on the features of the pension plans involved; the development of this treatment has been a part of legislation covering employer treatment.   If the *employee* contributes to the pension plan, the general rule is that the amount of his contributions is held to come from his taxable income, but when he later receives benefits from the plan, only the amount over and above that which he has contributed is taxed.[22]   If the employer contributes to a non-qualified plan giving the employee nonforfeitable rights, the same rule holds.[23]   That is, the payment by the employer is considered as taxable income to the employee at the time the employer pays, but the pension plan receipts are income to the employee only to the extent that they exceed the amount previously taxed as income.   If the employer contributes to a non-qualified, forfeitable pension plan, the contribution is neither a deduction for the employer nor income for the employee in the year of contribution.[24]   The most common case, however, occurs when the employer contributes to a qualified pension fund; here the contribution is not considered as income to the employee until received as a benefit payment, although it is deductible by the employer in the year of contribution.   The different cases dealing with the tax treatment of the employee may be summarized, with some additions, as follows:

1. The contribution to a pension fund is not taxable income to the employee:
    (a) if it is made by the employer to a qualified plan,
    (b) if it is made to a non-qualified plan under which the employee's interest is forfeitable.

2. The benefit paid from a pension plan is not considered as income to him:
    (a) to the extent that it has already been taxed as income when paid in as premiums,

(b) but rather is considered a capital gain if paid in a lump sum,[25]

(c) if paid because of his death to his beneficiary or estate within one taxable year, up to a $5,000 limit,[26]

(d) if distribution is made in stock; the tax is levied only if and when the stock is sold.[27]

3. Degree of Tax-Preference Given to Pension Plans

In view of these results, it seems desirable to examine pension plans and their tax treatment with a view to determining to what extent tax preference is involved and whether some preferable alternative tax treatment can be found.

A cash wage would be held taxable with few questions asked, but should a payment by the employer made under the terms of a pension plan also constitute a taxable wage? The American Federation of Labor has argued that "a pension plan is not . . . [a] gift by the employer, but a *deferred wage* earned by current labor services. . . ."[28] "The amounts contributed . . . should therefore be an irrevocable payment which the employer cannot withhold or recapture, just as he cannot withhold or recapture cash wage payments."[29] Such a payment made under these conditions would accord with the usual economic definition of taxable income as given by Haig, Simons, and section 61 of the Internal Revenue Code of 1954. It is similar to a taxable cash wage in that both the contribution to the pension plan and the cash wage are paid by the employer in order to increase the employee's command over economic goods and services. The principal difference is one of timing. Yet the person who receives a cash wage, and decides to use part of these resources to provide himself with retirement income through the purchase of an annuity, will find the full amount of his present income subject to income tax. This feature is especially obvious in the case of contributory pensions, where both employer and employee contribute to the pension but where the employer's contribution is not taxable income to the employee, while the employee's contribution does come from his taxable income. Here only an artificial difference creates tax-preferred treatment. On the other hand, it may be argued that in most cases the employee receives no immediate command over resources, and, since most workers are covered by plans that are non-vested, even in the future the employee has no assurance that he will receive any economic benefits. And yet such a situation is similar to the case where the individual pays premiums for a non-refundable annuity or for term life insurance or even for fire insurance or accident insurance; these premiums come from taxable income, yet may produce only the peace of mind which comes from knowing that if some unfortunate event should occur, say death, fire, or cessation of income at retirement, funds will be made available.

The earnings of the pension trust fund escape personal income taxation until distribution of these earnings takes place. While these earnings operate to increase the pension trust fund, and therefore future benefits, they are treated like undistributed corporate earnings except there is no limit on accumulation. And amounts which might have been paid out as taxes are not so paid but are reinvested to give increased future earnings.

The benefits, when distributed, then become taxable income to recipients to the extent that the benefits are due to contributions of the employer and earnings of the fund that have not heretofore been taxed to the employee. Thus, income paid into or earned by the pension plan, is destined for eventual taxation at the time benefits are paid, but even here these distributions are favored. The distribution usually takes the form of annuity payments, and, under the life expectancy system inaugurated under the 1954 Code, it is possible for the annuitant to recover as tax-free income more than the cost of the annuity.[30] Second, if the benefit payment is made in a lump sum within one taxable year of the employee's death or separation from the firm, the amount that would ordinarily be taxable, that is, the amount not due directly to the employee's contributions, is treated as a capital gain.[31] Third, the distribution may be made in the form of securities of the employer corporation. When this is done no tax is levied on the amount of "net unrealized appreciation" in the value of the stock.[32] This treatment paves the way for eventual taxation, when the gain is realized at the time of sale, at the capital gains rate. Fourth, if distribution of the benefits takes place within one year of the death of the employee and payment is made to his beneficiary or estate, $5,000 of this disbursement is free of income tax.[33] And fifth, the income is received in the period of retirement, usually after the age of sixty-five, when incomes, and hence the marginal tax rates applicable to them, are normally lower and when favorable tax treatment begins to flower with the extra personal exemption, full medical expense deductibility, and retirement income credits. As an added bonus, if payment from a qualified pension plan is made to a beneficiary other than the pensioner's estate, the amount due to the employer's contributions, heretofore untaxed by the income tax, is also exempt from estate tax.[34] From this it can be seen that although pension fringe benefits are not tax-free, they are, relative to similar forms of receipt and expenditures of income, tax preferred.

4. Effects of Present Tax Treatment

This tax treatment gives a clear advantage to the noncontributory, qualified pension plan over privately financed retirement plans. The employer may take as a deduction amounts paid into the plan; if these contributions are controlled by a trust fund, the earnings are not subject to income tax when earned; the employee pays no tax on either the contribution of the employer or the earnings of the pension fund until he actually receives them, usually after retirement, and sometimes the benefits are not taxed even then. These advantages are known among both labor and management,[35] and so it is not unusual that this form of pension has grown most rapidly. This growth has been widely praised on the grounds that it supplements social security payments under old-age and survivors insurance and so helps provide workers with a more adequate income after retirement.

This encouragement of employers and employees to provide

for the retirement of employees should be expected to draw praise. Blum has realistically noted, "When one focuses attention on a particular economic activity it is only too easy to conclude that it should be encouraged." [36] Like all economic goods it should be encouraged; but what effects stem from this encouragement?

It is difficult to say just what are the effects of pension plans. There are different kinds of pension plans and they produce different effects; for example, it can be argued that non-vested pension plans reduce labor mobility, while vested pension plans have no effect on it. Thus it seems best to discuss pension plans in terms of the type or types which are most important. These plans may be divided into three categories: (1) the vested refundable savings pensions plan, where the premium paid for the plan vests to the worker and will be returned to him at retirement, death, or some other stated event, (2) the vested non-refundable pension plan, which vests premium payments in the worker's name but which the worker receives only if he lives to retirement, and (3) the non-vested pension plan which calls for premium payments in the worker's name but which the worker receives only if he remains in the employment of the contributing employer and if he lives to retirement. Any one of these can become "qualified" under the tax laws and so become eligible for favorable tax treatment, and all are presently or potentially important. The non-vested pension plan is the most prominent today in terms of both workers covered and dollars spent. There is effective pressure, however, to change these plans into vested non-refundable plans so that this type will likely be most important in the near future. The fate of the vested refundable type of pension plan hangs on the passage of a bill similar to the Individual Retirement Act of 1955. Favorable comment on this bill from a wide variety of sources portends early passage.

By postponement of tax as outlined above, the tax base in any one year is narrowed by the amount of premiums paid and interest earned less taxable benefits paid. The amounts of employer contributions and interest earnings were estimated to be $2.6 billion and $.6 billion respectively for 1954. It is estimated that by 1964 the two amounts will be $5.1 and $1.8 billions. It is estimated that benefit payments have been in 1954 and will be in 1964 a little smaller than the interest earned.[37] The tax-postponement rule will, therefore, noticeably narrow the tax base in the years ahead. For 1954 the reduction in the tax base appears to be at least as large as the $2.6 billion in premium payments. Hall has estimated the revenue loss to the government at $800 million, based on the 1954 figures.[38] The reduction in the tax base is relative to what it would be if employees individually purchased annuities like the ones received under the pension plans.

However, as usual, the existing reduction is not the only consideration. In accordance with the most-favored-taxpayer principle, others have asked for the same treatment as that at present received by the 14 million workers covered by pension plans. This led to the introduction of The Individual Retirement Act of 1955 (H. R. 10), which would have allowed all workers not then covered by pension plans to set aside funds, free of tax, for retirement. The Treasury estimated that losses in *tax revenue*, not tax base, would be between $1 billion and $3.4 billion if the bill were adopted, depending on the extent to which the bill was utilized by taxpayers; the loss could be reduced to $275 million if certain proposed changes were adopted.[39] The reduction in the tax base, with its effect on marginal rates and incentives and cyclical stability through changes in tax rates, is both actually and potentially sizable.

The departure from the equal treatment of equals has already been recognized by the introduction of H. R. 10 and has been discussed above. A person under a pension plan fringe benefit can have tax-postponed money set aside for retirement, while an employee without such a plan, or a self-employed person, must finance his retirement out of post-tax income. And not only is there this difference in treatment between employments, but the benefits may not be considered as having been distributed justly among those in the tax-preferred group. Here, as with most tax-preferred benefits, the tax saving varies directly with the recipient's tax bracket. Thus, tax postponement enables the employee in the 20 percent marginal tax bracket to put away 25 percent more than he could have done had he been paid an amount in taxable cash equal to the pension plan premiums; the employee in the 60 percent tax bracket can put away 150 percent more, and the employee in the 80 percent bracket can contribute 400 percent more. Evidence that this advantage is not being overlooked may be gathered from the observation that payments from qualified pension and profit-sharing plans running into six figures, "not only to executives but also to rank-and-file employees, are not unknown and are expected to become more common in the future." [40] It is possible that this was not the order of aid envisoned when the qualified plan was formulated.

Pension plans give tax preference to saving and might be expected to channel resources in this direction. Hall has found that pension plan reserves increased $2.8 billion in 1954, which was 15 percent of personal savings reported by the Department of Commerce.[41] However, adjusting this figure of $2.8 billion for other factors, such as changes in government fiscal policy and a reduction in other forms of saving by those covered by pension plans, he estimates that total saving was increased by only $1 billion to $1.7 billion.[42]

There is not only this shift from consumption to savings, but there is also a shift in the control over these savings. The possibility that this may give rise to a change in investment patterns has been recognized and discussed, but the effects, both present and future, are still largely a matter of conjecture.[43] One last characteristic, which has been pointed out by the American Federation of Labor in its handbook on pensions, is the inflexibility of this form of savings. These funds are usually available only on retirement and are not available to meet other needs which might unexpectedly appear.[44]

As for cyclical stability, three items appear to be worthy of consideration. First, the fact that savings are increased is a desirable feature if inflation is the threat, but it is undesirable if the problem is deflation. Second, if pension premium payments are fixed amounts, not varying with changes in wages, the built-in stabilizing effect of the income tax is not impaired; in fact, it is increased. Third, outright efforts to achieve stability through changes in tax rates would be hindered somewhat because of the smaller tax base, which would require larger changes in rates to produce a given effect.

The effect of pension plans on the mobility of labor is a frequently mentioned topic when pension plans are discussed. It is pointed out that pension plans have a restricting influence on the mobility of labor which stems from the non-vesting provision of plans.[45] When an employee has a fund of money available to him at retirement contingent on his continued employment with his present employer, the larger the fund and the nearer he approaches its receipt, the less willing he is to leave.[46] This has led Hall to comment that the most pressing need in pension plans today is a need for fuller vesting provisions.[47]

A joint result with the immobility of labor might also be the immobility of capital. For example, if workers are covered by a non-vested pension and, after some years, have built up what is to them a sizable potential interest in the fund, then not only can they not afford to leave the firm, but they also cannot afford for the firm to go out of business. Thus, if this hypothetical firm were suddenly to find itself in difficulty because of, say, the introduction of lower priced imports, the usual pleas of the industry for protection should be seconded by the employees with increased emphasis. An increased pressure for inflexibility might be expected.

These conditions may aid in a better evaluation of the policy of encouraging pension plans through tax preference. Against the benefits of more retirement plans with higher benefits must be set a tax base smaller by at least $2.6 billion in 1954, with a much higher potential reduction as time goes by; inequity in treatment of workers drawing the same income but in different capacities and among workers drawing different incomes; a decreased mobility of labor and a possible reduction in capital mobility; and increased saving with inflexible characteristics, in some cases returnable only upon the occurrence of certain events. Other effects, both good and bad, doubtless also follow from this fringe benefit, but these appear to be the most important.

5. Proposals for Tax Treatment

The discussion so far indicates that there is little question that pension plans give rise to income; the question is more one of timing; that is, when is it income? Groves, dealing with annuities, insurance, and pension plans, notes two alternative treatments, (1) to tax employees when employers contribute, or (2) to tax employees when benefits are received, but concludes: "The tax-policy questions involved in the so-called pension-trust movement are substantial." [48] Accordingly, it is not surprising to find proponents of both of these alternative plans. Walter, for example, after citing some of the effects of pension plans on economic activity, concludes that tax-favor is unjustified and argues that "company contributions should be regarded as income to the employee for tax purposes." [49] Robbins, on the other hand, argues that the original contribution to the fund is not income because the employee has no control over it to spend or dispose of as he sees fit, and so taxation should be postponed until the final benefit is received.[50]

The answer to these questions depends on *when* these payments become income. With either a spendings tax or some forms of cumulative, long-term averaging under the present income tax, the problem would disappear. In fact, the lack of an averaging device was partly responsible for the use of pensions before 1942 when they had been sometimes set up to include "as beneficiaries only small groups of officers and directors who are in the high income brackets." [51] Where the employee's income does not remain in the same marginal tax bracket throughout his lifetime, a tax saving is possible under most averaging schemes. It is one of the aims of the various retirement plans to eliminate this tax differential on uneven incomes. The disadvantage with pension plans as a form of averaging is that they afford relief only to those who are covered by these plans and only to the extent of the sum involved. As a result, this is a piecemeal approach to the averaging problem as exemplified elsewhere in the law by provisions dealing with carry-backs, the distinction between expenses and capital improvements, capital gains, undistributed profits, and a host of other problems. Hence, although averaging is the preferred solution, a unified program affecting all income of all taxpayers is what is meant, rather than a system affecting only some of the income of some taxpayers.

Even among averaging systems there are differences. Under Vickrey's cumulative averaging system postponement of income, as is done under pension and retirement plans, will not alter the tax paid,[52] but under a system like Simons's five-year averaging system delay of income receipts can be profitable.[53] Still, until a unified averaging scheme is inaugurated, is there any other tax treatment that might be preferred to the present one? Here the problem and the answer vary with the vesting provisions.

Where payments are fully vested and will be returned to the employee when he leaves the company, at retirement, or at death, as is the case with most employee contributions but with only a few employer contributions, the contributions increase the economic power of the individual; they are a form of savings vested in his name, and so they fall within the definitional bounds of income. In this case taxation would be called for when the contributions are made. The argument against taxing them is that the worker has no control over these funds, which is true to some extent where he cannot withdraw the benefits until he leaves the company, retires, or dies. But perhaps this is a benefit to some who yield easily to the temptation to withdraw savings; if it is an undesirable feature, taxation should encourage the substitution of cash wages or provision for refunding.

The earnings of the pension fund, if they become the vested property of the individual members, should also be considered as income to the members and taxed as such. However, if it is from these earnings that the funds for providing insurance are accumulated, then the earnings should be treated like the insurance element of non-refundable, vested pensions discussed below. The eventual payment of benefits from the fund should be treated as are annuities under the present law; that is, part of the benefits should be considered a nontaxable return of capital, while the balance should be considered as taxable income.

This treatment is in accord with the theoretical treatment called for by the economic definition of income cited above and in section 61 of the Internal Revenue Code of 1954. It is also in accord with the treatment of comparable forms of saving, such as refundable annuities and retirement insurance. This treatment would remove the tax preference from this form of income and so remove the difficulties stemming from preferential tax treatment of pension plans as enumerated above. It would also mitigate the problem arising with lump sum benefit payments, because the sum subject to tax would be smaller than under the present system where the entire amount of the benefit payment, if only the employer has contributed to the pension plan, has not previously been taxed. The cost of this plan would be reduced incentives to save for retirement, but this reduction, due to the loss of tax favor, is smallest for the group usually considered as being in greatest need of encouragement, that is, the lowest income group.

Pension plans which have non-refundable, vesting provisions provide a more difficult problem. The difficulty is evident from the inconsistencies in the present tax treatment of insurance and annuities; these become magnified when non-refundable, vested pension plans are considered. This difficulty stems from the fact that insurance and annuities are, as Vickrey points out, made up of three parts which call for two different treatments.[54] Part of the payment into these policies represents savings and so should be taxed at the time the premium is paid. Another part represents pure insurance against loss of income and this should theoretically be treated as a deductible business expense when paid and as income when received.

A third component is the overhead or expense involved in the transaction, and this, too, should be deductible.

These differences have been largely ignored in formulating policy for tax treatment of insurance and annuities, and as a result the general treatment has been as though the entire amount were savings. In the case of a refundable annuity, the present treatment has not presented too great a problem since the annuitant is assured that the amount put into the annuity will be returned. The refundable annuity is similar to the refundable, vested pension plan described above. In the case of a non-refundable annuity the problem is different, but evidently it has not been considered of great economic importance. It is this type of annuity which is similar to the usual vested or non-vested pension plan; but when the same treatment is accorded the relatively large sums of money going into these plans, the problem assumes greater economic importance and calls for more careful consideration.

Under a non-refundable annuity the annuitant pays to the insurance company a certain amount, either in a lump sum or in periodic payments, for the assurance that if he reaches retirement age, or if some other contingency occurs, he will receive a certain sum periodically. If he dies before this event or before he collects an amount equal to what he has paid in, the policy is canceled and no payments or no more payments, as the case may be, are made. The tax treatment of this plan under present tax law holds that the annuity premiums are paid out of taxable income,[55] that if the taxpayer collects on the annuity, the gain as calculated under the life expectancy rule is taxable income,[56] and that if the taxpayer fails to recover the full amount he has paid for the annuity, the loss is not deductible.[57] This system can be supported by holding that the taxpayer received income, that he chose to spend it in a way which would give himself protection at a price determined in the market, and that this expenditure gave him both utility (peace of mind) and economic power (a possible claim on future wealth). Thus the purchaser who did not collect did receive income to the extent of the annuity premium. The annuitant who did collect was taxed on the total amount he received, composed of the premiums he paid plus the excess over this amount which he received when the contingencies developed. Thus it appears that everyone was taxed on his income. Only the annuitant who collects and lives past the life expectancy as given in the tables for taxing annuities receives tax-free income.

The principal criticism of this type of treatment is that the amount of income subject to tax is greater than the amount of income earned. Assume, for example, that 100 people pay $1,000 each for non-refundable annuities and, to simplify matters, that this money is not invested but is returned to the annuitants at retirement. If 60 percent of the annuitants fail to reach retirement age, then the fund is divided among the 40 remaining annuitants. If each of the annuitants shares equally in the allocation, then each will receive $2,500. The tax treatment of these persons under the present law will call for tax to be paid by each of the 100 annuitants on his $1,000 contribution. The 40 who survive will be taxed on the amount of the annuity exceeding their individual contributions, or $1,500 each. Thus taxes would be levied on $100,000 in contributions plus $60,000 in taxable benefits, while actually only $100,000 was income in the sense of goods and services produced and money received; the other $60,000 was merely a transfer of part of this $100,000. The problem may be observed in another light by noting that the income, from which the premium payment is made, is considered as increasing the net worth of the annuity purchaser, but, if the annuitant fails to collect, no allowance is made for a reduction in this net worth. The disadvantages discussed would apply to non-refundable vested pension plans if the plans were accorded the tax treatment just described.

An alternative tax treatment is to consider the premium payment as pure insurance of income and therefore to treat the payment as a deductible expense. This would be in accord with the treatment suggested by Vickrey and would avoid the problems just described. Under this treatment the amounts paid as premiums would be considered deductible expenses and the entire amount received as the annuity would be considered as taxable income.

This would eliminate taxation of the person who invested in the annuity but never qualified for the benefits. It would also eliminate the double taxation of the income. In fact, this treatment would reduce the tax base by the amount of expense involved in administering the fund. In other words, although $100,000 earned by the participants and paid into the fund might have been potentially taxable, only this amount less expenses would be paid out and taxed. This is the usual treatment of expenses connected with other forms of saving or investing; the costs of administering the fund or plan are subtracted, thus reducing the return.

Two types of vested pension plans have been examined and two different tax treatments have been recommended. But this is because two essentially different economic products are involved. In the case of the refundable, vested pension plan the worker desires an income if and when he retires, but if he should die before this time, he also wants a payment made, equivalent to the amounts which have been contributed in his name. Perhaps these payments are wanted to take care of his widow, educate his children, or do any one of a hundred things. On the other hand, in the case of the non-refundable pension plan, the worker desires to take care of his retirement by guaranteeing that a sum will be available if and when he retires. If he should die before that time or shortly thereafter, his need for funds will cease. Hence he desires funds only under more restricted conditions and so should be able to purchase this product at a lower price.

This difference in product means not only a cheaper product, but also a product which requires a different tax treatment because of the uncertainty of its ever rendering to the employee a command over consumption goods or an increase in his net worth.

The non-refundable, vested pension plan requires some system for transferring with a worker, in the event that he decides to accept employment somewhere else, the benefits that have accrued to him. This might possibly lead to a realization of the funds which have been contributed to the pension plan and so necessitate taxation at this point. There are several alternative methods available for handling the problem. Since these funds have been set aside and held nontaxable on the premise that they represent insurance of income against the absence or reduction of income at retirement, the accumulated fund should continue to be used for that purpose. This could be achieved by (1) purchasing a non-refundable annuity for the worker with the amount credited to his account at the time of leaving, (2) transferring the fund with the worker to the new employer if the new employer maintains the same type of pension plan, or (3) leaving the amount with the old employer's pension fund as a deferred, non-refundable pension to be paid to the employee at retirement. If, on the other hand, it is considered desirable to permit the employee to withdraw his accumulation when he changes employers, the amount should become fully taxable income in the year withdrawn, but even so, the individual would have benefited by tax postponement. Possible remedies for this situation might be to tax this income at the next highest marginal rate or alternatively to forbid capital gains treatment or section 1301 averaging over the period earned.

The proposed treatment of non-refundable, vested pension plans corresponds to the existing treatment of employer contributions to this type of pension plan. The effects of pension plans on certain facets of the economy and on public finance have been listed above, but it should be recalled that these dealt primarily with the effects of non-vested pension plans and vested, refundable pension plans. It is desirable to try to determine what effects might follow from a continuation of the present tax treatment of non-refundable, vested pension plans. The tax base would be reduced from what it would be if these plans were treated as the similar non-refundable annuity plans are treated under existing law, but it has been argued that the treatment of these annuity plans is not theoretically correct. Therefore the measure of the reduction of the tax base will depend on the definition of income adopted. The extension of this tax treatment to insurance might, however, lead to a reduction in the tax base. Yet insurance at present is subject to such tax preference that, if a consistent, logical treatment were adopted, the result could easily lead to an increase in the tax base.

This treatment of non-refundable, vested pensions would create an inequity in the treatment of non-refundable annuities, but it is argued above that the present treatment of privately purchased annuities leads to overtaxation of income, and so the change should be made in the taxation of private annuities.

The prevailing opinion that vested plans do not hinder the mobility of labor has already been pointed out. A non-refundable, vested pension plan is basically term insurance over a term longer than one year. Use of this good would be encouraged by its being offered as a fringe benefit. The effects on cyclical stability appear to be minor.

The last type of pension plan to be dealt with is the type referred to as non-vested. Here benefits are dependent not only on retirement but also on continued employment with the employer who grants the pension. This latter requirement is considered by many economists to be an undesirable feature because of its restriction on the mobility of labor. Since in all other respects the non-vested pension is similar to the non-refundable, vested pension plan, the good results sought from pension plans may be attained if non-vested plans could be transformed into non-refundable, vested plans by dropping the requirement of continued employment with one employer.

The cost of making this transformation has been estimated at 15 percent to 20 percent of the present premiums for non-vested plants.[58] Thus, for an extra outlay of 15 percent to 20 percent or a reduction in benefits by that amount, the worker can be assured of receiving a pension at retirement even if he should change his job. To workers who do not change employers this might not be a benefit of great value, but to others who do it might be well worth the cost.   Under present non-vested pension plans, although both groups of workers mentioned are covered by the pension plan, only the workers who do not change jobs receive the benefits.   Since the workers who do change jobs are usually engaging in an activity calculated to increase productivity, it seems odd that they should be, in a sense, taxed to provide pensions for the former group.

For this reason the non-vested pension plan does not seem to warrant any favorable treatment from the tax laws, and it has been urged that these plans be converted into vested pension plans.   According to the definition of income which has been suggested as a basis for examining fringe benefits, it can be argued that the premium payments into non-vested pension plans should be treated as income to the covered employee at the time the contribution is made.   It has been suggested above that non-refundable, vested, pension-plan contributions be deducted from taxable income because they are a form of pure insurance of income.   Insurance policies may take many forms and it may be questioned whether this non-vested form of pension plan is not also income insurance.   It is suggested, however, that the non-vested pension plan does not qualify since, although it does insure income in the event of retirement, the policy also includes other contingencies.   If this type of policy were considered as income insurance, then there would seem to be no limit to the conditions or contingencies which might be included in so-called income insurance policies.   The policies could easily degenerate into lottery or gambling devices, where the income tax questions encountered are sufficiently complex already.   These non-vested policies have the disadvantage cited above of appearing to offer the employee a retirement benefit, but then adding certain requirements before the employee may qualify.   The requirement that has been added in the past has been continued employment with the same employer, and this, many writers feel, has led to a decline in the mobility of labor.   At the same time, a ready substitute is available in the form of a vested, non-refundable pension plan. This type of pension plan is not a form of refundable savings but offers the employee a pension contingent on only one event: retirement. It offers all the advantages of the non-vested pension plan and at the same time does away with the major disadvantage of reduced mobility of labor. It is true that the recommended substitute, the vested, non-refundable pension plan, has higher costs, but this is because non-vested plans achieve a saving by promising a worker a pension at retirement and then declining to pay if the worker has changed employers.[59]

Consequently, it is recommended that the premium payments under non-vested pension plans be considered as income to the covered employee on the grounds that these are payments by the employer made on behalf of the employee, which payments could be taken by the employee in the form of cash or a vested pension plan or some other form if he so chose and which would, at some time, be considered as taxable income; and that, as has been stated, they do furnish utility and potential wealth to the recipient, the value of which is determined in the market. The earnings from the fund accumulated should also be taxed to the individual if it is possible to allocate the earnings; if it is not, they should be taxed at the time the benefit is distributed. This benefit could receive the same annuity treatment accorded qualified pension benefit payments today.

The tax treatment here recommended for pension plans may be summarized as follows. There appear to be three principal forms of pension plans which may receive two different kinds of treatment. First, the refundable, vested pension plan is frequently a form of saving and should be taxed as savings are today. Second, the non-refundable, vested pension plan is fundamentally a form of insurance and the tax treatment should permit the deduction of premium payments and the inclusion of the benefit payments. This is roughly the treatment accorded it today. Third, the non-vested pension plan, although not a form of saving, because there is no assurance of a return of capital, should, nevertheless, not be classified as insurance because of the undesirable inclusion of contingencies other than retirement for collection. The lesser evil here calls for taxation of the contribution and annuity treatment of the benefit, with the hope that this will encourage the substitution of other forms of pension plans for non-vested plans.

It may be argued that this treatment is complicated, but evidence indicates that the problems are not beyond solution. It is probable that the proposed tax treatment of non-vested pension plans will encourage a shift to one of the vested plans, which, it may be felt, will require an impossible amount of bookkeeping. Yet the existence of both refundable, and non-refundable, vested pension plans and the trend toward these vested plans indicate that this problem is not considered serious by the companies adopting them. There are other forms of payment which also require this type of bookkeeping and it seems likely that the technique of handling vested interests in a fund is being perfected. Two examples are the supplemental unemployment benefits negotiated in the glass industry to provide for full vesting of contributions [60] and some of the area- or industry-wide pension plans, which vest the employee's interest in the fund even though he moves from employer to employer. Examples of the latter are those run by the International Ladies Garment Workers Union and the Toledo Area Pension Plan.[61] Groves has commented on accounting problems in general in noting that the income tax would not have been possible in 1870 because accounting was in its infancy, but that the situation is changed today. "It is an open question whether the income tax owes more to the accounting profession or the reverse!" [62]

Additional support for the above suggested treatment may be derived from a comparison with the treatment accorded fringe benefits in two other cases. For one example, Canada allows the premiums paid by employers *and employees* under approved pension plans, up to $1,500 per year, to be deducted from income and the benefits to be included in income, but there are vesting requirements to be met before a pension plan is allowed that treatment. Pension plans which are non-vested receive treatment similar to that recommended above.[63] The second example is the tax treatment which has been accorded the new supplemental unemployment benefits plans. Here, when the plan has called for payments to the employee only if he becomes unemployed, the premium payments are not income for income tax purposes, but the benefits are income.[64] This corresponds to the pure insurance of income except that the purpose is to provide for unemployment rather than retirement. In the glass company type of supplemental unemployment benefit plan where the employer's contribution vests in the worker's name and will definitely be paid to him at some time in the future, this has been treated like savings and the premium payment has been held as income to the employee.[65] This treatment parallels the proposed treatment for pension plans.

Relative to the present tax treatment of pension plans, what changes in the effects discussed above might be expected if the proposed tax treatment were adopted? With respect to the tax base, it would be enlarged, although probably not greatly. Contributions to refundable, vested pension plans would become taxable, but these are at present minor—although potentially large. Contributions to non-vested plans would also become taxable, but it is expected that this type of plan will be abandoned for the non-refundable, vested pension plan. Thus from this source there should be little change in the tax base; this contributes to the ease of transition in tax treatment.

Should refundable, vested pension plans ever become economically important, as they might under bills resembling the proposed Individual Retirement Act of 1955, the amount involved might become important and the difficulty of changing the tax treatment would be multiplied. These considerations plead for early adoption of the proposed tax treatment.

The tax base might be broadened by a change in the tax treatment of pension plan benefits so that these benefits may not escape taxation. This would call for the inclusion in taxable income of benefits distributed in the form of securities. These could be evaluated and included in income at the market value or some approximation of it; under present treatment it is possible for this admitted wage to completely escape taxation. A second alteration would call for complete taxation of benefits paid to the pensioner's beneficiary. Although only the first $5,000 is so exempt now, the fact that the balance is subject to tax is indicative that this form of benefit is income. If death is a situation warranting tax preference, it would be more equitable to extend tax favor to all rather than to such a limited group. A third feature sometimes mentioned as constituting tax favor is the capital gains treatment of lump sum payments. Although capital gains treatment is subject to criticisms for such reasons as a lack of progressivity above certain income levels, nevertheless, capital gains treatment is probably a good substitute for normal income taxation in this case, since such a lump sum payment is due to accumulation over a number of years—possibly the full working life of the recipient. If, however, this treatment draws objection, a substitute treatment of this income as section 1301 income might be used, whereby the lump sum payment would be subject to a form of income tax averaging by considering the total amount as earned over a period of years and taxed accordingly.[66]

There are no figures showing the amount of payments received in these special forms. However, since total benefit payments are at present relatively small,[67] any increase in the present tax base would doubtless be insignificant. Such treatment deserves consideration rather for two other reasons. First, benefits will grow as more employees become eligible to receive these benefits and as the size of the benefits grows. The future size of this form of payment is potentially large. Second, the present tax treatment violates the principles of equitable treatment, since taxation depends on the form of income receipt. Pension benefits amounting to sums running into six figures have been cited; potential inequity here is considerable.

In the realm of equity, the proposed treatment would eliminate some inequities and create others. Those few who have refundable, vested pension plans, which are one form of saving, would find them treated like other forms of saving. Those who have non-refundable, vested pension plans would find these plans more favorably treated than privately purchased non-refundable annuities. To eliminate this newly created inequity in treatment, it is argued that the privately purchased non-refundable annuities should be accorded the same tax treatment as their related pension plans and for the same reasons.

The proposed tax treatment of pensions would probably lead to a change in the allocation of resources from their present uses, but it may be argued that these changes derive from a tax treatment that is closer to being neutral in effect. A shift from refundable, vested pension plans might be expected, but these, it may be argued, were a form of savings which had been encouraged by the postponement of tax. The fact that non-refundable, vested plans have increased under present tax treatment and would probably continue to flourish under the continuation of this treatment may be explained by pointing out that prior to this tax treatment such retirement plans, usually privately purchased, were more heavily taxed. This arose because all purchasers paid premiums from taxable income. In addition, benefits, in part a return of those premiums, were taxable income to recipients to the extent that the benefits exceeded the premium paid by the recipient.

Labor mobility would be encouraged relative to its present situation if the proposed tax treatment operates to discourage the use of non-vested pension plans and to increase the use of vested plans. Since a vested pension plan could be considered in the same light as a wage, these plans would seem to have the same effect on labor movement that wages would.

The effect on cyclical stability will depend, as in the examination of other effects, on which situation the proposed treatment is compared with. The factors to be considered in this respect are the level of savings, the automatic flexibility of the tax yield in response to changes in income, and the response in terms of tax yield to given changes in tax rates. Relative to the situation which existed before pension plans became an important part of wages, it has been argued above that savings have been increased; the effect on automatic flexibility has been uncertain since the removal of some of the employee's pay from the tax base will operate like a homestead or increased personal exemption to make the tax more sensitive to changes in income, while the fact that some of the changes in wages are in the form of pension plan premiums operates to reduce this sensitivity; and the response to tax rate changes has diminished due to the lower tax base. However, relative to the situation as it exists today, there would seem to be little change in store.

The tax treatment of pension plans recommended above appears to be consistent with the definition of income implied in the Internal Revenue Code and advocated in the "accrual" definition of income. It also appears to be practical to institute. The statements as to the difficulty of deriving a consistent tax treatment for pension plans appear to stem from a lack of realization that there are three different basic types of pension plans, rather than only two, in use at the present. The attempt to find a consistent treatment for vested pension plans seems doomed to failure so long as all vested plans are viewed as a single type of plan rather than the two, refundable and non-refundable, types which they actually are. Seldom is this distinction, which is important for tax purposes, pointed out, and there are evidences that many writers on the subject are not aware of the difference.[68] However, once this difference is recognized and once the non-vested pension plan is changed into one of the vested forms, a logical tax treatment appears possible. The recommended change in the treatment of pension plans should be made now before the savings type of plan becomes quantitatively important, as it may become if a measure similar to the Individual Retirement Act of 1955 is adopted. Also, the change in the treatment of certain benefits should be instituted soon, before benefits become an important part of retirement income. The larger the quantities involved—and both are destined to grow—the more difficult will be the change.

B.   PROFIT-SHARING PLANS

Profit sharing has been defined as any procedure under which an employer pays employees, in addition to regular pay, special current or deferred sums based on the prosperity of the business as a whole.[69]   There is considerable similarity between the type of profit-sharing plan that offers deferred payments and pension plans, in that both of these call for payments to be made today into funds from which benefits will be paid to employees at some future time, usually retirement, and both may qualify for favorable tax treatment under the same sections of the 1954 Internal Revenue Code, sections 401–404 and 501. The figures given in the Statistics of Income showing deductions taken under section 23(p) (1939 Internal Revenue Code; section 404 in the 1954 Internal Revenue Code), the section providing for deductions for contributions to qualified pension, profit-sharing, and stock bonus plans, include deductions for contributions to all three of these plans lumped into one figure.   Furthermore, the separation of this sum into the payments into the various plans has not usually been undertaken. From 1946 to 1956 figures showing the number of plans qualified under the above sections were not separated into their components—pension, profit-sharing, and stock bonus plans—but were shown as one figure representing the total number of plans.[70]   In these respects, pension and profit-sharing plans are considered alike.

The principal difference between the two plans is that pension plans generally call for committed contributions to the fund while profit-sharing plans call for contributions which are based on the profits of the firm.[71]   The latter feature has been considered attractive by management, while labor has usually expressed a preference for the assured annual contribution.

One of the differences within the classification of profit-sharing plans, important for tax purposes, is that between current payment and deferred payment plans.   A current payment profit-sharing plan calls for frequent, usually annual, payments to the employees of the amount of profit to be shared.

This type of plan does not receive tax favor in that, although the employer's payment is treated as a deductible expense, it is treated as taxable income to the employee. Such a plan is preferred by employees of firms where the average age of employees is low and the labor turnover is relatively high; such people usually seek cash wages. The deferred payment profit-sharing plan, on the other hand, if it meets the requirements for qualified plans, is accorded the tax treatment given to the qualified pension plan. Deferred payment plans are concentrated among large companies, and, according to one sample, cover over three fourths of all workers under profit-sharing plans.[72] Since these are the plans which receive tax favor, they are the ones which will be considered below.

The history of profit-sharing plans parallels that of pension plans. Studies of these early plans, going back to the latter half of the nineteenth century, have been summarized in two conclusions: (1) at no time has anyone been certain as to how many profit-sharing plans there were in operation in the United States, and (2) nevertheless, only a small percentage of all firms appears to have made use of these plans.[73]

Since 1942, however, with the change in the Internal Revenue Code and Treasury regulations plus other factors such as the excess profits tax and wage controls, there has been a marked increase in profit-sharing plans as well as pension plans. One study of 311 profit-sharing plans in 1953 found that 234 had been formed since 1942; the median age of these plans was seven years, while the average age was ten years.[74] Of these 311 plans, 182 were deferred plans, the ones likely to carry tax preference, and of this number 148, or over 80 percent, were formed since 1942.

The current extent of profit-sharing plans expressed in the number of plans, number of workers covered, amounts being contributed by employers, and amounts being received by employees is, again, difficult to determine. The difficulty arises for the reason that few extensive studies have been made, and where figures have been calculated, they have usually included several forms of deferred compensation as in the Statistics of

Income figures. When figures have been obtained the following dimensions appear. The estimated number of plans in 1954 varied from 9,000 [75] up to 21,000 [76] with about 50 percent to 60 percent of this number being completely or partially deferred.[77] The number of workers covered was estimated to be between 1.5 million and 2 million.[78] Of this number a large majority, probably around 75 percent, was covered by deferred payment plans.[79]

A figure representing the amount of money involved does not appear to have been calculated as a sum apart from pension and stock bonus plans. Thus reliance must be placed on the figures just given adjusted for the information which is available. For example, the Chamber of Commerce reported that fringe benefits in the form of pension plan contributions in 1953 were 6.8 cents per payroll hour while contributions to profit-sharing plans were 1.1 cents per hour.[80] If of this latter figure two thirds is for deferred payment plans while, say, all of the pension plan contribution is for qualified pension plans, then about eleven percent of the amount shown in the Statistics of Income as a deduction for qualified plans would be for profit-sharing plans. For 1954 figures this would be about $310 million.[81] Evidently this figure is within reason, since the Treasury is reported to have calculated the net increase in profit-sharing reserves in 1954 at $300 million.[82] This figure may appear small and so not worthy of consideration but it is only a very rough guess, and, from the way it is calculated, the smaller it is, the larger is the amount going to pension plans.

An indication of the growth of deferred payment profit-sharing plans may be gained from recent Treasury figures. In 1956, for the first time since 1946, the Treasury broke down deferred payment plans, which had just become qualified, into pension and profit-sharing classification. In the three years 1956, 1957, and 1958, new profit-sharing plans approved numbered 1,600, 2,500, and 3,100, covering 87,000, 145,000, and 154,000 employees respectively. Thus coverage would seem to be increasing by over 100,000 workers a year and perhaps at an increasing rate.[83]

The history of the tax treatment of profit-sharing plans parallels that of pension plans. The laws covering tax treatment have usually covered pension, profit-sharing, and stock bonus plans at the same time. Thus the tax treatment has been one of deferred taxation since 1921, with more qualifications added in 1942 as a requirement for tax deferment. Today payments into those plans meeting the requirements of sections 401–404 receive the same tax treatment as the qualified pension plans described above, while the earnings of the trust funds are not subject to tax until distributed as provided in section 501.

Some of the effects described above in Chapters II and III are due to the present tax treatment of profit-sharing plans. Once again these should be examined in order to determine the costs and benefits of the particular fringe benefit. In the field of public finance the effects on the tax base appear to be at present rather small, but increasing. Administration of tax laws applying to profit-sharing plans should be easier than those applying to pension plans because practically all profit-sharing plans call for either current cash payment to the employee, which is definite and clearly taxable, or payment into a plan with some arrangements for vesting, either immediate or future.[84] Thus the amount involved is credited to the account of the individual employee, and, if it becomes irrevocably his and the decision is made to tax this amount, it could be determined with relative accuracy.

With regard to narrowing the tax base, and so necessitating an increase in tax rates in order to raise a given amount of revenue, profit-sharing plans do not appear too important at first glance. The annual contribution by employers, which at present is not taxed to employees when the contribution is made, was in 1954 apparently only about $300 million a year, which, if taxed at a minimum 20 percent rate, would change tax revenues by only about $60 million. Here, however, the rate of growth and the influence on the taxability of other forms of income are important. Hall has estimated that the annual contribution to pension and profit-sharing plans will double between 1954 and 1964.[85] Since the rate of increase in profit-sharing plans seems slightly greater than the rate of increase in pension plans and since some of this increase might be taxable at a slightly higher marginal tax rate, the figures representing potential tax revenue will probably more than double in this period.

The most important effect, however, of this tax treatment is its effect on the taxation of other forms of income; exemption from present taxation here has led to requests for similar treatment for other forms of income. Thus the exemption from present taxation serves to support the exemption granted qualified pension plans and the potential exemption of large sums under legislation like the Individual Retirement Act of 1955. The narrowing of the tax base because of profit-sharing plans is currently small but potentially great.

On grounds of equity this tax treatment does not result in the equal treatment of persons with equal incomes, but rather results in treatment which varies with the form in which income is received. With an estimated 1.5 million to 2 million workers covered by profit-sharing plans and some 75 percent to 80 percent of these in deferred plans, these people are preferred to other taxpayers who do not have the opportunity to save under qualified deferred payment plans. Although there are about 14 million workers covered by qualified pension plans, an increasingly large number of these are covered by non-refundable, vested pension plans which, it has been argued above, are a form of retirement insurance and not a form of tax-preferred saving. But those who are covered by profit-sharing plans are usually saving rather than insuring, since the contribution to profit-sharing plans is more often vested in the worker's name and refundable to him. Thus, relative to other income recipients, they enjoy tax favor. Again among those benefiting from profit-sharing, the benefit, expressed in dollar terms, varies directly with the tax bracket of the recipient; in other words, progressivity, or even proportionality, is temporarily and in some cases permanently abandoned.

The incentive effects of profit-sharing plans may be divided into two separate forces. There is first the incentive effect from the tax treatment and second the incentive effect of the plan itself. The tax treatment may be expected to give the effects discussed above. That is, for those receiving the fringe benefit, the marginal tax rate is lowered through tax postponement or forgiveness. This is especially likely to result in increased incentives to work when the fringe benefit is tied to increased productivity and is given as a wage increase. Profit-sharing plans, which are tied indirectly to increased productivity, fit this condition well.

Besides the effects of the taxes involved on incentives, there is also the effect of the fringe benefit on incentives. It is one of the principal arguments in favor of profit-sharing plans that they result in increased effort on the part of workers. It should be understood, however, that the deferment feature is not a requirement for this incentive effect; current-payment plans, which provide for frequent payments that are fully taxable, are praised just as much, if not more so, for increasing productivity.

Profit-sharing plans will also affect allocation, mobility, and stability very much as do the general class of fringe benefits discussed in Chapter III. More specifically, however, if the use of profit-sharing plans is encouraged by tax preference, then there would not be a changed allocation among present consumer goods but between present and future goods. For those who prior to the introduction of the profit-sharing plan were not savers the shift is toward increased saving; for those who previously were savers, allocation may not be affected, since they may liquidate some of their other forms of saving, substituting the new profit-sharing.

Mobility of labor is affected in the same way as by pension plans. The lack of full immediate vesting operates as a deterrent to labor mobility. Even though practically all profit-sharing plans have some form of vesting, most plans granting deferred full vesting do so only after 10 to 15 years of service.[86] Hence there is still a restraint on mobility of labor.

With regard to cyclical stability, profit-sharing plans have an advantage over many other fringe benefits. Since contributions are based on profits, an element of flexibility is introduced into the rewards to labor. The other effects of higher levels of saving and greater required changes in tax rates when stabilization is a goal as discussed under pension plans are also applicable to profit-sharing plans.

The general arguments applying to fringe benefits apply to profit-sharing plans modified by the considerations that in the few cases where full immediate vesting occurs, mobility is not hampered and that some flexibility in wages is introduced.

The benefits and costs associated with the existing tax treatment have been discussed above. If it is felt that the benefits exceed costs, then this tax treatment should continue. If, on the other hand, the costs, both present and potential, are felt to outweigh the benefits, then the tax preference, where it exists, should be ended. The argument presented above has been that the costs are largely hidden, as is true in the case of most subsidies, but that when they are uncovered they are sufficiently large to call for tax reform. The alternatives for tax treatment include, once again, a system of averaging and a system of taxation based on the savings and insurance attributes of the particular plans involved.

Under a plan that grants refundable, vested rights, the amount contributed increases the net worth or economic power of the employee-recipient by the amount vested. This contribution is analogous to savings made out of income and so could be taxed as income to the recipient at that time. The interest, dividends, or profits received by the fund increase the employees' claims by the total earnings less expenses. Such payments are often allocated to the members of the plan so that each member knows what was his share of the earnings of the fund, or loss, for the year.[87] Earnings of the fund, if they are vested in the names of individual workers, should be included in each employee's income, while losses incurred by the fund should qualify as deductions from other earnings. At the time of distribution, the amount distributed would be considered a return of capital and so would not be taxable.

If a profit-sharing plan is not set up on a refundable basis but is rather a non-refundable type of retirement insurance, the tax treatment should parallel that suggested for similar pension plans. That is, the plan should be considered as a form of retirement insurance with contributions to the plan not considered as income, but benefits paid by the plan should be included as taxable income.

The results which would follow from the proposed treatment are largely similar to those cited in the case of pension plans. The principal differences are that profit-sharing plans involve a smaller amount of money and so are less significant in this respect, that these plans appear to be more like savings than like insurance and so the improvement in equity would be greater, and that tax favor is not so often cited as a cause for their adoption.[88]

· V ·

Life Insurance and Death Benefits

A. LIFE INSURANCE

EMPLOYEES may have problems of providing for their retirement which may be at least partially met by the pension and profit-sharing plans just described. A related problem facing employees is providing for the care and welfare of surviving dependents after death. The traditional method of meeting this difficulty is the purchase of life insurance. If life insurance is an economic good generally desired by workers, it meets the first requirement of a potential fringe benefit. If, in addition, this fringe benefit is given favorable tax treatment, the reasons for granting it are increased.

The present tax treatment of privately purchased life insurance is often characterized as favorable in that the Internal Revenue Code specifically exempts proceeds of life insurance policies from the income tax.[1] Funds used to pay life insurance premiums are not allowed as deductions and so this amount is subject to tax. But if the final amount paid as insurance benefits exceeds the amount paid as premiums, this excess escapes income taxation. It may be argued that this tax treatment is no more favorable than that accorded capital gains at death, but, relative to provision for survivors through periodic savings that earn and accumulate interest, this treatment of insurance may be described as favorable.

Favorable as this tax treatment might be, life insurance as a fringe benefit became the recipient of even more favorable tax treatment as early as 1920. In that year the Treasury issued a ruling modifying L. O. 528 which had held that group life insurance premiums were deductible expenses for the employer and were income to the employee.[2] This new ruling continued the deductibility to the employer but removed the contribution from the taxable income of the employee. The reasoning behind this change was that the benefits did not accrue to the worker but to his heirs and were contingent upon his continuing employment, and the insurance was not a gain to the employee since he could not convert it into cash. "It is paid by the employer not as compensation to the employee, but as an investment in increased efficiency. It is therefore not income to the employee." [3]

Although premiums paid by the employer for group term insurance were held not to be income to the employee, if the premiums were paid on an individual life insurance policy where the employee could name his beneficiary or where benefits were to be paid to the employee's wife or other dependents or to his estate as determined by his employer, the premium constituted taxable income.[4] Another type of insurance fringe benefit, known as group permanent insurance, attempted to combine the group insurance feature with the paid-up insurance feature. In ruling on this plan the Treasury held that premiums which gave the employee an increasing paid-up value of insurance would be held taxable income to the employee.[5]

If an individual purchases life insurance, either ordinary or term, the premium is considered as a personal expense and is consequently not deductible. However, if the employer pays this premium on a group term policy covering the employee, the employee never reports this amount as income and neither his beneficiaries nor his estate report the benefit as income. In addition the amount spent on insurance is exempt from tax under the Federal Insurance Contributions Act [6] and the Federal Unemployment Tax Act.[7] In this way the group term insurance policy is favored relative to a privately purchased term insurance policy. Most other forms of employer-furnished insurance apparently receive the same tax treatment as if they were privately purchased. Consequently, discussion will be confined to the group term type of policy.

Group life insurance has been used since before the First World War, and the amount of insurance in force has grown rather steadily with annual increases of one billion dollars or less up until the 1940s. During the first three years of the 1940s and in the period following the Second World War, the number of workers covered and the amounts involved rose greatly along with other forms of fringe benefits. From 1946 to 1956 the number of workers covered by group insurance increased 270 percent from 13 million to 35 million and the amount of insurance in force increased over 430 percent from $27 billion to $117 billion.[8] Thus, while more workers were being covered, the amount of coverage per worker was also increasing, from about $2,100 per insured worker in 1946 to about $3,350 in 1956. This amount grew to $3,580 in 1957.[9]

Coverage is not, however, confined to the rank and file of workers. One survey of the use of insurance by business firms found that group term insurance policies included coverage as high as $100,000 for top executives in 10 percent of the companies surveyed while one third of these companies provided as much as $25,000 for their key personnel.[10]

Benefits paid under group insurance policies have also increased since 1946; the number of persons receiving benefits and the total amount of benefits increased 300 percent and 380 percent respectively between 1946 and 1956. About $680 million was paid out in benefits with an average payment of almost $2,500 in 1956.[11]

The effects stemming from this fringe benefit are largely the same as those outlined for fringe benefits in general. The tax base is narrowed, with a resulting influence on increased tax rates and reduced incentives; there is an inequity in the tax treatment of persons who purchase term insurance; there is an increased consumption of insurance as an economic good. The effect on the level of economic activity is uncertain and would depend on: (1) whether the reserve fund were being built up or merely maintained, (2) the use made of the reserve fund, and (3) the use that would have been made of the money by the insured party had he received cash wages, compared with the use made by beneficiaries and those who receive economic income for furnishing these factors of production.

The narrowed tax base makes it more difficult for the government to stabilize activity through tax-rate changes, and the inflexibility of the fringe benefit contribution will tend to encourage not only wage and price stability but also employment instability. Labor mobility should not be reduced, since receipt of the fringe benefit, i.e., coverage by the insurance policy, is immediate and is not contingent on continued employment. The forfeitable, group permanent policy would be an exception to this.

The tax treatment of group term life insurance given as a fringe benefit may be broken down into two parts. One part deals with the present tax treatment of life insurance in general. This treatment is often criticized because it fails to tax the interest which is earned by the insurance company and paid to the insured's beneficiary.[12] The second part concerns the tax preference accorded term insurance premiums when paid by an employer. This is the problem arising from the use of insurance as a fringe benefit, but any consideration of the problem arising from the fringe benefit treatment must also include the problem of tax treatment of insurance in general.

It is axiomatic that persons similarly situated receiving equal incomes and having equal coverage by term insurance should pay the same income tax. Since this situation does not exist at the present, a uniform treatment should be sought. The argument which has been presented above has been that term insurance policies closely resemble pure insurance of income, and so the premiums should be tax exempt while the benefits should be taxable.[13] Gordon reaches the same conclusion but on slightly different grounds.[14] He comments, "Certainly no one has ever suggested that the mere existence of a contractual right to a payment on the occurrence of stated conditions constitutes income to a cash basis taxpayer in the absence of the occurrence of the conditions and the receipt of the payment." [15] While this treatment of the *premiums* might not be so difficult to institute, since it corresponds to present tax treatment of insurance given as a fringe benefit, changing insurance *benefits* from a status of nontaxable to taxable would doubtless encounter opposition. However, this change in treatment of benefits would not only work toward a solution of the problem arising from the different treatments accorded group term insurance and privately purchased term insurance, but it would also work toward the solution of the problems arising from tax preference of insurance in general.

It should be noted that this suggested treatment is recommended only for term insurance. Ordinary life insurance may be considered closer to a form of saving than to a form of pure insurance, and so the law requiring premiums on these policies to be paid from taxable income should be retained. The proposed treatment of insurance *benefits* recommended here might be adapted for use in the case of ordinary insurance; that is, the benefit might be considered as taxable income to the extent that it did not represent a return of capital which had already been subjected to tax. Since such treatment is similar to that which is used in the taxation of annuities and pension plans at the present time, this proposed treatment should not encounter much in the way of difficulties in administration, but it would require a seemingly drastic change in the attitude toward payments made at the time of death.

The present legislative attitude toward income realized at death appears to be that such income does not benefit the deceased and so should not be taxable to him. Thus capital gains accrued at time of death and insurance realized at death are not subject to income tax. Yet at death the same use is made of this money as is made of monies earned previously and subjected to tax. Thus an individual who has, among his many wants, a desire to provide for his survivors will find this need best met, in many cases, by the purchase of insurance. The incentive to make use of insurance for this purpose varies directly with the marginal tax rate of the individual involved. It is often argued that the individuals with the largest resources are the ones best situated to undertake the most risky investment, but in this case the existing tax structure guides them into investment in insurance; correspondingly the degree of risk assumed by insurance companies in their investments is limited by both custom and law.

It is recommended, then, that the tax treatment for group term insurance and privately purchased term insurance should be similar; that such treatment is both logical and administratively feasible; and that such treatment can be of use in solving some of the problems often cited with regard to ordinary insurance.

As a result the tax base would probably be expanded, since funds now going into group term insurance are never taxed but, under the proposed treatment, would be taxed when the benefits are received. In 1956 the benefits paid under group life insurance amounted to almost $683 million; [16] the tax base would be increased by this much. At the same time the tax base of persons who have privately purchased term insurance would be reduced slightly by the amount of the expense of the insurance company in handling this type of policy. Under the present tax treatment premiums come from income which has been fully taxed. Benefits are equal to these premiums less the expenses of the insurance company; therefore, if benefits rather than premiums serve as the tax base, the tax base would be reduced by the amount of expenses of operation. This observation abstracts from the time and interest considerations which arise because they should be of small importance. If benefits paid under group term insurance policies exceed expenses of administering privately purchased term insurance, the tax base will be increased. If the proposed treatment of insurance benefits were eventually extended to ordinary insurance and then to capital gains, the tax base would increase even more. A step toward the equal treatment of equals would be taken by this tax treatment.

Problems in administration might arise from the suggested change in tax treatment. Taxpayers could be counted on to list insurance premiums as deductions, but there might be a tendency to take all life (or other) insurance premiums as deductions rather than just the term insurance premiums. This difficulty might be mitigated by requiring life insurance salesmen to inform the insured of the deductibility of his premiums and requiring life insurance companies to include in the policies sold a conspicuous statement concerning tax deductibility. And on the tax form at the place where a deduction for insurance premiums might be listed, a space could be left for listing the type of insurance carried. At the time of benefit payments it is possible that executors of estates might fail to include the benefits in the deceased's income. But again, insurance companies might be requested to include with the benefit payment a statement as to its tax status. In fact, a system of withholding, possibly at the lowest marginal rate, might be instituted, as has occasionally been recommended for dividends.

Removal of tax preference for group term insurance might lead employees and employers into choosing a form of remuneration, cash or other fringe benefits, that would be more in accord with the allocation of resources which would occur in the absence of tax preference. The influence of the government on cyclical stability through tax policy would be improved through the presumably larger tax base, but other effects on stability would apparently be minor. Mobility of labor would remain unaffected. Any change should be largely concentrated among the higher income groups, for it is to these groups that insurance is sold on its tax advantage. And if insurance is to be encouraged, some system of doing this other than by making benefits progressively related to income could be devised.

It is therefore recommended that the existing treatment of group term insurance and privately purchased term insurance be altered as outlined above. Not only would there be an improvement in tax base, equity, allocation, and cyclical stability, but a foundation would be laid for the solution of other problems connected with insurance. The change appears to be justified.

B. SOCIAL SECURITY

A prominent part of the retirement or insurance program of most workers today is federal old-age and survivors insurance. This program collects premiums in the form of taxes from both the employer and the employee and makes payments either to the worker when he retires or to his surviving dependents at his death. Since part of the expense of this program is paid by the employer, while the employee is the recipient of the benefits, this payment qualifies as a fringe benefit.

The present income tax treatment of old-age and survivors insurance contributions calls for payments made by the employee to come from his taxable income [17] while payments made by the employer are not included in the taxable income of the employee and so are not subject to federal income taxation. Contributions made by the self-employed are made at one and one half the rate levied on the employee, and, like the employee's tax, these contributions are not considered as deductions from taxable income.[18] The benefit payments made by the plan to retired employees or to their survivors are not subject to federal income taxation.[19] Employers are permitted to deduct their contribution as an excise tax which is an ordinary and necessary expense.[20]

This tax treatment results in tax preference for the program in that only a little over half the total contributions are subject to federal income tax (the employee's contribution plus the contribution of the self-employed) while the employer's contribution plus interest earnings of the fund escape taxation. The net amount which escapes tax is equal to the employer's contribution plus interest earnings less administrative expenses.[21]

The growth of old-age and survivors insurance as a fringe benefit has largely paralleled that of other fringe benefits but the reason for its development is slightly different. While other fringe benefits arose primarily from bargaining between employers and employees, old-age and survivors insurance was legislated into existence, and its growth has been a result of this same force which gave it birth. Its growth, however, in either dollar terms or percentage terms can rival that of any other fringe benefit.

The Social Security Act was enacted in 1935 with a provision for old-age insurance, and in 1939 survivors insurance was added. At the end of 1940, 222,500 beneficiaries were receiving monthly payments under this part of the Social Security Act; monthly and lump sum payments to beneficiaries totaled $35.4 million during 1940. By the end of 1946 the number of beneficiaries had risen over sevenfold to 1.6 million and benefits paid had risen almost elevenfold to $378 million. Eleven years later these figures showed almost 11 million beneficiaries, nearly a sevenfold increase over 1946, and payments of $7,347 million, almost a twentyfold increase over 1946.[22] Although these amounts are held to be not subject to federal income tax, still other figures are necessary in order to determine the tax preference involved.

Figures for the year 1957 show that the income of the old-age and survivors insurance trust fund came from two sources: contributions to the fund were $6,825 million, while interest on investments amounted to $557 million.[23] A little less than half of these contributions, $3.2 billion, was made by employers and was not subjected to federal income taxation,[24] while the entire amount of income on investments was not included as taxable amounts. It would appear, then, that approximately $3.7 billion entered the trust fund without having been taxed under the federal income tax.

Not all this amount, however, is destined to appear as income to old-age and survivors insurance beneficiaries. In the same year, 1957, expenditures by the trust fund were divided into benefit payments amounting to $7,347 million and administrative expenses amounting to $162 million.[25] If it is argued that the administrative expenses here should be treated like those incurred in other forms of income insurance, then administrative costs might be subtracted from tax-free contributions and interest on investments when computing the amount that went into the trust fund without having been taxed. These calculations would show that approximately $3.6 billion was never taxed and yet is destined to become nontaxable income to old-age and survivors insurance beneficiaries.

The effects of this fringe benefit are similar to those which have been discussed above. The existing tax treatment of old-age and survivors insurance narrows the tax base and thus leads to higher tax rates. It violates the sense of tax equity in that some recipients of this fringe benefit receive some tax-free income, while others may find their retirement income entirely taxable.[26] Furthermore, among those who receive the benefit, the income value of the benefit varies directly with the marginal tax bracket of the recipient. It changes the allocation of the employee's income toward increased saving and toward a particular form of saving or insurance. Since the fringe benefit moves with the employee when he changes jobs, it does not restrict the mobility of labor except where the transfer is from covered to non-covered employment. With regard to cyclical stability, the present tax treatment forces higher tax rates on income under the federal income tax; this makes stabilization through tax rate changes more difficult. However, benefits under old-age and survivors insurance are usually looked on as a counter-cyclical tool. That is, in the event of a depression they would not fall with other income and would probably increase as a larger part of the population over sixty-five retired. In addition, these benefits could be increased by legislation. However, these counter-cyclical features could still be retained even if old-age and survivors benefits were taxed. With respect to legislated changes in benefits for counter-cyclical purposes, old-age and survivors insurance differs from pension plans.

As is true in the case of some other fringe benefits, the principal effect is not that which has stemmed directly from the particular fringe benefit, but rather the result it has led to in related matters. In the case of old-age and survivors insurance the fact that the benefit paid is exempt from taxation has led others to request the same tax treatment for other forms of retirement income. One result has been the enactment of section 37 of the Internal Revenue Code of 1954, which allows a tax credit against other forms of retirement income. Thus the tax favor granted to one fringe benefit has spread to other forms of income which are not fringe benefits and has further narrowed the tax base.

At the same time this additional tax favor is greater than

could have been supported on grounds of equity. It has been argued above that about half the net receipts of the old-age and survivors trust fund have been subjected to federal income tax, and so the benefits represent to the extent of about 50 percent a return of capital which, according to the principles of income taxation, should be returned tax free. Therefore, in actuality only a portion of the old-age and survivors benefit is actually tax preferred, but in the granting of the tax credit to other forms of retirement income, the credit was granted on $1,200 of retirement income (at the lowest marginal tax rate), although at the close of 1953, just prior to enactment of the retirement credit, the average old-age and survivors benefit payment was just over $500 per year,[27] and it is argued that approximately half of this represented a return of capital.

While old-age and survivors insurance has been responsible for directly removing certain income from the income tax base and indirectly responsible for the exemption of other retirement income from the tax base, still further plans for tax exemption have been presented. A bill, H. R. 11764, introduced in Congress in 1956, called for more favorable treatment of contributions made under the railroad retirement system, which is similar to the old-age and survivors insurance system. Specifically the bill called for continued exemption of the contribution by the employer, and proposed that the contribution by the employee also be exempt from income tax; no mention was made of including benefits in taxable income. Under this treatment the entire contribution plus earnings of the fund less administrative expenses would be tax free. In 1957 employers contributed $305 million and the interest income of the fund was an additional $109 million, both tax free, while administrative expenses were $8 million. Thus just over $400 million entered the fund untaxed, and benefits when paid from the fund are not considered as taxable income. The proposed bill would also make tax exempt the other $305 million contributed by employees. It has been noted that, once granted, such treatment would be likely to spread to old-age and survivors insurance and then to pension plans. The cost in income tax loss was estimated at $800 million if this treatment were extended to the former and $2 billion if given to all three types of retirement plans.[28]

Recognizing some of the weaknesses of the present tax treatment, the Treasury in 1947 mentioned two alternatives.[29] One possibility was to tax old-age and survivors benefits like pensions and annuities by considering a part of the benefit a return of capital. A second was to exempt the employee's contribution from tax but to tax the benefit received. This second possibility was rejected because it ran counter to the prevailing concept of taxable income and because it would likely lead to pressure for similar exemption of contributions to pension plans, other retirement plans, and perhaps eventually to all forms of saving.

It has been argued above that there is a difference between income insurance and saving and that the exemption of income insurance premiums from taxation does not logically lead to exemption of savings from taxation. Old-age and survivors insurance appears to fall into the classification of income insurance in that under certain circumstances it promises income in the event of retirement or death. It is possible that nothing or only a nominal sum might be received.

These considerations would call for a change in treatment. Like other forms of income insurance, premiums could be considered as deductible expenses while benefits would be included in taxable income. This treatment would be consistent with the principles outlined above and with the treatment recommended in the case of pensions, profit-sharing, and life insurance. Difficulties would arise during a transition period, but during this period benefits could be treated as annuities are presently treated, i.e., part of the benefit payment would be considered a return of capital.

The results of this proposed tax treatment would be varied but, it is argued, would constitute an improvement over present treatment in several respects. The tax base might be reduced at first, but it would be broadened in the long run.

Benefits at the present time exceed the taxable contributions of employees and the transition treatment would require that these benefits receive the treatment accorded annuities with some portion of these benefits considered a return of capital. In 1957 about $3.7 billion of contributions came from employees or self-employed and was taxable; at the same time benefits were about $7.3 billion.[30] Thus, if over 50 percent of benefit payments is considered a return of capital, the tax base will be reduced. However, in the long run the tax base will be increased, since taxable benefits will include employer's contributions, which are at the present not taxable as personal income. This proposed tax base figure will doubtless become more important in the future not only because wages are rising but also because an increasing percentage of wages is scheduled to be allocated to old-age and survivors insurance.

The charge of inequity in tax treatment has been met by the retirement income credit provision in the Internal Revenue Code of 1954. However, existing law still does not provide the same treatment for old-age and survivors insurance and other forms of retirement income. For example, a person who has $1,200 retirement income from investments may take a tax credit at the lowest marginal tax rate. Meanwhile the recipient of a like amount of old-age and survivors benefits finds himself with tax favor equivalent to a tax credit computed on this payment at his highest marginal tax rate.[31] Treating all retirement income as taxable, or all as subject to the retirement credit at the same marginal tax rate, will more closely approach the goal of equal treatment of equals.

Other effects of the proposed tax treatment appear to be of less importance. For example since the old-age and survivors insurance program is compulsory, the changed tax treatment would cause little effect on the allocation of resources. And since coverage under the program is almost 100 percent, labor mobility should not be retarded by either the present treatment or the proposed treatment. Cyclical stability would be affected by increased tax revenue, which the government might forego by lowering rates, and by the broadened tax base which would make it easier to stabilize economic activity through tax rate changes of a smaller magnitude.

C. WIDOW'S BENEFITS

The retirement and death benefits which have been discussed call for contractual payment at death or retirement. They are usually a result of legislation, bargaining, or agreement between employer and employee. Consequently, they are seldom classified as gifts from the employer, which would exempt them from income taxation. A fringe benefit that has gained prominence recently appears to resemble retirement and death benefits, being paid at the death of the employee, while largely escaping income taxation, being classified as a gift rather than compensation. This new fringe benefit is a payment made by an employer to the widow of a deceased employee; it is sometimes referred to as a "widow's benefit."

In practice this benefit has been given by continuing the salary of the deceased employee for a limited period of time by means of payments made to his widow. At the same time, it is usually stated that the payment is made in recognition of the services of her husband. This has many of the earmarks of taxable compensation, and as a result it might be expected that efforts would be made to include these payments in taxable income.

Actually, the tax treatment of this type of payment has varied through time. Orginally these payments by the employer to an employee's family were held to be gratuitous and therefore tax exempt.[32] Subsequent rulings by the Treasury Department tried, on the one hand, to bring the widow's benefit within the fold of taxable income by holding that exemption from income tax would apply only if payment were made *by* one to whom no service had been rendered.[33] Yet on the other hand it ruled that payments to a particular widow were a tax-free gift because they were made *to* one who had performed no service.[34] In 1950 the Treasury attempted to remove all doubt as to taxability and ruled that any payment by the employer to the widow of a deceased employee, if made in consideration of services, should be included in gross income.[35] The Revenue Act of 1951 and the 1954 Code altered this somewhat by declaring that up to $5,000 per employee paid on a non-contractual basis to the deceased employee's beneficiaries should be excludable from taxable income.[36]

The above rulings and statutes would seem to bring receipts by beneficiaries within the fold of taxability, at least after the initial $5,000 per worker. Yet the courts have taken a different approach which has, for all practical purposes, annulled the Treasury's rulings. The courts have held that the 1950 Treasury ruling, I. T. 4027, was not applicable where a gift was involved, with which the Treasury would doubtless agree, and then they have proceeded to classify most payments by employers to employees' widows as gifts.[37] In fact the Tax Court has held that a payment to the widow can still be a gift even though given " 'because of' or 'in recognition of' or 'in consideration of the services of the deceased employee." [38] The Court also considered it unimportant that the corporation deducted the amount paid as an expense and that the amount corresponded to the husband's salary.[39]

In line with considering employer payments to employee dependents as gifts, the courts at one time extended the principle by ruling that employer payments to a retired employee, through the purchase of an annuity, was a gift.[40] In another case [41] the retired employee died before receiving the entire amount of the pension, in this case presumably taxable, and the balance was paid to his widow; the court held these remaining payments to constitute taxable income.

In view of the diversity of Treasury rulings, statutes, and court decisions, there has been some question as to what to expect in the way of tax treatment in cases involving payments to widows of deceased employees. Yohlin has attempted to summarize the tax treatment by pointing out that payments appear to be taxable if (1) payments are made to the employee's estate rather than to his widow, (2) payments are made pursuant to statute, as in the case of firemen and policemen, because it is felt that employees regard these fringe benefits as additional compensation,[42] (3) payment is made pursuant to a voluntary plan, and (4) payments are not ratified by stockholders.[43] On the other hand, these payments appear to qualify as a gift if (1) there was no obligation on the part of the employer, (2) the corporation derives no benefit from the payment, (3) the widow performs no services, and 4) the services of the husband to date were fully compensated.[44] The employer will usually find his payments considered as deductible expense if (1) payments are made "for a limited period," and (2) they are made "in recognition of the services rendered" by the deceased.[45]

It appears from the above that there are three distinct attitudes toward the widow's benefit. The Treasury considers the benefits additional compensation and therefore taxable; the legislative branch, Congress, has also considered such payments as taxable income, but it has wished to grant some relief, presumably because of transitional problems at the time of death, and so has allowed a portion of the payment to be received tax free; and the courts have looked on these payments primarily as nontaxable gratuities.

The uncertainty of tax treatment may have discouraged the extensive use of this fringe benefit. Since payments appear to be made on an individual, voluntary basis, and since payments are deducted by the employer along with other expenses while not reported by the recipient, being considered as gifts, there seems to be no natural turnstile where the amounts of transactions involved might be recorded and computed. An analysis of what seem to be most, if not all, of the cases that reached federal district courts between 1949 and 1957 and were decided in favor of the taxpayer has been made and offers some concept of size. Eighteen cases are cited, with the amounts involved given for seventeen of these. These cases involved just over $482,500 in total, with individual amounts ranging between $5,000 and $72,000 and averaging about $28,400 per case.[46] Thus the total amount involved appears to be quite unimportant, but the amount involved per person cannot be so described. In most of the cases where the information is given, the widow or her family held a controlling interest in the corporation.

The use of this fringe benefit appears to be limited at the present, but the number of cases has grown from about one case every other year in the period 1949 to 1954 to five cases in 1956 and seven cases in 1957. Furthermore, if favorable tax treatment becomes established, the use of the benefit may be expanded to widows of employees who own little or no stock in the corporation. The potentialities for growth are significant.

The increased use of this particular fringe benefit could be expected to have certain consequences for both taxation and economic activity in general. If these payments are additional compensation, as the Treasury contends, then it may be argued that the tax base will be narrowed, with resulting effects on the level of economic activity, the ability to effect cyclical stability, and incentives to work. There would be a departure from the goal of equal treatment of equals, for some would receive payments from employers as taxable pension plans while others would receive equal payments from employers as non-taxable gifts. A concomitant result might be a restriction on the mobility of labor if it should become evident to employees that these benefits are being awarded to employees with long service with the company; the effects would be similar to those flowing from a non-vested pension plan. This type of payment has the same purpose as life insurance, a payment at death, and to the extent that it is expected with relative certainty, it would lead to the abandonment or reduction of other life insurance carried by employees.

A fundamental problem, necessary of solution before any fruitful evaluations can be made, is whether or not these payments are gifts as contended by the courts or compensation as contended by the Treasury and, apparently, by Congress. Granted that it is possible for businesses to bestow gifts on others and that employees may be among the recipients of this largess, nevertheless, such a practice is potentially dangerous as far as the personal income tax is concerned. Among the motives usually guiding the giving of gifts are sympathy for persons, either individually or collectively, desire to promote a cause, and friendship. These relations may also exist between employer and employee, but the market is customarily presented as being impersonal, and so relations between employer and employee, who customarily deal with each other at arm's length in the market, might not be those calculated to give rise to gifts.

Although genuine gifts might flow from employer to employee, or in the reverse direction, the more normal flow is that of taxable income in the form of wages. In view of this and the fact that classification of the transfer as a gift will give rise to a tax saving, any such transfer should be treated prima facie as an income payment. A similar situation has developed between two other participants in the operation of the market. Some buyers and sellers of goods have discovered that the abandonment of arm's-length bargaining can lead to larger after-tax income. Thus, if a buyer is presented with the choice of buying certain goods from seller A or seller B, it may be more profitable to buy from the seller with the higher price. For example, if seller A's selling price is $100 higher, the buyer will report $100 less income if he purchases from seller A than if he purchases from seller B. His income tax, however, will also be reduced thus giving him a net loss less than the $100. If seller A now expresses his appreciation for the business given him by giving the buyer a $100 gift, the buyer receives this gift tax free. The buyer thus loses $100 of taxable income but gains $100 of nontaxable gifts. Transfers of goods, services, or money, garbed as gifts, between parties who represent themselves as participants in arm's-length bargaining in the market should from the outset be suspect.

The above considerations call for the inclusion of widow's benefits in taxable income. Guttentag *et al.* have suggested that widow's benefits be included in taxable income at the time insurance premiums are paid and that the final benefit be excluded from taxable income by raising the amount which is tax exempt.[47] To the extent that provision is made for payment of widow's benefits through insurance and to the extent that these payments are vested in the name of the employee, this procedure would be consistent with the treatment recommended in the cases involving other types of retirement and death benefits. However, in most of the recorded cases of widow's benefits, payment was awarded after death of the employee and therefore before insurance could have been purchased. Hence the most appropriate time for taxation is at the time the benefits are received. This treatment is consistent with the treatment recommended above for life insurance and other retirement and death benefits.

D. MISCELLANEOUS DEATH AND RETIREMENT BENEFITS

Some of the more widely used fringe benefits which are realized at death or retirement have been discussed, but this list does not exhaust the ways in which employees may be given extra tax-preferred pay at retirement or at death. Some of these additional benefits are similar to those that have been discussed, while others entail different problems.

Federal employees, for example, are covered by the Civil Service Retirement Act which includes in taxable income amounts withheld as contributions from wages and treats the benefits paid to retired workers or their survivors as annuities. This type of plan is similar to other pension plans and the suggested tax treatment would depend on the vesting provisions of the plan.

Similar to old-age and survivors insurance is the plan set up by the Railroad Retirement Act. One important difference is that instead of only $2\frac{1}{2}$ percent of wages being contributed by each of the employees and employers, as under old-age and survivors insurance, the Railroad Retirement Act calls for contributions of $6\frac{1}{4}$ percent by each employee and employer. Thus the amounts involved per person are considerably larger. An interesting development in this field has been the introduction in Congress of two bills, one that would increase the contribution of both employer and employee to $7\frac{1}{4}$ percent each and another that would exempt from taxation the employee's contribution in addition to the employer's contribution.[48] Since at present the employer's contribution and the benefit payment are already exempt from income taxation, this bill would make exemption complete, thus moving away from the treatment suggested above for old-age and survivors insurance.

In recent years some fringe benefits designed to give highly paid executives income at lower tax rates have been introduced.[49] One of these has taken the form of deferred compensation, which calls for payment to be made to the employee after he retires from work in return for his agreement not to work for competitors of the present firm and for his availability as a consultant. Many observers feel that this is in effect a postponement of present salary from a time when it would be subject to high marginal tax rates to a time when the marginal rate would be reduced. In effect, then, this is an attempt at averaging income.

Another fringe benefit designed to aid the highly paid executive is the restricted stock option. The employee is given the right to purchase stock in the employing company at some time in the future at a price determined today with reference to today's market price. If, in the intervening time, the price of the stock rises and the stock is purchased at the lower option price and then held for a certain minimum period of time, the gain, when realized, is taxable at the long-term capital gains rate. The aim is said to be to give the employee a proprietary interest in the firm and to give him a source of income which will leave him with more after-tax income.

A newer variation of the stock option plan is the stock purchase plan under which the executive obligates himself to purchase stock in the employing company at the current market price. The stock purchase plan differs from the stock option plan is that under the newer plan the company lends the executive the money to buy the stock, charging only a nominal rate of interest, and applies dividends from the stock to repay the loan. Any gain from the stock will be taxable at the capital gains rate provided it has been held for the minimum six month period.[50]

These latter three fringe benefits—deferred compensation, stock options, and stock purchase plans—are generally used as special plans to fit particular situations. Perhaps as a result, the relevant tax law appears uncertain. Thus it is pointed out that "the taxability of the employee with respect to deferred compensation under these contracts is not clearly defined in the code or in the regulations." [51] The tax treatment of stock options has been incorporated into the Code,[52] but variations in the form these options take have given rise to many court cases.[53]

These fringe benefits are not so widely used as the ones which have been discussed previously, although stock plans embracing all regular workers are being increasingly used.[54] Nevertheless, the general principles which have been outlined as applying to fringe benefits apply here as well as elsewhere. Consequently, a plan for tax treatment consistent with points made above is desirable. To the extent that the use of such plans is broadened, the need for a consistent tax treatment will also increase.

· VI ·

Unemployment and Health Insurance

THE specific fringe benefits which have been discussed have been those which are received by the employee or his survivors at his death or retirement. In addition, there are a number of benefits that call for payment before retirement or death, generally in the event of unemployment or illness: for example, unemployment insurance, supplemental unemployment benefits, health and accident insurance, disability insurance, workmen's compensation, medical insurance, hospitalization and surgical insurance, catastrophe medical insurance, and wage continuation plans.

Most of these fringe benefits are insurance against particular events and thus subject to the considerations already laid down. Two of them will be considered in detail, as representative of the group.

A. UNEMPLOYMENT INSURANCE

Unemployment insurance is provided workers under Chapter 23 of the Internal Revenue Code of 1954. This chapter, known as the Federal Unemployment Tax Act, calls for co-operation between the federal and state governments in administering the program. The Act calls for a compulsory payment to be made by the employer to the state and federal governments, and from the fund thus built up, for payments to be made to workers who are covered by the Act in the event of their unemployment.

The treatment under the federal income tax of these payments has been determined by regulation rather than by statute. Thus the federal unemployment insurance tax has been held as an excise tax and so qualifies as a deduction for the employer calculating his income for tax purposes.[1]   The contributions to the state unemployment insurance funds have also been held deductible as either a tax or a business expense, depending on the particular state law.[2]   Two states, Alabama and New Jersey, have required contributions from employees; these, too, have been held to be deductible as taxes.[3]   The contributions made by the employers (or employees) to the funds are thus not subject to federal income tax.   In addition, the benefits paid to unemployed workers are not taxable.[4]

Although this fringe benefit is granted under federal and state statutes, not all employees are covered by these statutes. The Internal Revenue Code of 1954 taxed only employers of eight or more employees and only that portion of the employee's income not exceeding $3,000.[5]   However, the trend of legislative bodies has been to broaden the coverage and benefits of the law.   In 1955, for example, Congress brought an estimated additional 365,000 employers and 1.7 million employees under the Act by extending coverage to employers of four or more employees.   In the same year four states raised the maximum taxable wage from $3,000 to $3,600, and thirty-five states increased their maximum benefits by an average of $4.50 per week.[6]

Through time both contributions and benefits have tended to increase.   In 1940 contributions amounted to $959 million for 23 million workers, while $519 million was paid in benefits to 5.22 million unemployed workers.   In 1957 employers contributed $1,873 million for 43.2 million workers, while 5.65 million workers drew benefits amounting to $1,766 million, an average of about $310 per worker.   Contributions by employers to both federal and state governments have hovered around $1.6 billion from 1950 through 1957, while benefit payments have averaged about $1.34 billion, fluctuating from just under $1 billion to just over $2 billion.[7]

Here, then, is a payment made to an employee by his employer, or employers as a group, channeled through the government.   The payment appears to meet the general definition of income as outlined by economists and the Code.   Yet it has been considered desirable to exempt it from tax, possibly because it is received at a time of transition and tribulation.

As usual, such tax preference is likely to have certain effects on economic activity. Of interest is the departure from the principle of equal income taxation of equal incomes. For example, a person earning $3,600 a year might find himself unemployed for one fourth of the year and draw unemployment insurance at a rate equal to half his normal rate of pay. His total money income in this case would be $3,150, made up of $2,700 regular pay and $450 unemployment insurance. He would pay the same tax as a similar individual earning $2,700 in wages, although his cash income marks him as more like an individual earning $3,150 a year. At the same time the unemployed individual may possibly enjoy an additional item sometimes classified as income; he will find himself with additional leisure. It is possible that the unemployed individual will actively be seeking new employment and so there will be no additional leisure, but it is also possible that he will allow others to do his seeking for him, either the United States Employment Service or a private employment agency (an expense which is deductible); or, if the unemployment is known to be temporary, the time may prove to be leisure to the same extent as a vacation.

Unemployment insurance, as it is administered under the Federal Unemployment Tax Act, is given as a fringe benefit because the law decrees it and not because of tax favor accorded it. Consequently the present tax treatment should have no effect on the use of such insurance and hence the allocation of resources. Among the privately negotiated supplementary unemployment benefit plans, however, favorable tax treatment might operate to encourage payment in this good rather than in cash or some other good.

Two other economic effects which have been discussed above with other fringe benefits are those concerned with mobility of labor and cyclical stability. Since unemployment insurance is not dependent on tax favor, the proper question might more appropriately be to what extent the effect of unemployment insurance on these two economic phenomena would be changed if tax favor were withdrawn. Unemployment insurance is usually considered as an aid to increasing mobility of labor in that workers find that there will be some income during the period when they are changing jobs. To the extent that these payments were subjected to income taxation, this would make less money available and presumably reduce the amount of mobility.

This feature could be avoided by having the unemployment insurance payments included in taxable income but not subjecting them to withholding. In this way, the amount available at the time of unemployment would not be reduced. At the same time, since withholding taxes for persons who draw no salary or a smaller salary for a part of the year have a tendency to exceed total income tax liability, this foregoing of withholding might still not result in a net additional tax payment at the end of the tax year.

The benefits of unemployment insurance in reducing cyclical instability are also often cited. Consequently taxation of these benefits might be opposed. But again, unlike most other fringe benefits, unemployment insurance is not likely to be abandoned because of taxation of the proceeds, since it is instituted by law. Taxation would, however, reduce somewhat the counter-cyclical effect of this benefit. But, as just mentioned, the tax money need not be collected before the end of the recipient's tax year, and if further counter-cyclical tax reduction is then desired, it could be obtained through a reduction in tax on all income rather than through a reduction granted only to those individuals fortunate enough to be covered by governmental unemployment insurance.

The disadvantages of a narrowed tax base and an unequal treatment of persons who have similar amounts of income can be overcome, accordingly, without sacrificing mobility of labor or cyclical stability. This fringe benefit is a form of insurance and the principles of taxation applicable to insurance as outlined above would appear to be applicable here. The payments by the employer do not vest to the credit of any individual employee, so there is no element of individual saving here but rather a form of pure insurance. The tax treatment recommended in this case is for contributions not to be considered as taxable income to the employee, since no employee is guaranteed payment except under certain contingencies, and for benefit payments to be included in taxable income of the recipient. This treatment is easily applicable in the case of governmental unemployment insurance.

While this tax treatment includes unemployment benefits in income, if it is felt that unemployment is a situation warranting favorable tax treatment, an equitable solution might provide for a deduction equivalent to some fraction of normal weekly pay times the number of weeks of unemployment. This would give tax favor both to the recipients of unemployment benefits and to those who receive no unemployment benefits at all.

As is true with other fringe benefits, the proposed tax treatment may not only help overcome some of the difficulties cited but it may aid in avoiding their spread. While it is likely that the present trend toward increased coverage by the benefits from unemployment insurance will continue, new forms are being adopted. Severance pay has received more attention as entire plants have moved to new locations and as automation has led to job changes. The late 1950s have seen increased use of supplemental unemployment benefit plans. Both of these are forms of unemployment insurance.[8]

Under supplemental unemployment benefit plans the employer contributes to a fund from which the employee draws when he is unemployed.[9] The tax treatment of this fringe benefit has closely conformed to the principles outlined above. Thus payments made by the employer but not vested in the name of the workers are not taxed to the employee until received, when they must be included in taxable income although they are not subject to withholding.[10] When payments are vested in the name of the employee, as in the glass company type of supplemental unemployment benefits, the payments are taxed to the employee at the time the company contrib-

utes.[11]   The fact that the treatment of this form of unemployment insurance and the treatment of severance pay correspond
with the principles outlined for taxation of insurance type
fringe benefits may make changes in the treatment of govern-
mentally sponsored unemployment insurance less difficult to
institute.

B. HOSPITALIZATION AND SURGICAL INSURANCE

In addition to the forms of unemployment insurance just
discussed there are other forms of insurance which provide for
contingencies such as illness and accident.   Several forms of
fringe benefits have been offered by employers to take care of
these contingencies: examples are medical insurance, hospitalization insurance, surgical insurance, health and accident insurance, wage continuation plans, and workmen's compensation.   Although these provisions might appear to offer considerable protection against illness and accident, there have been
hints that new but similar fringe benefits are in the offing.
Unions have intimated that in the future they will add to this
list major medical insurance to cover major illnesses, dental
insurance, and diagnostic insurance.[12]   These fringe benefits,
given and proposed, are similar in their purpose and their tax
treatment and so an examination of one of them may suffice
as an evaluation of them all.

Hospitalization insurance, one of the most widely granted
fringe benefits in this group, insures the employee against hospital expenses connected with accident or illness by providing
for certain payments to be made for room, drugs, and other
hospital services at prescribed rates.   These payments may or
may not cover the entire hospital bill, but in most cases will
cover a substantial portion of the total bill.   The cost of this
insurance, a prescribed premium, is paid either by the employer or by both employer and employee.

Allowance of a deduction for unusually large medical expenses was introduced in the Revenue Act of 1942,[13] and this
was interpreted to include insurance premiums for hospital insurance.[14]   Early in the life of this deduction the way was

paved to encourage its use as a fringe benefit when it was held that employees receiving hospitalization insurance paid for by the employer did not have to include the premiums in their taxable income.[15]

The tax treatment of the benefits from hospitalization insurance is covered in the Internal Revenue Code of 1954, and appears to hinge on the tax treatment which was accorded the premium payments. In general, if premiums were paid by the taxpayer, benefits are excluded from gross income;[16] if premiums were paid by the employer, benefits are included in gross income.[17] In the latter case, however, benefits used to pay for hospital or medical expenses are excluded from gross income to the extent of the expenses incurred. The practical difference between the privately purchased hospitalization insurance policy and the employer-furnished one is that *all* benefits are tax free if the employee purchased the policy, while benefits are tax free only to the extent of actual expenses if the employer furnished the policy.

The effect of this fringe benefit on equality of tax treatment is a subtle one which is likely to escape notice. Both the private purchaser and the fringe benefit recipient appear to escape taxation on amounts spent for hospitalization insurance. However, assume an employee earning $5,000 a year and itemizing his deductions. He will be allowed a deduction for his expenditures for hospitalization insurance only if total medical expenditures exceed 3 percent of his adjusted gross income, $150. In some years this amount may materialize but in others it may not. In addition, his total deductions must exceed 10 percent of his adjusted gross income or it will not pay him to itemize his deductions. Thus his use of this deduction is contingent on the above conditions. The taxpayer who receives his hospital insurance as a fringe benefit, however, does not include the premium payment in even his gross income and so he is assured that this amount will escape taxation. If his employer gave him, say, $100 of hospitalization insurance instead of an equal amount of salary, the fringe benefit recipient would report only $4,900 of gross income. It may also be noted that this taxpayer, if he itemizes, finds that 3 percent of his adjusted gross income is, in this case, a smaller figure.[18]

The taxpayer who finds it more profitable to use the optional standard deduction will also find himself with lower tax liability if he is given hospitalization insurance. Assume once more a worker with a salary of $5,000 per year. Using the optional standard deduction and assuming two exemptions, the worker would find his taxable income to be $3,300. If he purchased $100 of hospitalization insurance, but this was still not enough to make itemization of deductions profitable for him, his taxable income would remain unchanged. If, on the other hand, the employer gave the hospitalization insurance as a fringe benefit, reducing the salary by an amount equal to its cost, the worker would find himself with only $4,900 cash income. He could deduct his optional standard deduction of $490 and his two exemptions of $1,200. His taxable income would be $3,210, or $90.00 below that of his similarly situated neighbor.[19] This inequality arises from declaring that certain expenditures are the basis for a standard reduction in taxable income and then adding that under certain conditions these expenditures do not have to be included in income, yet may still be taken as deductions.

These examples show that the aggregate tax base is reduced by the sum of (1) 90 percent of the amount of hospitalization insurance given as a fringe benefit to taxpayers using the optional standard deduction, and (2) at least 3 percent of the amount of hospitalization insurance given to taxpayers who itemize their deductions and have enough other medical expenses to take a medical deduction.[20]

The allocation of resources might be expected to be shifted since it is now possible for a worker to receive this particular service at a smaller cost to himself if it is given as a fringe benefit than if he purchases it. To what extent tax favor has been responsible for the growth of health insurance fringe benefits is difficult to determine, but it is clear that their growth has been considerable. For example, over the ten-year period, 1941 to 1951, hospitalization insurance coverage increased by

33 million in Blue Cross, 23 million in private group insurance, and 20 million under individual insurance. At the same time surgical insurance increased its enrollment by 23 million in Blue Shield, 24 million in group insurance, and 15 million under private insurance.[21] It can be seen from these figures that increased coverage under group plans was more than two and one half times as large as the increased coverage under individual contracts for hospitalization insurance, and the figure for surgical insurance was more than three times as large.

Once plans have been introduced and adopted, future expansion in this type of fringe benefit seems to be through expanded coverage of dependents, retired workers, and their dependents, and through increased benefits.[22] The cost of a plan covering dependents is usually higher than that of one which covers only the employee. If two workers, then, perform the same task and draw the same wage plus a fringe benefit in the form of hospitalization insurance, and if one worker is single, while the other is married, then the worker who is married may be said to draw the higher rate of pay if fringe benefits are considered a part of the worker's reward. This leads to a situation where a worker's pay depends not only on his marginal productivity but also on his marital and dependent status. Most insurance policies of this type have only two classifications for insurees: those without dependents and those with dependents; thus any discrimination from this source arises principally between these two classes of workers.

It might be argued that hospitalization insurance operates like other insurance and constitutes an increase in saving, thus affecting the level of national income and the ability to maintain cyclical stability. However, this argument overlooks the point that this type of insurance is, like term insurance, a type of pure insurance and therefore involves no net saving on the part of the insured as a group. Unless there is a net accumulation in a fund for future contingencies, the amount put aside by those who do not consume hospital services is used to pay for the excess of hospital costs over insurance premiums of those who do use hospital services during the year.

This fringe benefit should not have any effect on labor mobility and should cause changes in jobs in the same way that a difference in wages would. If one employer offers a certain wage plus this fringe benefit, he may be expected to attract workers from other employers offering only the same cash wage but no fringe benefit. This, however, is only a difference in wages which, while it may cause workers to change jobs, does not affect mobility per se.

Hospitalization insurance is a form of pure insurance, and under the principles outlined above the recommended tax treatment would exclude the premium payment from the recipient's taxable income and include the benefit in his income. The recommended tax treatment changes the treatment of premiums for privately purchased plans, relieving them of taxation, and of benefits received under both privately purchased and employer-furnished plans, calling for inclusion of these amounts in taxable income and allowing a deduction only when actual expenditures warrant.

An objection might be raised against this proposed treatment on the grounds that it levies a tax on the recipient of insurance benefits at a time when he is burdened with unusual hospitalization or medical expenses. Congress has indicated that such circumstances as illness, retirement, old age, accident, and unemployment all entitle the taxpayer to special consideration in tax treatment. The taxation of insurance benefits appears to violate this principle. However, inclusion of insurance benefits in gross income does not necessarily mean that they will be taxed, since the medical deduction is still available for those who itemize their deductions and the optional standard deduction for all others.

The proposed treatment does create a discrepancy between the amounts reported as income under the various tax and regulatory laws dealing with wages. The amount reported as income for income tax purposes would be cash wages plus benefit payments from insurance policies but not including amounts paid by the employer as premiums for hospitalization insurance. The amount reported as income under the Federal

Insurance Contributions Act and the Federal Unemployment
Tax Act includes only cash wages and excludes both premiums
on and benefits from hospitalization insurance when purchased
by the employer as a fringe benefit.[23]

What has been said above about hospitalization insurance
also applies to other forms of health insurance: medical insurance, surgical insurance, health insurance, accident insurance,
major medical insurance, and possibly several additional forms
of insurance.   The trend appears to be toward a more widespread use of all of these forms of insurance as a fringe benefit,
and this may tend to reduce the number of private purchasers
who are discriminated against at present in their purchases of
these forms of insurance.   At the same time, there appears to
be an increasing number of forms of health insurance which
may open up new areas for difference in tax treatment.   Thus
the problem does not appear to be decreasing in quantitative
importance.

The proposed tax treatment will have some effect on the
efficiency of present withholding provisions.   This arises from
the fact that, although it is proposed that insurance benefits be
included in gross income, no provision is made for withholding.   This weakness might be mitigated by having the insurance companies send at the end of each year some form similar
to the present W-2 form to those persons to whom payments
have been made during the year.   Since it is probable that
the benefit will be used for medical expense purposes and possibly be deductible, it is not recommended that actual withholding be used with regard to these benefits.

For the fringe benefit recipient who is already itemizing his
deductions and taking a deduction for medical expenses, the
proposed tax treatment will not significantly alter his tax from
what it is now.   For the recipient who uses the optional standard deduction because this and other deductible expenses are
not sufficient to justify itemization, his tax will be increased.
This proposed tax treatment, perhaps, does not accord with
some ideas of justice, but it seems to be consistent with Congressional intent that there are certain levels of expenses for

specific purposes which are considered "normal" and only when expenses exceed this level do they justify deduction. Present tax treatment, however, allows a deduction for medical expense, no matter how small, so long as it is covered by insurance.

This chapter has dealt with some of the fringe benefits given in the form of insurance. It has pointed out that these fringe benefits usually receive more favorable tax treatment than privately purchased insurance. In some cases—for example, supplemental unemployment benefits—the tax treatment of the fringe benefit is in accord with the taxation of income as defined by economists and by the general definition in the Internal Revenue Code. In most cases, however, this accord of principle and practice is not found. Here, then, is an area where a fundamental reexamination of concepts needs to be undertaken in order to arrive at a logical, consistent, and equitable tax treatment. It is felt that the principles laid down in this chapter would lead to such a solution.

· VII ·

Fringe Benefits in Kind

A. INTRODUCTION

THE fringe benefits which have been discussed have been those which give payment to the employee if certain contingencies occur. Such contingencies, on the whole, have been illness, unemployment, retirement, and death. Payment may be made by the employer's taking out insurance or by direct payments from employer to employee. Generally, however, the employee receives a cash payment, as in the case of retirement benefits and unemployment benefits, or perhaps a receipted bill, as sometimes is the case under hospitalization insurance, for services used.

There is, however, another class of fringe benefits which is composed of goods and services given directly to employees. Cases of employers furnishing employees housing, as in mill villages, and food, as in hospitals, plus many other examples, predate the federal income tax. The Federal Income Tax Law of 1913 presumably included these goods and services in the concept of taxable income by including the phrase, "in whatever form paid." Subsequent Treasury rulings introduced the "convenience of the employer" rule, which removed some of these goods from taxable income.[1] The history of the tax treatment since that time has been rather varied. Generally, still, income in kind is taxable income to the recipient, but Congressional action, Treasury rulings, and court decisions have removed some of these goods and services from income when certain conditions are met. Then, too, the sands of opinion have shifted, at least in Treasury rulings, as conditions have changed, with the result that items that at one time would have escaped taxation have found themselves included in taxable income at a later time.

The reasons for giving payment in kind are difficult to ascertain. Doubtless most early cases arose because of what was called "convenience of the employer." Since receipt of these goods benefited the employer, since the value of the goods to the employee was questionable, as Kleinwachter demonstrated, and since the use of such benefits was not widespread, some of these benefits were given tax favor in the form of tax exemption. With the advent of higher tax rates in the 1930s and thereafter, these benefits took on an added attractiveness, being equated to a higher level of cash, taxable income, the amount varying directly with the marginal tax rate. This has led employees in higher tax brackets to search for goods and services which might be received tax free; when these benefits have been discovered, companies have appeared to be eager to cooperate in giving them and in many cases have extended them to workers in lower marginal tax brackets.[2] As a result, the variety of goods and services offered by companies includes the following items and appears to be expanding: meals, housing, medical care, education, recreation, moving services, commuting facilities, credit (interest-free), clothing, employee discounts, and use of company property such as cars, yachts, lodges, and similar goods. There are doubtless other economic goods involved, but these appear to have attracted the most attention.

Three of these fringe benefits will be discussed at length in order to discover what problems are associated with their tax treatment and what principles are involved. Features peculiar to certain other fringe benefits in kind will then be analyzed.

B. MEALS

To qualify as a fringe benefit, a good should be desired by employees. On this ground, food doubtless ranks high. Thus an employer furnishing meals to his employees might be relatively safe in assuming that this is a good which employees would have desired strongly enough to have purchased if he had not furnished it. And although differences in tastes may affect pleasure in its receipt, there are innumerable goods where differences in tastes appear more pronounced.

Peculiarities of the industry, rather than tax treatment, appear to have been the stimulus originally leading to the furnishing of meals to employees. Thus, in cases where the employee was forced to work at a physical location some distance from commercial eating places, such as on ships, in logging camps, or on farms, the employer customarily furnished food. Also, when employees were on duty for extended lengths of time, as in hospitals, their food was customarily furnished. The general principle evolved that whenever it was to the employer's benefit that the employee be fed at the place of work, the value of the food received should not be considered as taxable income to the employee.

For most employees the taxability aspect probably at first carried no weight since exemptions were relatively high and first bracket tax rates were relatively low. However, as most employees have joined the ranks of taxpayers, and at the minimum marginal tax rate of 20 percent, an additional reason for granting free meals has developed. This feature does not seem to be cited as a reason for granting free meals, but the facts that there have been several court cases concerned with the taxability of meals, that the Treasury has been called upon to issue rulings on the taxability of free meals, and that Congress has seen fit to legislate, for the first time, on the taxability of free meals in the 1954 Internal Revenue Code all tend to point to the importance of the tax treatment.

The history of the tax treatment of meals given by the employer has been one of changing laws and regulations and seemingly inconsistent court decisions. Early apparent inclusion of meals as income "in whatever form paid" and subsequent exclusion when for "convenience of the employer" have already been cited.[3] Later Treasury rulings applied this latter principle to different occupations, pointing out the limitations of its applicability.[4] In 1925 the Court applied the principle in a case brought before it.[5]

In 1950 the Treasury departed from its previous path with the issuance of Mimeograph 6472 which held that meals and lodging furnished by the employer would be taxable to the employee if these benefits were considered as compensation— whether or not they might also be considered as given for the convenience of the employers.[6] This shifted the emphasis away from the convenience of the employer, but it still left important questions to be decided, such as how is it possible to determine when meals and lodging are considered as income and when they are not?[7] Still, it was felt in some quarters that the courts in subsequent cases were following the new ruling.[8]

The 1954 Internal Revenue Code, however, brought another reversal in direction. Section 119 of the Code stated that meals are to be excluded from the income of the recipient when furnished by the employer if they are furnished for the convenience of the employer and if they are furnished on the premises of the employer. Thus meals meeting these conditions are tax free even if considered as part of the compensation. The cycle of tax treatment seems to have run its course for the second time: starting with taxability of income "in whatever form paid," to exemption from taxation when given "for the convenience of the employer," returning to taxation when intended as compensation, and changing again to exemption when given "for the convenience of the employer" and given on the premises.

The amount of money involved in the purchase of this particular fringe benefit is difficult to determine, but it appears to be small. The Chamber of Commerce includes free meals in a miscellaneous classification along with a few other minor fringe benefits and estimates the cost of all these at about 1 percent of the total cost of fringe benefits. (See Appendix III.) At the same time, in the case of an individual worker the amount involved may be of sizable proportions.[9] Should, however, the practice of furnishing meals spread—and this trend is indicated by news stories and observation—the amount involved will be large, not only for the employee-recipient but also in total amount.

This type of fringe benefit given in kind, like other fringe benefits, can be expected to have certain effects on the tax system and on economic activities. If meals given to employees are considered as a form of income to employees—and the implication of section 119 is that meals are normally income—then the exclusion of these meals under certain conditions serves as an additional source of erosion of the tax base. The effect of the narrowed tax base on tax rates and incentives has been discussed above, but free meals deserve special mention from the standpoint of incentives to work. Break, in commenting on this subject, has noted that giving meals to workers reduces their fixed obligation to provide themselves with food and also their incentive to work.[10]

Another consideration in the evaluation of the present tax treatment of meals is the correspondence to the concept of equity. The question here would center on whether or not meals that were provided primarily for the convenience of the employer might also be of convenience, or income, to the employee.

In this light, the implication that something which benefits the employer is precluded from being a benefit to the employee does not appear to be well founded. It is also in the employer's interest that he pay money wages to the employee so that the employee may purchase goods which maintain him as a healthy, happy, and efficient worker, but this does not mean that the money wage is reduced in its worth to the employee. It is true that the employer may purchase a good that he would like the employee to use and the employee may consider the good as not worth its market price. But the preferred solution in this case may not be tax exemption to the recipient, in addition to deductibility to the employer-donor.

Where a good is as widely purchased for consumption purposes as is food, it would seem almost axiomatic that the supplying of meals to employees by employers would furnish usances to the employees and so would fall within the bounds of income. Vickrey notes that, even when the work to be done is in a remote area, the quarters (and presumably meals, too) furnished would seem to be more for the convenience of the employee than the employer.[11] Treasury rulings for other taxes based on wages note that although the "convenience of the employer" test is used in determining whether meals and quarters are income for income tax purposes, it is not relevant when computing income for Federal Insurance Contributions Act and Federal Unemployment Tax Act purposes. Under these laws the value of meals and lodging may be considered income, even when furnished employees on a vessel or in an isolated locality.[12]

There are other writers and other court cases which hold that meals are income to the employee even though the serving of these meals may also be construed as benefiting the employer. Kletzing[13] and Guttentag et al.[14] both argue that meals are income to the employee, although they advocate taxation at some value lower than cost. The judge in the Hyslope case ruled that a reimbursement made to Hyslope, an Indiana state trooper, for meals purchased while on duty, should be taxable because Hyslope was in no different position from other workers who were unable to have their meals at home.[15] In another case Martin, a wireless operator on a seafaring dredge, was ordered to include in his taxable income the value of food and lodging received by him while the dredge was at sea. The key fact in this case was that the employer paid Martin a salary from which was deducted an amount for food and lodging.[16] In the light of these arguments meals constitute income and their exemption from income taxation constitutes an inequity in tax treatment.

Tax favor for meals has also been the cause of a noticeable shift in the allocation of resources. In the case of meals furnished by the employer, one of the results has been increased expenditures on meals. This shift has occurred, as might be expected, through an increase in quality rather than quantity of meals consumed.   Evidence of this change may be gathered from the observation that much of the money spent in the most expensive restaurants is furnished by the employer for expense accounts.   This observation may be coupled with another: that the spenders do not customarily buy the same priced meals when using their own, after-tax money.[17]

There is another aspect to the subject of quality.   Since one of the reasons free meals are furnished is in order to improve the good will of the employees, the meals, unless they are of a quality at least equal to what the employee would have furnished for himself, will not create much good will.   Therefore, if error is to be made, it will likely be made in the direction of higher quality.   This assumption is also made by those writers who, although advocating taxation of meals as a form of income, propose that these meals be taxed at less than their cost because the employee will probably value them below cost.

The effect of the present tax treatment on labor mobility and on cyclical stability would appear to be negligible.   One other effect, however, intimated by the phrase "convenience of the employer," deserves mention.   It has been pointed out above that in an occupation the disutility associated with which is generally considered as being rather high, some tax-preferred fringe benefit might be justified as an offset to this disutility.   The phrase "convenience of the employer" may in some cases carry the connotation that the job has what would ordinarily be considered some unusual unpleasantness in the working conditions.   In these cases the allocation of resources would be improved by exemption from taxable income of the fringe benefits, perhaps meals, given to offset the unpleasant conditions.   However, the selection of occupations deserving this tax treatment is fraught with so many difficulties that it would probably be better left out of the considerations until more definite work has been done on this point.

The above-mentioned effects on the tax base, incentives, and tax equity have led to expressions of dissatisfaction with the present tax treatment.   Vickrey, for example, proposes that meals be included in income, but with some arbitrary reduction in the cost of the meal, because it is likely that the employer will furnish more expensive food than the employee would have voluntarily purchased.[18] Guttentag *et al.* argue for inclusion, since meals as a fringe benefit nearly always replace a personal expenditure, but at an arbitrary price.[19] Kletzing argues that meals should be partially nontaxable.[20] The Canadian Income Tax Act states that income shall include the value of board and lodging received by an employee [21] except when he is required by his work to be away for a period of twelve hours or longer from the municipality where he ordinarily reports for work. Meals consumed during the period of absence are not taxable income.[22]

In view of the effects of the present tax treatment of meals and the above proposals for a change, it would seem that a better treatment of meals could be found. The proposals for taxation at a fraction of the cost would work toward elimination of the effects on the tax base, incentives, and equity which have been discussed. However, inclusion at full value or cost could improve on this. This latter treatment would increase the tax base and reduce the disincentive effect relative to either complete exemption or partial exemption of meals. The difficulty of complete inclusion apparently arises from considerations of equity. It would be considered improper or inequitable by most persons to tax an employee on some good that he received but did not want. Therefore proposals have been made to tax the employee on some portion of the value of the meal, a portion that represents what the employee would have voluntarily purchased.

While partial inclusion will work toward the solution of this problem of equity, it fails to eliminate either it or another problem, the changed allocation of resources. The fact that part of the value of the meal is still untaxed means that as long as the worth of the untaxed part of the meal to the employee exceeds what would be his after-tax income if he were paid in cash instead of the meal, it pays him to take the meal.

This leads to the use of resources valued at a relatively high price to give to the employee utility which could have been purchased in a different mix to give the same utility with the use of fewer resources. The relationship may be set down in a formula with the following variables: let d be a fraction less than one, representing the value of the tax free portion of the fringe benefit in question to the employee-recipient divided by the market value of the fringe benefit; let r be the marginal tax rate of the employee. If, then, r is greater than $1 - d$, it will pay the employee to accept the fringe benefit; if r is less than $1 - d$, it will pay him to accept cash wages instead. This formula points out that where r is high or where d is high there will be pressure to secure payment for work in the form of fringe benefits with a resulting change in the allocation of resources from that which would exist if all payments were in cash and subject to tax. The result is that the person selecting the fringe benefit is able to increase his share of consumption, which in a full employment economy must come at the expense of some other consumer, the government, business, or some combination of the three.

Since partial inclusion of meals in the tax base does not completely solve the problem of equal treatment of persons similarly situated, would complete inclusion constitute an improvement? Under complete inclusion the argument that the taxpayer would be taxed on goods which he did not value highly would be true if he continued to receive those goods. However, if the employee were being taxed on goods which he did not value so highly as the market, it would seem that he would request that his employer give him cash instead of the not-so-desirable goods. In other words, there would be a force, taxation, encouraging the employee to move from the malallocation obtaining under the granting of tax-free fringe benefits. At the same time the tax base would be broadened either by the inclusion of the marginal fringe benefit heretofore excluded or by the inclusion of cash which was substituted for the less desirable fringe benefit.

Accordingly a tax policy of inclusion in the tax base at full value or cost, at least in the case of meals, would constitute an improvement in the tax base, incentives to work, equitable treatment, and allocation of economic goods.

C. HOUSING

The use of housing as a fringe benefit largely parallels that of meals, since in many cases both board and lodging have been furnished employees. And, as in the case of meals, the tax treatment of housing has turned on the "convenience of the employer" doctrine, with housing generally being held as a form of taxable income unless it was given for the convenience of the employer.[23] The 1950 Treasury ruling [24] narrowed the "convenience of the employer" doctrine as it applied to lodging, but section 119 of the Internal Revenue Code of 1954 restored some of the nontaxability by stating that lodging would not be includable in the taxable income of the employees if he were "required to accept such lodging on the business premises of his employer as a condition of his employment."[25] Thus it is possible for this economic good, which is usually purchased for use as consumer good, to be received by an employee and yet not be considered as part of his taxable income.

The comments which have been made above with regard to the effects of the present tax treatment of meals furnished by an employer are equally applicable to housing similarly furnished. Again, the results that might be expected are a reduced tax base, reduced incentive to work relative to those which would exist if all income received were subject to tax, an increased use of the product, and a more favorable tax treatment for those receiving this benefit than for those who pay for their housing out of after-tax income. The argument that home owners are the recipients of tax favor in being allowed the deductibility of interest and property taxes and in not having to report imputed income from this investment may narrow the gap between the recipient of the fringe benefit and the home owner but, even so, a gap remains.   And it widens between the employee who receives tax-free housing and the employee who rents his housing.

In view of this situation, those who have proposed that meals furnished by employers be included in the taxable income of the employee have also made similar recommendations concerning the tax treatment of housing.[26]   Here again concern has been voiced about the equity of taxation of the full value of the fringe benefit furnished because of a lack of freedom of choice on the part of the employee-recipient and because he may be given more expensive quarters than he would have voluntarily chosen.   But here, too, taxation at full value would be more equitable vis à vis other income recipients, and it would highlight the problem created by giving the employee better quarters than he would have chosen.

There is, however, one important respect in which a fringe benefit in the form of housing differs from a fringe benefit in the form of meals.   This difference arises in the case where an employee maintains a residence and the employer provides him with quarters in addition to this regular residence.   In such a case there is less reason to believe that this good is provided by the employer as a form of extra income to the employee and less reason to believe that the good is highly valued by the employee as extra income.

Solution of this problem requires a reexamination of the reasons an employer has for making payments for certain goods and services, and of how these payments relate to personal income.   Some of these payments are made for goods and services which will be embodied in the product being produced; they are not considered as furnishing the employee any utility, pleasure, or usance.   Examples might be the raw materials purchased, tools to work with, and fire insurance on the factory. Some other expenditures may be made in order to make the plant a pleasant place in which to work.   These benefit the employee and so might be considered as taxable income, but for various reasons they are usually classified as conditions of work and left untaxed.   Examples might be heat and air conditioning in the plant, an attractively painted or decorated work place, music piped in to the work area, and attractive rest rooms. Finally, the employer may make payments to or on behalf of his employees in such a manner that these payments are considered of significant benefit to the employee and are taxed as income to the employee. Unfortunately there is no sharp line between these three classifications,[27] and it is the cases which lie on the margin, especially between the last two classifications, which give trouble when tax treatment is being determined.

When the employer furnishes to the employee housing which is his only place of residence, this seems to properly belong in the third classification of income to the employee. On the other hand, provision of quarters by an employer when the employee already maintains a residence may tend to move the fringe benefit out of the classification of income and into the classification of conditions of work or expenses of the employer.[28]

However, there are arguments which may be advanced to indicate that, even in this case, quarters furnished by the employer are income to the employee. For example, the fact that the employee is provided with housing for a good bit of the time may make it possible for him to maintain smaller or less expensive quarters, or to operate his regular residence with smaller expenditures, than he otherwise would have been able to do.

A second consideration stems from the federal income tax concept of commuting expenses. These are considered personal expenses by the tax law in that they arise from the employee's choice of location for his home. If the employer provided transportation to work, as is sometimes done in Great Britain,[29] this expenditure would doubtless he included in the employee's taxable income. If, on the other hand, the employer provided a residence at the place of employment, this might be considered in fact a substitute for commutation expenses. In some cases this is the cheapest way to commute. Wealthy people, especially, sometimes maintain a residence at some place of their own choosing and in addition a house, apartment, or room near their place of work. Both of these residences are considered personal expenses.

There are thus advantages to be gained by the employee even when he maintains his own separate residence, and under these circumstances it would be proper to tax this benefit as income. However, when this is the case, much more so than when the employer is providing the employee with his only residence, a portion of the expenditure can properly be described as benefiting *only* the employer, very much like the purchase of tools for the employee to use. Here, then, it would seem proper to tax the benefit at something less than full cost or value. The tax could be levied on some value based on cost and age of the building, or on some value calculated as a percentage of the wage received,[30] or at some percentage of the value of the housing.

At least one additional condition should be laid down: that the value of the housing maintained by the employee should exceed in value the housing furnished by the employer. Without this provision, it would be possible for the employee to own or pay rent on a sub-standard dwelling place and then have the employer furnish him more expensive, tax-preferred quarters. The administration of this rule would be in the vein of the 1950 Treasury ruling.[31] That is, housing furnished an employee should be considered as compensation unless the taxpayer can prove that he already maintains more expensive quarters from his own funds; then taxation might be based on some lower value.

The tax treatment of housing is more complicated than that of meals, since it is possible for a person to profitably receive two houses, but hardly two meals, within the usual period of consumption. Nevertheless, the proposals made are similar to those that have been made by others, and it is felt that increased difficulties in administration, if they should develop, would be more than offset by improvements in equity, the tax base, lowered tax rates, and the allocation of resources.

D. MEDICAL CARE FOR EMPLOYEES

In addition to health, medical, hospitalization, and surgical insurance, which many employees are receiving from their employers, employees are the recipients of other, more direct goods and services aimed at preserving their good health. Many companies are taking steps to provide medical care or diagnostic services for their employees in their plants or at medical centers, and some employers who feel their plants are not of sufficient size to bear such an expense alone have entered into cooperative medical programs.[32]

Since medical services are usually purchased by consumers as a personal consumer good, any provision of these services by an employer would appear to be a form of income in kind It is, of course, true that expenditures for these goods or services are permitted within limits as a personal deduction in the computation of taxable income, but the inequities which arise from leaving these expenditures out entirely have already been pointed out in the discussion of hospitalization insurance. Like hospitalization insurance, then, medical care received directly from the employer should be a part of the recipient's income. There is, however, an additional problem here. The difference between employer expenditures for goods and services giving no benefit to employees, expenditures to improve employee working conditions, and expenditures to increase the income of employees has been mentioned. It is probable that in the cases of medical care and education these three types of expenditures merge more smoothly into one another than in any other employer expenditures which might be considered as a fringe benefit. It would be agreed by most persons that, in the event an employee is injured at work, medical care should be available for him and its receipt should not constitute income to him. On the other hand, a person receiving medical care for an illness or injury not connected with his earning a livelihood would be considered by most as receiving income. The dividing line between these two cases, however, may be a very indistinct one. Who can trace with certainty the cause of a cold, asthma, allergies, heart trouble, strained muscles, certain diseases, or even psychiatric disorders? Are these ailments congenital, or are they contracted at home, at play, at work, from overwork, or just how?

Plant medical facilities may range from the first aid stand with no paid attendant to elaborate hospital facilities.[33] In addition to in-plant medical care, companies may furnish medical care on other, perhaps more inviting premises.[34] Estimates of the cost of these medical programs range from just under $10.00 per employee per year for in-plant medical care in large firms [35] to about $300 per employee for a diagnostic examination given by Life Extension Examiners, an organization in the business of providing this fringe benefit.[36]

There are, therefore, several difficulties attendant upon the taxation of this fringe benefit. The amount involved per employee in most cases is relatively small; there is the difficulty in determining what part of the expenditure stems from the job of the employee and what part is merely a form of personal consumption; the expenditure is allowable as a personal deduction within limits and so, in many cases, if it were included in the employee's income he could also list the expense as a deduction from adjusted gross income; it would entail additional difficulties in administration, since employers would have to make a calculation of the amount of the fringe benefit received by each employee and the employee would have to include this amount in his income. Not a difficulty of taxation but what might be considered a benefit of nontaxation is the possible encouragement of increased use of medical resources that, it is sometimes argued, give better health not only to the recipient but also to his neighbors, since in many cases the health of an individual depends to no small extent on the health of his neighbors.[37]

Arguments for taxation which may be set against those just mentioned are the arguments which were cited in connection with hospitalization insurance: the tax base is narrowed; tax rates are necessarily increased, with effects on economic activity; taxpayers similarly situated are not similarly treated by tax laws; and there is a shift in the allocation of economic goods toward an increased consumption of medical services.

The tax treatment of this fringe benefit will depend on how these two sets of arguments are evaluated. One solution has been instituted with regard to the tax treatment of this fringe benefit under the social security laws. Here it has been held that facilities and privileges such as entertainment, medical services, or discounts on purchases, are not to be taxed if they are small in amount and are furnished by an employer "as a means of promoting the health, goodwill, contentment, or efficiency of his employees." [38] Since the furnishing of health, goodwill, contentment, or efficiency can also be accomplished by taxable wages, the key feature of this ruling is probably the requirement that the expenditure be small in amount.

The tax treatment of medical care furnished by the employer will depend on the values placed on all the arguments for and against taxation of this fringe benefit. It is suggested, however, that in general these expenditures be included in the gross income of the employee. One exception to this general rule might be that when the amount involved is "small," say around $15 to $25, which would change the tax of the lowest marginal rate taxpayer by only $3 to $5, the payment not be included in the employee's income. Furthermore, when it can be shown that the medical service is furnished as a result of injury or illness due to the employee's work, then this sum should be allowed as a deduction from the employee's gross income. This treatment should meet two of the more important arguments against taxation: the high administrative cost relative to the tax yield and the unjustness of taxing as income services received because of a business-incurred expense. At the same time it recognizes the arguments for taxation of this fringe benefit along with many other fringe benefits.[39]

E. OTHER FRINGE BENEFITS IN KIND

The three fringe benefits in kind discussed above are not the only ones offered to employees today; perhaps they are not even the most important ones. While there have been, since the beginning of the income tax in the United States, examples of income in kind to worry those who deal with the income tax, the importance, for tax purposes, of these fringe benefits has been increased as a result of recent developments: the broadened coverage of the tax through reduced exemptions, increased tax rates which increase the importance of every non-taxable dollar of income, a social conscience which holds that persons should be assured of having certain goods, such as medical care and, increasingly, higher education for their children, and intermittent wartime wage controls which restricted payments in cash but left other avenues open. Payment of wages in goods has, in many cases, tended to meet one or all of these objectives. The resulting increased use of fringe benefits has been not only in increased quantity but in increased quality, with a wider variety of goods coming within the pale of the fringe benefit classification. A few of the goods which are frequently used as fringe benefits for employees may be briefly described.

Education is a fringe benefit with a wide range of applicability. It is given to employees by hiring teachers to come to the plant to teach after hours or on company time, by the company's setting up its own instructional institution, or by paying the employee's tuition at some educational institution.[40] Instruction is at many levels, including in-plant instruction on the job, in-plant instruction concerning hobbies and entertainment activities,[41] general and vocational education in company schools,[42] courses at accredited colleges,[43] graduate work, including acquiring a Doctor of Philosophy degree,[44] and specialized executive training courses at some of the nation's leading universities.[45] Educational benefits are not confined to employees, but are also being bestowed on dependents of employees.[46]

Planned recreation for employees financed by employers is another type of expenditure which is growing and which is considered by some as a fringe benefit. The expenditures may take many forms, ranging from the mere provision of grounds where athletic contests may be held to the provision of directors of recreation, expensive recreation facilities, and equipment, and even to allowing employees to engage in these activities on company time.[47] In this field, as in medical care, unions are also taking steps to provide services financed primarily by payments direct from the employer to the union and by tax-exempt union dues.

Another fringe benefit, the use of which has increased recently, is the provision of moving services for the newly hired employee. Some examples of this and some comments on the effect of this fringe benefit on the mobility of labor have already been given.[48] So far this benefit appears to be confined to employees with skills which are in relatively scarce supply, i.e., those who draw wages much higher than the average wage or those who are hard to find at going wage rates,[49] and it is at the present considered as personal, taxable income by both the Treasury and the courts; thus it can hardly be considered an important example of tax favor. However, continued use with possible preference appears likely when it is noted that: (1) the benefit will likely continue to be used to attract particular persons to employment, (2) a good case can be made for nontaxability on grounds both of equity and resource allocation, (3) the court, while calling for taxation, has recognized the argument of inequitable treatment, and (4) legislation has been introduced to remove this fringe benefit from taxation.[50] Pressure for changed tax treatment of the fringe benefit may eventually lead the way to a closer correspondence of the income tax to a tax on income.

Discounts on goods sold by employers to employees have attracted the attention of writers on taxation,[51] and in some cases these discounts doubtless are of sufficient size to warrant consideration of their tax treatment.[52]

A fringe benefit which has not enjoyed as widespread use in this country as abroad is the provision of commuting facilities. In England and Scotland there are instances of workers being carried to and from work for distances up to twenty miles in company buses.[53] In this country the provision of parking space for commuting employees would be a corresponding fringe benefit. This benefit would in most cases be of negligible value,[54] but space furnished in the heart of a crowded city might not be so unimportant.[55]

A fringe benefit enjoying increased use is interest-free loans by the employer to the employee. These loans are often made to employees for the purchase of either stock in the company or a personal insurance policy by the employee.[56] Like the medical type of fringe benefit, expenditures for interest qualify as a personal deduction. Thus there is a change only with regard to taxpayers using the optional standard deduction. In the event that the deduction for interest is ever abandoned, this fringe benefit would take on more importance.

Less definite but probably more widely employed than most of the benefits just discussed is the use of company property for personal consumption purposes by employees. Although the employee may not be given ownership of the property, as is usual in the cases cited above, he is given the right to consume the property, and this is basically what is purchased when the ownership of property changes hands. Thus companies have found that they can reward employees by permitting increased use of company property, with the same effect as by increasing wages,[57] and employees, especially in the high marginal tax brackets, have come to look for this type of benefit.[58]

The application of the principle is broader than the use of only physical property. In some cases the use of services of other company employees is allowed as a fringe benefit. Thus some companies provide personal counseling in law, investments, taxes, real estate, and some other areas.[59] An attempt to deal with more extravagant uses of company property and services was made in H. R. 7893, introduced May 16, 1952. It proposed to include in the Code, "Any person (1) making any payment of anything of value to or on behalf of any officer, employee, partner or shareholder of such person or (2) making any service, property or facility available to any person described in (1)" shall report such payments to the Secretary of the Treasury, provided the sum of these payments exceeds $200 during a year.

The discussion in the present study has been confined to fringe benefits as defined therein: those payments, over and above cash wages, for something which furnishes utility to the employee, paid by the employer to or on behalf of the employee. This has been interpreted as meaning the purchase of some good which is given to the employee or the arrangement with some firm selling a good or service for delivery of the good, service, or money to the employee at some time in the future. In practice this definition of fringe benefits excludes what appears to be one of the growing ways of benefiting employees by employer payment: the system whereby a labor union furnishes the benefit to the employee, while the money to finance the good or service is furnished by the employer. In this case it appears that the union is the donor of the benefit and so it is not usually considered in the class of other fringe benefits. Nevertheless, from a tax standpoint it should matter little whether the employer purchases the good for the employee or gives the money to the union for the same purpose.

An example of this type of benefit is the hospitalization and medical service furnished by the United Mine Workers to its members. This particular project calls for the construction of ten hospitals in three states for the purpose of furnishing miners with free medical service. Payments to physicians for services are also to be made by the union. Thus the employee is to be furnished with goods and services which he might otherwise have to purchase from his regular wage income. The costs of this project are to be borne by the United Mine Workers Welfare Fund, which at present receives a forty cent royalty on each ton of coal produced, paid by the employers to the Welfare Fund. In the first ten years of the Fund's existence, it took in almost one billion dollars.[60]

When this process is subjected to closer examination, it can be seen that here is a payment made by employers to the union, and, that since this payment does not go directly as personal income, it is not subjected to personal income taxation. Later, when the payment is turned into goods or services that benefit the employee, it is possible that the benefit will not be counted as income to the recipient. In one case involving a pension given by the union to retired union members and financed by union members, the contribution was held nontaxable while the benefit was held to be taxable income.[61] But the regulations hold that pensions paid by those to whom no service has been rendered are not taxable to the recipient,[62] and so the possibility of nontaxability is ever present.

So long as the payments to the union members are in the form of medical services, it may be argued that the actual change in the amount of taxable income will be minor. This may be true, but some consideration should also be given to the equity aspects as outlined above. Union-furnished goods and services appear to be growing,[63] and here is a potentially important source of income to the recipient. If this is coupled with the present allowance of union dues as a deduction from income, it is possible that in the future unions could furnish members with many of the goods and services they now buy with their after-tax income. These goods, if financed with nontaxable employer contributions or tax-deductible employee dues, could be considered as nontaxable gifts, and so completely escape income taxation. The initial steps along this path appear to have been taken.

There are doubtless other fringe benefits in kind than the ones that have been mentioned, but these have been selected for two reasons: they have all at some time been given tax treatment which is preferential if they are considered as forms or personal consumption, and they have all been considered by one or more writers as warranting discussion and recommendations for alternative tax treatment. Thus, both individually and collectively, as another part of the body of fringe benefits, their tax treatment should be reexamined.

· VIII ·

Summary and Conclusions

THE role of fringe benefits in economic life today has been described above, with an attempt to explain why fringe benefits have become so important a part of the present scene and what might be expected with regard to the growth and use of fringe benefits in the future. The effects of these fringe benefits on economic activities and on various aspects of public finance have been discussed.

In general it can be said that the use of fringe benefits has arisen for a number of reasons, only one of which has been their preferential tax treatment. However, with the advent of the Second World War and increased tax rates and the coming of postwar court decisions broadening the scope of collective bargaining, the tax status of fringe benefits has become much more important. This tax status has been important in the growth of fringe benefits and, reciprocally, the growth of fringe benefits has been important in the increased interest in their tax status.

The problems connected with the use of fringe benefits and the tax treatment accorded them have been discussed, and an attempt has been made to suggest an improved tax treatment for each of the benefits. In general this has entailed an attempt to determine whether or not the fringe benefit might be considered as income to the recipient and, if it could be so considered, then to determine when it is income, how the tax might be levied, and what effects might be expected from the proposed change in tax treatment.

Although this process might be considered a piecemeal solution to the problem of the taxation of fringe benefits, unified results are achieved by adhering to a general set of principles.

In the first place, the taxation of fringe benefits is only one part of a larger problem of the tax treatment to be accorded many other payments that are classified as income by many economists and writers on public finance but are specifically excluded by certain provisions in tax laws and tax rulings. This is the problem of the erosion of the tax base, which concerns capital gains, depletion allowances, the income of farmers, and many other deductions and forms of receipt as well as the several forms of fringe benefits that have been discussed. The solution of this problem requires basically the determination of a definition of income to be taxed and then a stricter adherence to the definition. The reason for the present state of affairs regarding taxation and tax exemption of the abovementioned forms of income possibly arises because a good case can be made for the favorable tax treatment of almost any particular receipt in order to encourage its use. What has been overlooked, however, is the effect of this tax favor on other forms of receipt and other economic activities. If encouragement of some economic condition is desired, tax policy may be used, but such treatment fails to spotlight its subsidization aspect, and tax preference is often presented as a relatively costless process. An increased awareness of the costs of tax preference should encourage a closer adherence to the impartial taxation of income.

Closely related to the problem of defining income, but nevertheless sufficiently different to warrant separate classification and discussion, is the problem of separating wages, as a form of taxable income, from conditions of work, generally considered as contributing to the well-being of the employee but not to his income. Although no definite and widely accepted answer to this problem seems to have been advanced in the literature, this important problem must be considered in order to arrive at a general principle regarding the tax treatment of fringe benefits. Accordingly an attempt has been made to list the factors that seem most important in determining the boundary between wages and conditions of employment. With a general definition of taxable income and with a general guide for separating wages from conditions of work, the tax treatment of fringe benefits can be determined so as to become a logical part of a consistent tax system. Without these general rules, the tax treatment will continue on its decision-by-decision basis, with resulting inconsistencies.

As a guide to the tax treatment of fringe benefits it has been suggested that the definitions of income given by Haig and Simons come closest to corresponding to the general intent of the federal income tax as expressed in the Internal Revenue Code. Haig defined income as "the money value of the net accretion to one's economic power between two points in time." [1] Accordingly the tax treatment of fringe benefits should be determined within this frame of reference, and Haig's warning that departures from this definition will create anomolies and injustices in income taxation should be emphasized.

To attempt to separate wages from conditions of work has been more difficult. Here there seems to be no sharply drawn line, but it has been suggested that benefits accruing to workers are more likely to be considered as conditions of work when the benefits flow naturally from the particular type of work, or when goods and services purchased by the employer are consumed by all or most employees, in about the same quantities and qualities at the place of employment, with low marginal cost per employee. In fact, considerations determining the taxability of these benefits are likely more important in determining what might be called "conditions of work" than the conditions are in determining the taxability.

With the guideposts of a definition of income and a general concept of conditions of work, the examination of the tax treatment of particular fringe benefits has been undertaken. Several fringe benefits have been examined in this light, and an attempt has been made to determine how the present taxation affects certain aspects of economic activity, such as the allocation of resources, mobility of labor, and cyclical stability, and certain aspects of the operation of the tax system, such as the size of the tax base, incentives to work, equitable treatment of taxpayers, and administration of the tax. In this way the effects of the present taxation of the fringe benefit may be compared with the effects that may be expected from other tax treatments and some conclusion reached as to the preferred tax treatment.

As a result of this type of analysis, the tax treatment of pensions is held to rest on the insurance and savings aspect of the plan. If the benefit payment by the employer goes for insurance and does not give the employee a paid-up refundable claim for future payment, the contribution should not be taxed, but the final benefit payment should. If, on the other hand, the contribution by the employer goes for a paid-up insurance policy, annuity, or pension, the contribution resembles saving, and should receive the same tax treatment as other forms of saving. These very general observations may be applied to particular fringe benefits like pension plans, life insurance, old-age and survivors insurance, widow's benefits, unemployment insurance, health insurance, and several other similar benefits. In most of these cases the proposed tax treatment marks a departure from present treatment.

Besides the general classes of insurance and saving type fringe benefits there are fringe benefits that are given in kind. For these goods the important considerations are to what extent they are given to offset unpleasant working conditions and to what extent they might be considered as having the attributes of conditions of work. Ordinarily, however, if they consist of goods normally purchased as consumption goods, a better case can be made for their taxability. Here, again, there are important examples of their present exclusion from taxation, indicating that the proposals for taxation would lead to a change in tax treatment.

The individual fringe benefits discussed may appear to be of small value and therefore relatively inconsequential, but their past growth has been cited, their collective importance stressed, and their future growth predicted. A 1956 study of the erosion of the income tax base lists several deductions, exemptions, and forms of income and expenditures which are not taxed but which, from the general concept of taxable income, apparently belong in taxable income. Fringe benefits are one of these exclusions mentioned and, according to the estimates made, account for the second largest amount of tax loss of the classifications made, second only to the standard deduction.[2]

One final factor contributing to the solution of the problem deserves mention. The fringe benefits that have been discussed above are largely those that are given to most or all employees. However, a few of these, such as widow's benefits, stock options, stock purchase plans, and deferred compensation, are generally confined to the higher-paid employees. The reason often cited for the use of these benefits is that they help minimize the employee's income tax by spreading his compensation over a longer period of time when his earnings, at the later dates, might be lower. If this is done under a progressive income tax, a more evenly spaced income will result in a smaller tax.

The problems created by an arbitrary choice of the year as the accounting period for calculating income taxes have been widely publicized in both the popular press and the learned journals. As a result, the subject has received the attention of writers in the field of public finance, and several proposals for solving the problem have been advanced.[3] In fact, a few unsuccessful attempts at averaging have been made by some government units in the past.[4]

The problem of averaging has wide application, affecting many baseball players, movie actors, physicians, graduate students, casual laborers, business executives, and others. One of the solutions, perhaps unexpected, to this problem has been the introduction of certain fringe benefits, and these fringe benefits appear to be the ones wherein a decision with regard to tax treatment is most difficult.[5] Consequently the adoption of some form of averaging is recommended to remove the pressure for granting these benefits and to furnish a policy for taxation of both the benefits and other forms of income which vary markedly from year to year. A system of averaging might also forestall the normal tendency of fringe benefits to spread from higher income workers to lower income workers [6] and discourage the introduction of new averaging-type fringe benefits. The effect of a system of averaging in checking the spread of fringe benefits is another advantage, one not often mentioned, in favor of averaging as a part of the income tax system.

Fringe benefits have become an increasingly important part of wage contracts and, as such, an increasingly important part of compensation for labor. There are few if any signs that either their growth in dollar terms or their rate of growth is likely to diminish in the near future. Expenditures of this magnitude cannot be ignored by the tax system. It is hoped that the observations and principles discussed in this study will contribute toward a tax treatment of fringe benefits which will result in an improved federal income tax.

Appendix I

A. Pay for time not worked

1. Vacations
2. Holidays
3. Lunch periods
4. Sick and maternity leaves
5. Medical care time (at the plant)
6. Personal excused-absence time
   a. Death in family; b. Shopping time; c. Medical and dental care time (away from plant)
7. Jury duty time
8. Voting time
9. Wet-time (time lost due to inclement weather)
10. Witness time

B. Monetary awards and prizes for special activities and performance

1. Anniversary awards
2. Attendance bonus
3. Plant neatness bonus
4. Service bonuses and awards
5. Quality bonus
6. Prize awards in employee contests relating to safety, waste reduction, morale, and other subjects
7. Suggestion plan awards
8. Other non-production bonuses or awards requiring some special employee activity or service

C. Bonuses, contributions, and profit sharing, for which the employee renders no direct regular or special service

1. Current profit-sharing payments (not related to provision of retirement income)
2. Stock (thrift) plan contributions
3. Stock purchase plan contributions
4. Sale of company stock at less than current value
5. Christmas or year end bonus

6. Separation allowance (dismissal, severance, or terminal pay)
7. Layoff pay or allowance
8. Military induction bonus
9. Military service allowance
10. Supplements to unemployment or workmen's compensation
11. Family allowance
12. Educational subsidies or tuition or expense payments (when not related directly to the employee's job)
13. College scholarship awards to employee's sons and daughters

D. Payments to provide employee security and financial protection against various hazards and contingencies

1. Legally required payments
   a. Old-age and survivors insurance; b. Unemployment insurance; c. Workmen's compensation; d. State disability insurance
2. Other payments to provide protection (by insurance or otherwise) against
   a. Death; b. Nonoccupational accident, sickness, and dismemberment; c. Hospitalization expense; d. Medical expense; e. Surgical expense; f. Retirement (pension, and in some cases deferred profit-sharing plans)
3. Employee welfare fund contributions
4. Administrative costs of employee benefit programs

E. Practices and services that benefit employees primarily

1. Credit union facilities
2. Food service costs or losses
3. Employee discounts
4. Music lessons, golf instruction, and other services rendered at reduced cost or at no cost to employees and dependents
5. Garden plots
6. Vacation, health, and hospital facilities provided at low cast
7. House financing

Source: C. W. Sargent, *"Fringe" Benefits: Do We Know Enough About Them?* (Hanover, New Hampshire: Amos Tuck School of Business Administration, 1953), pp. 14–15.

Appendix II

A. Fringe benefits listed by the survey

1. Bargaining and grievance time
2. Bonuses
3. Cafeterias
4. Credit unions
5. Gifts and other awards
6. Holidays
7. Insurance (includes life, hospitalization, medical-surgical, sickness, and accident)
8. Old age and survivors insurance
9. Unemployment compensation
10. Workmen's compensation
11. Lunch periods (paid)
12. Payment to jurors, National Guard, etc.
13. Pensions
14. Profit sharing
15. Recreational activities
16. Rest periods (paid)
17. Severance pay
18. Vacations
19. Wash-up time
20. Welfare funds (money, flowers, etc.)
21. Miscellaneous

B. Fringe benefits added under "miscellaneous" by the companies surveyed

1. Anniversary award
2. Canteen
3. Clean-up time
4. Coffee—milk
5. Death in family pay
6. Dispensary
7. Down time allowance
8. Early closing before holidays
9. Electric rate discount
10. Employee discounts
11. Employee education
12. Employee newspaper
13. Employee relief
14. Eyeglasses
15. First aid
16. Gloves
17. Income tax service
18. Indoctrination and training

19. Laundry
20. Lost time for lunch wagon visitation
21. Medical
22. Military gratuity
23. Military separation pay
24. Non-interest loans
25. Nonoccupational disability pay
26. Parking facilities
27. Physical examination, annual
28. Purchases at discount
29. Safety shoes
30. Safety supplies
31. Seniority bonus
32. Shower allowance
33. Sick leave plan
34. Suggestion awards
35. Tardy allowance time
36. Uniforms
37. Work clothing
38. Miscellaneous item not explained

Source: Associated Industries of Cleveland, "Employee Benefit Survey" (February 17, 1954, unpaged mimeograph).

Appendix III

FRINGE PAYMENTS BY TYPE OF PAYMENT, 1953 and 1957

	Total companies		Total manu-facturing		Total nonmanu-facturing	
	(in percent of payroll)					
	1953	1957	1953	1957	1953	1957
Legally required payments (employer's share only)						
Old-Age and Survivors Insurance	1.3	2.1	1.3	2.0	1.3	2.1
Unemployment Compensation:						
0.3% tax to Federal Government	0.3	0.2	0.3	0.2	0.3	0.2
State tax (net)	0.8	0.8	0.9	0.9	0.7	0.6
Workmen's Compensation (including estimated cost for self-insured)	0.7	0.7	0.9	0.9	0.4	0.5
Railroad Retirement Tax, Railroad Unemployment Insurance, state sickness benefits insurance, etc.	0.1	0.1	*	0.1	0.1	0.1
Total	3.2	3.9	3.4	4.1	2.8	3.5
Pension and other agreed-upon payments (employer's share only)						
Pension-plan premiums and pension payments not covered by insurance-type plans (net)	3.8	4.1	2.6	3.1	5.8	5.9
Life insurance premiums, death benefits, sickness, accident, and medical-care insurance premiums, hospitalization insurance, etc. (net)	1.8	2.2	1.8	2.3	1.8	1.9
Contributions to privately financed unemployment benefit funds		0.1		0.2		*
Separation or termination pay allowances	*	*	*	*	*	*
Discounts on goods and services purchased from company by employees	0.1	0.1	*	*	0.3	0.3
Miscellaneous payments (free meals, compensation payments in excess of legal requirements, payments to needy employees, tuition refunds, savings and stock purchase plans, etc.)	0.2	0.3	0.1	0.2	0.4	0.5
Total	5.9	6.8	4.5	5.8	8.3	8.6

FRINGE PAYMENTS BY TYPE OF PAYMENT, 1953 and 1957
(Continued)

	Total companies		Total manu-facturing		Total nonmanu-facturing	
	(in percent of payroll)					
	1953	1957	1953	1957	1953	1957
Paid rest periods, lunch periods, wash-up time, travel time, clothes-change time, get-ready time, etc.						
Total	2.0	2.3	2.1	2.4	1.8	2.0
Payments for time not worked						
Paid vacations and bonuses in lieu of vacation	3.3	3.8	3.2	3.9	3.6	3.7
Payments for holidays not worked	2.1	2.3	1.9	2.2	2.4	2.3
Paid sick leave	0.6	0.6	0.2	0.3	1.2	1.3
Payments for State or National Guard duty, jury, witness and voting pay allowances, payments for time lost due to death in family or other personal reasons, etc.	0.2	0.2	0.1	0.1	0.4	0.4
Total	6.2	6.9	5.4	6.5	7.6	7.7
Other items						
Profit-sharing payments	0.6	0.8	0.6	0.7	0.7	0.9
Christmas or other special bonuses, service awards, suggestion awards, etc.	1.0	0.8	0.6	0.6	1.8	1.2
Special wage payments ordered by courts, payments to union stewards, etc.	0.3	0.3	0.2	0.2	0.4	0.3
Total	1.9	1.9	1.4	1.5	2.9	2.4
Total fringe payments as percent of payroll	19.2	21.8	16.8	20.3	23.4	24.2
Total fringe payments as cents per payroll hour	34.6	47.4	31.5	44.9	40.0	50.8
Total fringe payments as dollars per year per employee	720	981	667	940	809	1,035
Number of companies	940	1,020	594	656	346	364

* Less than 0.5%.

Sources: Chamber of Commerce of the United States, *Fringe Benefits 1953* (Washington: Chamber of Commerce of the United States, 1954), p. 10.

Chamber of Commerce of the United States, *Fringe Benefits 1957* (Washington: Chamber of Commerce of the United States, 1958), p. 9.

Appendix IV

TOTAL QUALIFIED PENSION, PROFIT-SHARING, AND STOCK BONUS
PLANS IN OPERATION, 1930–1958

Period ending	Number of plans	Period ending	Number of plans
1930	110	June 30, 1951	14,671
1939	659	June 30, 1952	17,018
Sept. 1, 1942	1,947	June 30, 1953	20,675
Dec. 31, 1944	7,786	June 30, 1954	24,879
Aug. 31, 1946	9,370	June 30, 1955	28,160 (estimated)
June 30, 1947	10,399	June 30, 1956	32,300 (estimated)
June 30, 1948	11,258	June 30, 1957	38,050 (estimated)
June 30, 1949	12,154	June 30, 1958	44,540 (estimated)
June 30, 1950	12,925	Dec. 31, 1958	47,520 (estimated)

Source: Prentice Hall, Inc., *Prentice Hall Pension and Profit Sharing Service*
(New York: Prentice-Hall, Inc., loose leaf), par. 1012; supp. XVIII, pars. 9.6, 22.6.

Appendix V

A. The plan is one established by the employer for the exclusive benefit of his employees or their beneficiaries.

B. The sole purpose of the plan is to offer the employees (or their beneficiaries) either (a) a share of the profits of the business or (b) an income after retirement.

C. The plan is permanent.

D. The plan is in writing.

E. The plan is communicated to the employees.

F. The plan is in effect.

If a trust is involved, the following requirements relating to the trust must be satisfied as well:

G. It must be impossible *under the trust instrument* for any of the trust corpus or income to be used at any time other than for the exclusive benefit of the employees or their beneficiaries.

H. The contributions to the trust must be for the purpose of accumulating funds for distribution to employees or their beneficiaries in accordance with a plan qualified under the tax law, Sec. 401(a).

I. The trust is valid and existing under controlling local law.

Source: Prentice Hall, Inc., *Prentice-Hall Pension and Profit Sharing Service* (New York: Prentice-Hall, Inc., loose leaf), par. 1671.

Notes

NOTES TO CHAPTER I. HISTORICAL GROWTH AND QUANTITATIVE
IMPORTANCE OF FRINGE BENEFITS

1. Robert Murray Haig, "The Concept of Income," in Robert Murray Haig, ed., *The Federal Income Tax*, pp. 22–23. In discussing its breadth, Haig said, "It is by all odds the most theoretically perfect income tax law extant, from the point of view of its general scope" (p. 22).

2. U. S., *Internal Revenue Code of 1954*, sec. 61 (a).

3. William S. Vickrey, *Agenda for Progressive Taxation*, pp. 48–52; Henry C. Simons, *Personal Income Taxation*, pp. 52, 111.

4. Vickrey, *Agenda*, pp. 24–26; Donald B. Marsh, "The Taxation of Imputed Income," *Political Science Quarterly*, LVIII (1943), 515.

5. The Department of Commerce computes and publishes figures representing the value of some forms of imputed income. For example, for 1954 the imputed rental income from owner-occupied houses was estimated at $5.4 billion, while food produced and consumed on farms was estimated at $1.7 billion. U. S., Office of Business Economics, *Survey of Current Business*, July, 1956. p. 23.

6. Cf. Austin M. Fisher and John P. Chapman, "Big Costs of Little Fringes," *Harvard Business Review*, XXXII (1954), 35–44; Joseph H. Guttentag, E. Deane Leonard, and William Y. Rodewald, "Federal Income Taxation of Fringe Benefits: A Specific Proposal," *National Tax Journal*, VI (1953), 250–72. The U. S. Bureau of Labor Statistics in one of its studies is wary of using such a nebulous term and so entitles the study, *Problems in Measuement of Expenditures on Selected Items of Supplementary Employee Remuneration*, Bulletin 1186 (1956), pp. v, 13.

7. J. Henry Landman, "The Taxability of Fringe Benefits," *Taxes*, XXXIII (1955), 173.

8. Harold Stieglitz, *Computing the Cost of Fringe Benefits* (Studies in Personnel Policy, No. 128, 1952), p. 5.

9. *Ibid.*

10. *Ibid.,* p. 6.

11. C. W. Sargent, *"Fringe" Benefits: Do We Know Enough About Them?,* pp. 14–15.

12. Associated Industries of Cleveland, "Employee Benefit Survey."

13. Stieglitz, *Computing the Cost,* pp. 8–9.

14. *Ibid.,* p. 25. The problem arises as to how all nine companies could agree that health and accident insurance and paid military time off should be included as fringe benefits while the Quaker Oats Company, one of the nine companies, did not include them. A letter from Mr. Stieglitz to the writer explains that the table is a consensus of what the companies felt *should* be included as a fringe in cost calculations. Subsequent discussion describes what the companies actually included in their own calculations. One reason for the discrepancy between what should be and what is included is the difficulty of obtaining cost figures for the individual fringe benefits.

15. *Ibid.,* p. 8.   16. *Ibid.,* p. 9.

17. National Labor Relations Act, as amended by the Labor Management Act of 1947, sec. 9 (a).

18. Fisher and Chapman, "Big Costs of Little Fringes," *Harvard Business Review,* XXXII (1954), 37.

19. U. S., Office of Business Economics, *National Income 1954,* pp. 210, 180.

20. *Ibid.,* p. 210.   21. *Ibid.,* pp. 211, 181.

22. *Ibid.*

23. Chamber of Commerce of the United States of America, *The Hidden Payroll,* p. 13. See Chamber of Commerce of the United States of America, *Fringe Benefits, 1957,* p. 28, for a comparison of studies made in 1947, 1949, 1951, 1953, 1955, and 1957.

24. *Inland Steel Co.* v. *N. L. R. B.,* 170 F (2d) 247 (1948).

25. U. S., Office of Business Economics, *National Income 1954,* p. 211.

26. U. S., Office of Business Economics, *Survey of Current Business,* July, 1957, p. 22.

27. Chamber of Commerce, *Fringe Benefits, 1957,* p. 28.

28. U. S., Office of Business Economics, *National Income 1954,*

pp. 181, 211; U. S., Office of Business Economics, *Survey of Current Business,* July, 1957, pp. 16, 22.

29. Evan Keith Rowe, "Health, Insurance, and Pension Plans in Union Contracts," *Monthly Labor Review,* LXXVIII (1955), 993–95.

30. Fisher and Chapman, "Big Costs of Little Fringes," *Harvard Business Review,* XXXII (1954), 39.

31. The Health Insurance Council, *Accident and Health Coverage in the United States as of December 31, 1951,* p. 16.

32. Blue Cross advertisement, *Business Week,* April 16, 1955, p. 89.

33. United Automobile, Aircraft and Agricultural Implement Workers, *UAW-CIO Collective Bargaining Handbook for Workers Security Programs,* pp. 11–13.

34. Doris M. Thompson, *Cooperative Medical Programs* (Studies in Personnel Policy, No. 134, 1953), p. 4.

35. U. S., Steel Industry Board, *Report of the President of the United States on the Labor Dispute in the Basic Steel Industry,* p. 17.

36. *Ibid.,* pp. 7–8.

37. Treasury Decision 5186 in U. S., Bureau of Internal Revenue, *Cumulative Bulletin,* 1942–2, p. 352. (Hereafter called *Cum. Bul.*)

38. James C. Hill, "Stabilization of Fringe Benefits," *Industrial and Labor Relations Review,* VII (1954), 222–23.

39. U. S., Office of Business Economics, *National Income 1954,* pp. 181, 211.

40. Hill, "Stabilization of Fringe Benefits," *Industrial and Labor Relations Review,* VII (1954), 223–37.

41. See Lloyd G. Reynolds, *The Structure of the Labor Market,* pp. 94–95; also statements by Leonard Lesser, note 45, Chapter IV, below.

42. See pp. 76–77 above.

43. United Automobile Workers, *Collective Bargaining Handbook,* pp. 26–27. (Italics in original.)

44. Charles L. Dearing, *Industrial Pensions,* p. 300.

45. *Inland Steel Co.* v. *N. L. R. B.,* 170 F (2d) 247 (1948).

46. *W. W. Cross & Co.* v. *N. L. R. B.,* 170 F (2d) 285 (1948).

47. *United States Machinery Corp.,* 96 NLRB 1309 (1951).

48. *N. L. R. B.* v. *Lehigh Portland Cement Co.,* 205 F (2d) 821 (1953).

49. *Weyerhaeuser Timber Co.,* 87 NLRB 672 (1949).

50. Some other factors encouraging the adoption of fringe benefits are discussed in Allan I. Mendelsohn, "Fringe Benefits and Our Industrial Society," *Labor Law Journal,* VII (1956) 380–81, and in Arthur M. Ross, "Fringe Benefits Today and Tomorrow," *Labor Law Journal,* VII (1956), 477–78.

51. The unusual nature of these benefits makes news, and so most of these examples are gleaned from news stories. See "Havana Jaunt for 132, All on the Boss," *Life,* December 16, 1957, pp. 125–26; "Car in Every Garage—Boss Puts It There," Atlanta *Journal and Constitution,* March 30, 1958, p. 10–A; "More Companies Teach Employees How to Read—and Absorb—Faster," *Wall Street Journal,* January 9, 1957, p. 1; "Hedco Gives Year's Paid Vacation for 10 Years' Work," *Tide,* June 20, 1953, p. 54.

52. "Insurance—New 'Fringe' on Executive Payrolls," *Personnel,* XXX (1953), 71. This survey also pointed out that some executives are the recipients of high value group life insurance policies. See p. 127 below.

53. The Health Insurance Council, *The Extent of Voluntary Health Insurance Coverage in the United States as of December 31, 1955,* pp. 12–13, 20–21.

54. " 'Vesting' Assures Workers' Rights," New York *Times,* June 18, 1955, p. 22. See also "Trends Changing in Pension Plans," New York *Times,* August 12, 1956, pp. 1–F, 2–F.

55. Dearing, *Industrial Pensions,* pp. 108, 122.

56. U. S., Congress, House of Representatives, Committee on Ways and Means, *Hearings, Individual Retirement Act of 1955,* H. R. 10, 84th Cong., 1st Sess., pp. 35, 44. See also "House Group to Hold Hearings on Taxing Voluntary Pensions," *Wall Street Journal,* June 17, 1955, p. 3.

57. F. Beatrice Brower, "Group Insurance for Employees and Their Dependents, 1945–53," *Management Record,* XVI (1954), 297–99.

58. See "Greenwich Sees the Ghost of 1656," New York *Times,* August 1, 1956, p. 25, which tells of the purchase of Great Captain's Island in Long Island Sound by the Aerotec Corporation of Greenwich, Connecticut, for use by its 200 employees as a holiday spot. They hope "eventually, to build overnight cabanas, adequate water and sewage facilities and, perhaps, a club house."

59. See "New Price Tag on Policymakers," *Business Week,* July

16, 1955, p. 45; "Physical Checkup—In Style," *Business Week,* September 23, 1950, p. 84.

60. Dearing, *Industrial Pensions,* p. 166.

61. Fisher and Chapman, "Big Costs of Little Fringes," *Harvard Business Review,* XXXII (1954), 44.

62. "Union Threatens Strike Unless General Motors Betters Ford Terms," *Wall Street Journal,* June 8, 1955, p. 7. See also "Unions Hint at Demands to Come," *Business Week,* September 3, 1955, pp. 89–90.

NOTES TO CHAPTER II. PROBLEMS CREATED IN
PUBLIC FINANCE

1. Irving Fisher, *Constructive Income Taxation,* especially pp. 3–17.

2. Haig, *The Federal Income Tax,* pp. 1–28.

3. Simons, *Personal Income Taxation,* pp. 41–58, particularly p. 50. For a good discussion of this topic see Paul H. Wueller, "Concepts of Taxable Income," *Political Science Quarterly,* LIII (1938). Part I, "The German Contribution," is found at pp. 83–110; Part II, "The American Contribution," is found at pp. 557–83.

4. Fisher, *Constructive Income Taxation,* pp. 207–8.

5. Haig, *The Federal Income Tax,* p. 7. Simons complained that, literally construed, this definition excluded consumption but that Haig did not intend this. Simons therefore defined income as an algebraic sum of consumption and change in wealth over a given period of time. Simons, *Personal Income Taxation,* pp. 62, 50.

6. Haig, *The Federal Income Tax,* pp. 13–15.

7. U. S., *Statutes at Large,* XXXVIII (1913), 167.

8. *Ibid.*

9. Haig, *The Federal Income Tax,* p. 27.

10. See Walter W. Heller, "Appraisal of the Administration's Tax Policy," *National Tax Journal,* VIII (1955), 25; Paul Strayer, "The Individual Income Tax and Income Distribution," *American Economic Review,* XLV (1955), 434; Joseph A. Pechman, "Erosion of the Individual Income Tax," *National Tax Journal,* X (1957), 1–3.

11. Dan T. Smith, "Two Years of Republican Tax Policy: an Economic Appraisal," *National Tax Journal,* VIII (1955), 7.

12. *Ibid.*

13. *Commissioner* v. *Wilcox et al.,* 327 U. S. 404 (1946).

14. *Towne* v. *Eisner,* 245 U. S. 418 (1918).

15. *Jones* v. *U. S.,* 60 Ct. Cl. 525 (1925).

16. *Van Rosen* v. *Commissioner,* 17 T. C. 834 (1951).

17. J. Henry Landman, "The Taxability of Fringe Benefits," *Taxes,* XXXIII (1955), 177.

18. U. S., *Statutes,* XXXVIII (1913), 167. This terminology remained part of the Internal Revenue Code until 1954 when the wording was changed to give a much briefer general definition of income, which said, "Except as otherwise provided in this subtitle, gross income means all income from whatever source derived, including (but not limited to) the following items:" after which are listed fifteen specific examples of income.

19. O. D. 265, *Cum. Bul.* 1 (1919), p. 71. It is interesting to note that in a series of decisions two years later the "convenience of the employer" rule specifically excluded some income that is today included under the rule. Although board and lodging furnished to employees in fisheries and canneries, to employees of the Indian Service, and to hospital employees was under certain conditions considered as being for the convenience of the employer, these services when furnished to ministers, army officers, and domestic servants were not so considered. *Cum. Bul.* 4 (1921), pp. 84–86. Today, however, board and lodging furnished the last three groups is considered as nontaxable—presumably because of the convenience of the employer doctrine.

20. L. O. 1014, *Cum. Bul.* 2 (1920), pp. 88–90, U. S., United States Internal Revenue, *Regulations 45* (1920), article 33.

21. *Revenue Act of 1921,* sec. 219 (f).

22. *Revenue Act of 1926,* sec. 219 (f).

23. For a list of rulings covering this see Commerce Clearing House *Standard Federal Tax Reporter,* vol. 571, paragraphs 631.1734 and 631.1736.

24. Dearing, *Industrial Pensions,* pp. 285–87.

25. *Revenue Act of 1942,* sec. 165.

26. Bureau letter of October 26, 1943, reprinted in *Standard Federal Tax Reporter,* vol. 433, paragraph 6587.

27. Mim. 6472, *Cum. Bul.* 1950–1, p. 15.

28. I. T. 4027, *Cum. Bul.* 1950–2, pp. 9–11.

29. U. S., Congress, Senate, Committee on Finance, *Internal*

Revenue Code of 1954, Report No. 1622, 83rd Cong., 2nd Sess., p. 19.

30. "Tax Men Eye Wage Fringes," *Business Week,* July 18, 1953, p. 120.

31. Guttentag, *et al.,* "Federal Income Taxation of Fringe Benefits: A Specific Proposal," *National Tax Journal,* VI (1953), 251.

32. Fisher and Chapman, "Big Costs of Little Fringes," *Harvard Business Review,* XXXII (1954), 38. The average referred to is the arithmetic average of the second and third quartiles.

33. The 11¢ per productive hour per employee is the sum of benefits classed as "employee activities" and "employee benefits" less the pension plan.

34. Fisher and Chapman, "Big Costs of Little Fringes," *Harvard Business Review,* XXXII (1954), 40. The remaining 23¢ per productive hour was composed of 8¢ for overtime shift premiums and about 15¢ for pay during vacations, holidays, and other time off.

35. Chamber of Commerce of the United States, *Fringe Benefits, 1953,* p. 10. The Chamber of Commerce figure does not include premium payments for time worked, which Fisher and Chapman found to be 7.86¢ per hour per employee and did include in their figures. If this amount is subtracted from their 41¢ per hour, we get 33.14¢ per hour per employee, which is not very different from the Chamber of Commerce figure. One minor point which widens the gap between the two sets of figures is the use of fringe benefits per employee per productive hour by Fisher and Chapman and fringe benefits per employee per payroll hour by the Chamber of Commerce. Productive hours are those that the employee actually spends at work in the plant; payroll hours are those hours for which he is paid, whether he is at work or not. The number of payroll hours will normally be larger than the number of productive hours by the amount of time-off given for paid holidays and paid vacations.

36. *Ibid.* The tax-free fringes were: legally required payments like OASI, UC, WC, railroad retirement, etc.: 3.2 percent; insurance premiums for life, health, medical care, etc.: 1.8 percent; discounts on goods and services: .1 percent; miscellaneous payments: .1 percent.

37. Philip Arnold Knowlton, *Profit Sharing Patterns,* pp. 16–21. Payments from deferred payments profit-sharing plans are at times

subject to capital gains treatment under the provisions of Sec. 403 (a) (2) of the *Internal Revenue Code of 1954.* This section holds that if a lump sum payment is made from one of these plans it is taxable at the capital gains rate. Distribution is therefore sometimes made to the employee in a lump sum, and the employee may use this amount to purchase an annuity or pension.

38. Some part of the .6 percent of payroll costs paid for sick leave will also be tax free in future years because of provisions in the 1954 code.

39. Chamber of Commerce, *Fringe Benefits, 1953,* p. 10.

40. *Ibid.,* p. 29; Fisher and Chapman, "Big Costs of Little Fringes," *Harvard Business Review,* XXXII (1954), 36.

41. Cf. "The Private Life of a Self Made Millionaire," *Look,* May 3, 1955, p. 44; "Car Makers Start Lavish Contests to Spur Sales, Cut Dealer Stocks," *Wall Street Journal,* May 16, 1955, p. 16; "Suit Is Filed Against 5 Thermoid Officers Charging Manipulation," *Wall Street Journal,* June 17, 1955, p. 13; "Beck Sells Union $160,000 Home and Now He Lives in It Rent-free," New York *Times,* July 25, 1955, p. 1.

42. J. K. Lasser and V. Henry Rothschild, "Deferred Compensation for Executives," *Harvard Business Review, XXXIII* (1955), 89.

43. Chamber of Commerce, *Fringe Benefits, 1953,* p. 10. For the view that this figure overstates the case, see " 'Costs' of Fringe Benefits," *AFL-CIO Collective Bargaining Report,* I (1956), 17–19.

44. U. S., Office of Business Economics, *National Income, 1954,* pp. 200–1.

45. Calculated from figures in U. S. Office of Business Economics, *Survey of Current Business,* July, 1957, pp. 16, 19, and July, 1958, p. 5; U. S., Bureau of the Census, *Statistical Abstract of the United States: 1958,* pp. 209–11.

46. Goldberg cites a case where the employer agreed to provide a water cooler to replace the one that had been provided by the employees through a 50¢ per month contribution per employee. See Arthur J. Goldberg, "Compensation Other Than Cash," paper presented before the Taxation Section of the American Bar Association, New York, September 18, 1951 (mimeographed), pp. 2–3.

47. A. C. Pigou, *A Study in Public Finance* (3rd rev. ed.), pp. 77–78.

48. Vickrey, *Agenda,* p. 43.

49. Simons, *Personal Income Taxation,* p. 123. Kleinwachter's

Flugeladjutant is a fictional character who is traditionally used to emphasize the problems connected with the taxation of income in kind. Of two service officers who are drawing the same pay, one is assigned to regular field duty while the other becomes the *Flugeladjutant* to the sovereign. In such capacity he enjoys quarters at the royal palace, dines on food fit for the king, has at his disposal servants for various duties and horses for sport, and attends the theater and opera with the sovereign. The question arises concerning the tax treatment of these perquisites, and the problem is magnified when it is brought out that the *Flugeladjutant* is a person who longs to live in the field and have the company of other soldiers and that he dislikes palace living, the theater, and the opera. See *ibid.,* p. 53.

50. *Ibid.*

51. Goldberg, "Compensation," p. 4; also quoted in Stanley S. Surrey and William C. Warren, *Federal Income Taxation, Cases and Materials* (Brooklyn: The Foundation Press, Inc., 1953), p. 89.

52. Goldberg, "Compensation," p. 5; also cited in Guttentag *et al.,* "Federal Taxation," *National Tax Journal,* VI (1953), 252. Goldberg also points out that both these elements need not necessarily be present. In the example he cites to illustrate this point he seems to emphasize the necessity for compensation to be proportional to work performed.

53. Guttentag *et al.,* "Federal Taxation," *National Tax Journal,* VI (1953), 252. Even Goldberg says of his position, "The line which I have suggested would seem to have none of the precision which is normally so desired in the tax field." Goldberg, "Compensation," p. 4.

54. The *Encyclopaedia of the Social Sciences,* for example, does not list "conditions of employment" as one of the terms to be discussed. In the discussion of "wages" there is no reference to a relationship between wages and conditions of employment. Under the discussion of "income," Irving Fisher does note that income includes not only wages but perquisites—"like board and lodging for a servant girl." There is no attempt to carry the discussion further.

55. *Regulations 106,* sec. 402.227 (a); *Regulations 107,* sec. 403.227 (a).

56. Cf. "Still other fringe benefits such as paid vacations and bonuses are, of course, taxable immediately," in Everett J. Mann,

"Deferred Compensation and Stock Option Plans May Be Legal, but Are They Ethical?" *The Journal of Accountancy*, XCIII (1952), 324.

57. Emanuel L. Gordon, "Tax Effects on Union Welfare Plans," *Tax Law Review*, VI (1950–1951), 51.

58. See p. 28 above.

59. Pigou, *A Study*, p. 6.   (Pigou's italics.)

60. Dearing, *Industrial Pensions*, p. 130.

61. Heller "Appraisal of the Administration's Tax Policy," *National Tax Journal*, VIII (1955), 26.

62. "Similarly situated" could mean that A and B had either the same adjusted gross income or the same net taxable income before fringe benefits.

63. This illustration may clarify the point:

Case I.   Before fringe benefits are granted:

	A	B
Adjusted gross income	$2,400	$4,800
Less exemptions	600	3,000
Income before deductions	$1,800	$1.800
Less deductions	480 (itemized)	480 (standard)
Taxable income	$1,320	$1,320

Case II.   With fringe benefits of $200 substituted for part of present cash wages:

	A	B
Adjusted gross income	$2,200	$4,600
Less exemptions	600	3,000
Income before deductions	$1,600	$1,600
Less deductions	280 (itemized)	460 (standard)
Taxable income	$1,320	$1,140

Case III.   With fringe benefits of $200 given in addition to cash wages:

	A	B
Adjusted gross income	$2,400	$4,800
Less exemptions	600	3,000
Income before deductions	$1,800	$1,800
Less deductions	280 (itemized)	480 (standard)
Taxable income	$1,520	$1,320

There are minor adjustments to the maximum contributions deduction and maximum nondeductible medical expense, but these are small relative to changes due to the introduction of fringe benefits.

64. Adam Smith, *The Wealth of Nations,* p. 777.

65. Solomon Barkin, "Financial Statements in Collective Bargaining," *The New York Certified Public Accountant,* XXIII (1953), p. 444.

66. Lasser and Rothschild, "Deferred Compensation for Executives," *Harvard Business Review,* XXXIII (1955), 97.

67. This point is made by both Surrey and Mann.   Stanley S. Surrey, "Policy Issues in Federal Taxation," in Current Business Studies, No. 10 (1951), pp. 25–26; Mann, "Deferred Compensation and Stock Option Plans May Be Legal, but Are They Ethical?" *The Journal of Accountancy,* XCIII (1952), 327.

68. Haig, *The Federal Income Tax,* p. 19.

69. Note the pessimistic conclusions in Strayer, "The Individual Income Tax and Income Distribution," *American Economic Review,* XLV (1955), 430, 437.

70. Quoted in Randolph E. Paul, *Taxation in the United States,* p. 82.

71. Computed from the tax rates as given in the *Internal Revenue Code of 1954,* Sec. 1 (a).   See also the tables comparing marginal and effective tax rates in the U. S., Congress, Joint Committee on the Economic Report, *The Federal Revenue System: Facts and Problems,* 84th Cong., 1st Sess., pp. 150–51.

72. U. S., Internal Revenue Service, *Statistics of Income for 1951,* Part I, p. 55.

73. Computed from *Internal Revenue Code of 1954,* Sec. 1 (a).

74. J. Keith Butters, Lawrence E. Thompson, and Lynn L. Bollinger, *Effects of Taxation: Investment by Individuals,* pp. 81–89. They cite a case from the 1946 *Statistics of Income* where there was one individual with adjusted gross income between $4 million and $5 million.   Normally this amount of income would fall in the 85.5 percent marginal bracket; *Statistics of Income,* on the other hand, reported his average tax rate at 49 percent; his actual average rate of tax on all his income was calculated by the authors to be 24.7 percent, pp. 85–88.

75. Cf. William S. Vickrey, *Theoretical Economics* (preliminary edition, mimeograph, 1949), p. 158.   When an excise tax is levied, the equilibrium position of the taxed good will shift from the point

of intersection of the demand and supply curves to a point to the left. The new equilibrium point is at the place where the vertical distance between the demand and the supply curves is equal to the new excise tax. The area of the triangle enclosed by the demand curve, the supply curve, and the vertical line representing the amount of the excise tax per unit is the loss in net social surplus. The area of this triangle is approximately one-half times the amount of the excise per unit times the reduction in quantity consumed. Where the demand and supply curves are approximately linear, the changes in the quantity consumed will be proportional to the tax rate. For example, if the tax rate is tripled, the reduction in number of units consumed (measured before and after the tax increase from the number consumed under a zero tax rate) is tripled. The product of these two changes, the increase in the tax rate and the reduction in units consumed, is increased nine times. So, too, is one half this product the loss in surplus. Thus the loss may be expressed as a function of the square of the tax rate. The amount of tax collected, however, will be somewhat less than in proportion to the tax rate since, if the rate were doubled, twice the tax per unit would be collected, but on a smaller number of units.

76. I am indebted to Professor Carl S. Shoup for this point.

77. George F. Break, "Effects of Taxation on Work Incentives," in U. S., Congress, Joint Committee on the Economic Report, *Federal Tax Policy for Economic Growth and Stability*, 84th Cong., 1st Sess., 1955, p. 195.

78. Mim. 5657, *Cum. Bul.* 1944, pp. 550–51.

79. Cited in Russell R. Kletzing, "Tax Treatment of Compensation in Kind," *California Law Review*, XXXVII (1949), 636–37.

80. "Columbus, Ohio, Rules Layoff Pay is Subject to City's Income Tax," *Wall Street Journal*, September 7, 1955, p. 2.

81. Rev. Rul. 56–249, *Cum. Bul.* 1956–1, pp. 488–92.

82. It is noted in *Tax Administrators News*, XIX (1955), 102, that during the past year "a number of states took further steps to make their laws conform to the Federal Internal Revenue Code." Iowa, for example, adopted the Federal Code definition of income.

83. See "U. S. Lifts One Bar to Lay-Off Pay Plan," New York *Times*, September 9, 1955, p. 48. This reports a ruling by the Secretary of Labor that employer payments under supplemental unemployment benefits plans will not be considered as wages within the meaning of the Fair Labor Standards Act.

84. "Foreigners Face Tax Rise in Japan," New York *Times,* June 5, 1955, p. 24; "It's the Same the World Over," *Life,* December 10, 1951, p. 36. For a brief description of some of the fringe benefits granted Japanese workers, see Boris S. Yane, "Wages in Japanese Mining and Manufacturing," *Monthly Labor Review,* LXXVIII (1955), 548–49.

NOTES TO CHAPTER III. ECONOMIC EFFECTS OF PRESENT TAX TREATMENT

1. *Business Week* points out that the requirement for "making the varsity" in business has been advanced from $10,000 a year to $20,000 a year, but that besides this $20,000 figure, "thousands of dollars worth of extras make up the package that gives the $20,000 significance" (p. 41). Among the benefits listed are: "deferred pay bonuses, stock option plans, extra-liberal expense accounts, a company car at all hours, or the use of the company plane or boat. Sometimes it's a few weeks at the company's Maine lodge angling for company trout, or weekends at the company's South Dakota preserve gunning for company pheasant. Then there's the occasional trip to Europe to study foreign markets of competition— trips on which the faithful corporate servant is accompanied by his wife and children . . . . And there are golf club, luncheon club, trade and professional association memberships . . ." (p. 45). It is pointed out that the recipients look for these extras; they know that extra salary is not half so good as these benefits (p. 46). "New Price Tag on Policymakers," *Business Week,* July 16, 1955, pp. 41–46.

2. This result is based on the additional assumption that the employee's disposable income is unchanged after the granting of the fringe benefit. That is, as part of his income is freed from taxation, the remaining part is subjected to higher tax rates.

3. The Health Insurance Council, *The Extent of Coverage, 1955,* p. 21.

4. Ernest Havemann, "The Expense Account Aristocrats," *Life,* March 9, 1953, p. 140.

5. *Ibid.,* p. 141.

6. "*Life* Goes to Houston's Paradise for Office Girls," *Life,* September 15, 1952, p. 150.

7. Regulations issued in 1936 and applicable to the new Social Security Act carried this provision in the definition of wages. *Reg-*

ulations 90, art. 207; *Regulations 91,* art. 14. SST 302, *Cum. Bul.* 1938–1, pp. 456–58, applied this rule to a specific case involving meals. In the same vein, L. O. 1014, *Cum. Bul.* 2 (1920), pp. 88–90, had earlier ruled that group life insurance was an investment in increased efficiency and therefore not income to the employee.

8. Thompson, *Cooperative Medical Programs,* p. 4.

9. *"Life* Goes to Houston's Paradise for Office Girls," *Life,* September 15, 1952, p. 150.

10. "Deputy Who Liked Work Quits over the Pay," Greenville (S. C.) *News,* October 24, 1958, p. 6.

11. Reynolds, *The Structure,* pp. 94–95.

12. It would be necessary to know the degree of similarity of the two jobs being compared, the amount paid for fringe benefits by the employer, the amount of these fringe benefits which were tax free, and the marginal tax bracket of the employee.

13. U. S., Bureau of Labor Statistics, *Digest of One Hundred Selected Pension Plans under Collective Bargaining, Winter 1957–58, Bulletin* 1232 (1958), pp. 15, 39.

14. Associated Industries of Massachusetts, *Survey on Fringe Benefits in Massachusetts Industry,* p. 33.

15. Allan I. Mendelsohn, "Fringe Benefits and Our Industrial Society," *Labor Law Journal,* VII (1956), 383. See also Fisher and Chapman, " Big Costs of Little Fringes," *Harvard Business Review,* XXXII (1954), 44.

16. Cf. Vickrey, *Agenda,* pp. 35–37; John F. Due, *Government Finance, an Economic Analysis,* p. 142.

17. For a discussion of the optimal properties of competitive operations, see William S. Vickrey, *Theoretical Economics* (revised), mimeograph, Part II, pp. 121 B-123 A.

18. Marsh, in discussing the absence of tax on many forms of imputed income, makes virtually the same point but in different terms. He states that because of the tax preference accorded some forms of imputed income the least aggregate sacrifice principle is violated. By curtailing investment in fields where the return is taxable and increasing investment in fields where the return is not taxed, the pre-tax return foregone exceeds the pre-tax return achieved. Marsh, "The Taxation of Imputed Income," *Political Science Quarterly,* LVIII (1943), 534.

19. One possible source of saving which would lead to a lower price per unit of product might arise from the inclusion of all

workers as consumers, whereas some of the workers might not turn out to be consumers of the product. For example, the cost of hospitalization and surgical insurance might drop if, by including *all* workers, some of the newly included are of the "I've never been sick a day in my life" type and so are not likely to use the service. Another example would be the reduction in the cost per person for recreation services if all contribute but only the ones presently using the service continue to use it.

20. This argument is subject to several qualifications. For example, the good concerned may benefit not only the consumer but others as well. That is, there may be external economies of consumption; medical care is the traditional example. Closely related to this is the possibility that utilities derived from a good are not independent of all other goods but are interdependent, resting to some extent on the quantities and qualities of these other goods held. A third possibility is that the employee-consumer did not have full knowledge of the market and so was not aware of the benefits which accrue from consumption of the fringe benefit or did not know where the good might be purchased cheapest. All of these factors would work to mitigate or annul the statement in the text. But it should be noted that each of these qualifications can cut both ways. A good acquired by a consumer may produce external diseconomies of consumption, a barking dog for a pet or a Christmas office party, for example; interdependence may render existing goods less valuable—as in the case of the employee who finds home furnishings and food rather drab after spending the working week on company expense money; and the employer is as subject to a lack of knowledge as the employee. Until these factors are more definitely evaluated, perhaps the safest conclusion is that they are of secondary importance to begin with and, furthermore, that they possibly tend to cancel each other.

21. Stieglitz, *Computing the Cost,* pp. 4–5. Also reported here is a situation in which a company that paid $1.81 per hour to certain employees reported that the fringe benefits raised the earnings to $1.97 per hour. Commenting on this a worker wrote, "I cannot pay my bills or live on average earnings. What I actually get is what counts and it's not $1.97" (p. 5).

22. Dearing, *Industrial Pensions,* p. 114. See also the similar comment on p. 53.

23. UAW-CIO, *Handbook,* pp. 3–5, 11–12.

24. American Federation of Labor, *Pension Plans under Collective Bargaining*, pp. 3–6. This difference may be observed in operation in the 1955 negotiations between the American Can Company and its unions. The Company and the CIO steelworkers unions at 32 plants signed a contract in August, 1955, calling for suplemental unemployment compensation for workers for 52 weeks plus a 13 cent per hour average pay increase. An official of the Federated Laborers Union (AFL) at American Can Company said that they would turn down an expected offer of supplemental unemployment compensation and bargain for "substantial wage increases plus increased holiday and vacation benefits." "AFL to Spurn Layoff Pay at American Can, Local's Official Says," *Wall Street Journal,* August 17, 1955, p. 21.

25. Mendelsohn, "Fringe Benefits and Our Industrial Society," *Labor Law Journal,* VII (1956), 326–28, 383. Some few contracts have allowed union members a choice between fringe benefits and cash. See the agreements reported in "Making SUP More Tangible," *Business Week,* September 17, 1955, p. 166; "TV, Movie Extras Get Salary Rises," New York *Times,* July 3, 1956, p. 17.

26. Due, *Government Finance,* p. 142.

27. Vickrey, *Agenda,* pp. 35–36.

28. Guttentag, *et al.,* "Federal Income Taxation of Fringe Benefits: A Specific Proposal," *National Tax Journal,* VI (1953), 267–68.

29. *Clifford Jones* v. *U. S.,* 60 Ct. Cl. at 577 (1925).

30. Nathan Belfer, "Hidden Costs in the Labor Agreement," *Labor Law Journal,* VI (1955), 409–10. Mendelsohn says that management estimates of the cost of fringe benefits will always include clerical and administrative costs. See Mendelsohn, "Fringe Benefits and Our Industrial Society," *Labor Law Journal,* VII (1956), 380–81. If these are extra costs due to the peculiar nature of fringe benefits, such costs, while they may not be looked on as bringing direct benefit to the worker, do constitute an opportunity cost that could, in many cases, be diverted into a cash wage.

31. Walter J. Blum, "The Effects of Special Provisions in the Income Tax on Taxpayer Morale," in U. S., Congress, Joint Committee on the Economic Report, *Federal Tax Policy,* pp. 253–59.

32. Haig, *The Federal Income Tax,* p. 2.

33. *Ibid.,* pp. 1–7.

34. William Wallace Hewett, *The Definition of Income and Its Application in Federal Taxation,* p. 9.

35. *Ibid.,* p. 24.

36. Vickrey, *Agenda,* p. 35.

37. Quoted in Yane, "Wages in Japanese Mining and Manufacturing," *Monthly Labor Review,* LXXVIII (1955), 548.

38. *Ibid.*

39. B. U. Ratchford, "Practical Limitations to the Net Income Tax—General," *Journal of Finance,* VII (1952), 211.

40. See Rev. Rul. 55–140, *Cum. Bul.* 1955–1, p. 317. See also *Baxter D. McClain* 2 BTA 726 (1925).

41. Although such tax-free treatment of this particular fringe benefit appears contradictory to the revenue ruling and the case cited above, some court cases have moved in this direction. See *Mills et ux.* v. *U. S.,* 57–2 USTC, par. 9766 and *Woodall et ux.* v. *U. S.,* 57–2 USTC, par. 9767 where reimbursement for moving expenses was held not taxable. These decisions were later reversed at 255 F (2d) 370 (1958), also in 1 AFTR 2d 58–1771. Some earlier cases dealing with the problem are less definite but seem to grant tax preference to employer-provided moving services. In *W. H. Pennington* v. *Commissioner,* 9 TCM 955 (1950), Pennington was hired in Memphis to work in California, and "he was furnished meals and transportation en route." From the facts of the case it appears that he did not deduct his moving expenses nor include in his income the value of meals and transportation furnished, and the Commissioner did not press for their inclusion. The same results appear in *Lawrence Perry and Mildred Perry* v. *Commissioner,* 9 TCM 602 (1950) where transportation was furnished from California to Saudi Arabia. See Boris I. Bittker, "The Individual as Wage Earner," *New York University Eleventh Annual Institute on Federal Taxation,* pp. 1166–70, where he concludes that transportation and meals were not included in income in the above two cases. He also includes a third case, *Russell Porter Dolan* v. *Commissioner,* 7 TCM 79 (1948), but this case is more complicated and seems of questionable value as an illustration of tax-preferred treatment. Also see p. 175, below.

42. The tax treatment of transportation has been discussed. Regarding company-financed education, sec. 117 of the 1954 Code exempts from income scholarships and fellowships. Sec. 1.117–4(c) of the regulations states that the amount paid for this purpose by a grantor will not be exempt if it represents compensation for services, either past, present, or future. The proposed regulations were

more limiting; sec. 1.117-4(d) removed from exempt status "any amount received by an individual from his employer or any entity related to the employer if such amount is because of the employer-employee relationship." The final regulations were issued without this provision. The Code and regulations leave room for tax-free education as a benefit to either employees or their dependents.

43. "The Real Estate Side of Executive Changes," *Business Week,* April 16, 1955, p. 126. But the story notes that this policy is not followed in the hiring of people who are sought after by employers.

"In New England, companies are bemoaning what's expected of them in hiring new engineers—not only on housing but on everything that goes with a change in homes. On the West Coast, electronics experts are like hen's teeth—and most anything goes for a good one.

"One man moving from San Francisco to Seattle had a stable of horses—and the company not only helped him find a house and wire it for 220 v. electricity for his new range, but boarded his horses and then paid their freight when he found a spot for them in Seattle" (p. 126).

44. Doris M. Thompson, *Tuition Aid Plans for Employees* (Studies in Personnel Policy, No. 151, 1956), pp. 29, 31–32.

45. Robbins, in commenting on the absence of vesting provisions in most pension plans, states, "Anyone who has given even casual attention to turnover statistics knows that a large majority of workers who have this presumed 'security' will never qualify for the benefits so carelessly tossed about in discussion and so heatedly contended for as slogans in the labor disputes." Rainard Benton Robbins, *Pension Planning in the United States,* p. 143.

46. Evan K. Rowe and Thomas H. Paine, "Pension Plans under Collective Bargaining," *Monthly Labor Review,* LXXVI (1953), 238–39. These results are similar to those found by Dearing in *Industrial Pensions* cited above. In late 1950 the Brookings Institution surveyed 340 firms with 4.5 million employees. Of this number, 3.8 million employees were covered by private pension plans, but only 22 percent of this number were covered by plans with vesting provisions. Among those plans with vesting provisions, full or partial vesting usually occurred only after 10 to 25 years of service, although three firms did offer a few workers full immediate vesting. pp. 69–76. At this time it was estimated that there were

8.5 million workers covered by private pension plans and that the annual contribution per covered employee averaged $247. p. 161.

47. Paul F. Brissenden, "Labor Mobility and Employee Benefits," *Labor Law Journal*, VI (1955), 766. This opinion is discounted somewhat by Howard D. Marshall in "Unions and Labor Mobility," *Labor Law Journal*, VII (1956), 86–89, 91. Both Brissenden and Rowe make the point that pension plans may also increase mobility of workers in that, if a new company begins operation and has a pension plan, this will attract workers from firms without such plans. This, however, seems to assume that the new company offers the same wages as existing firms plus the pension plan fringe benefit and so, in effect, higher wages. But measurement of mobility means the relative willingness or unwillingness of an employee to move, given a certain wage differential. The fact that the employee moves when there is a wage differential is not proof that mobility has increased.

48. From a letter from Peter Drucker to V. Henry Rothschild, a tax consultant, quoted in "Deferred Pay: Still No Law," *Business Week*, July 23, 1955, p. 44.

49. *Ibid.*

50. Chamber of Commerce, *Fringe Benefits, 1957*, p. 9. Of the 25 cents per payroll hour estimated as tax-preferred fringe benefits (see Chapter II, p. 28), only a small portion, probably not more than four or five cents per payroll hour, would be counted as going for immediate consumption goods. See second, fifth, and sixth items under "Pension and other agreed-upon payments" in Appendix III.

51. Randolph Paul observes that, while high income tax rates might be expected to lower the amount of investment, this has not happened. He says the explanation may be that the source of investment funds is no longer the individual but pension funds and other pools of capital owned in part by low income groups. Randolph E. Paul, "Erosion of the Tax Base and Rate Structure," in U. S., Congress, Joint Committee on the Economic Report, *Federal Tax Policy*, p. 229.

52. T. D. 5186, *Cum. Bul.* 1942–2, p. 352.

53. "Such adjustments [in fringe issues] have been made in many cases by the Board when it is determined that they are equitable and do not result in an appreciable increase in the level of production costs or do not furnish the basis for increasing prices." U. S.,

National War Labor Board, *Wage Report to the President on the Wartime Relationship of Wages to the Cost of Living,* p. 67. Gordon also states that employers were allowed to grant fringe benefits "because these were regarded as less inflationary than wage increases." Gordon, "Tax Effects of Union Welfare Plans," *Tax Law Review,* VI (1950–51), 1. For a review of wartime action with regard to fringe issues, see U. S., Department of Labor, *The Termination Report of the National War Labor Board,* I, 307–402. See also Gertrude G. Schroeder, "The 'Stabilization' of Fringe Benefits under the 1951–53 Wage Controls Program," *Southern Economic Journal,* XXI (1955), 319–29.

54. In this respect the introduction of the Social Security Act was ill-timed.

55. Mendelsohn reports that employers believe fringe benefits, once given, are psychologically important to employees and that wages should be cut before fringe benefits. Mendelsohn, "Fringe Benefits and our Industrial Society," *Labor Law Journal,* VII (1956), 379–80.

56. Harold M. Groves, *Trouble Spots in Taxation,* pp. 78–86.

57. See Robert A. Sigafoos, "The Municipal Income Tax—A Janus in Disguise," *National Tax Journal,* VI (1953), 188.

NOTES TO CHAPTER IV. THE TREATMENT OF
RETIREMENT BENEFITS

1. Prentice-Hall, Inc., *Prentice-Hall Pension and Profit Sharing Service,* pars. 1011–24, contains a good summary of investigations which have been undertaken. However, here too the lack of comprehensive treatment is decried. See also Daniel H. Brill, "Economic Impact of Private Pension Plans," in Dan M. McGill, ed., *Pensions: Problems and Trends,* p. 79, for a report that projects for the compilation of statistics on the many phases of operation of pension plans are under way at several government agencies. For proposals to remedy the lack of information, see the study prepared by Daniel M. Holland for the National Bureau of Economic Research, *Suggestions for Research in the Economics of Pensions.*

2. One study of pension plans reaches the conclusion that pension plans are already complex and growing in complexity. Specifically it is noted that in 327 companies surveyed there were 423 pension plans in operation—all different. F. Beatrice Brower, *Pen-*

sion Plans and Their Administration (Studies in Personnel Policy, No. 149, 1955), p. 9.

3. See Murray Webb Latimer, *Industrial Pension Systems in the United States and Canada,* I, 21.

4. National Industrial Conference Board, *Industrial Pensions in the United States,* p. 6. Of these workers 85 percent were employed in just three industries: metal working, railroads, and other public utilities.

5. *Ibid.,* p. 14.

6. *Ibid.,* p. 21.

7. *Ibid.,* p. 49.

8. Robert M. Ball, *Pensions in the United States* (A study prepared for the Joint Committee on the Economic Report), p. 11. For other studies of pension growth during this period, see Murray Webb Latimer and Karl Tufel, *Trends in Industrial Pensions,* pp. 3, 47.

9. Prentice-Hall, *Pension and Profit Sharing Service,* par. 1012. See Appendix IV of the present study. This figure represents "qualified" plans under sec. 165(a) of the 1939 Internal Revenue Code—sec. 401(a) of the 1954 Code—and so overstates the number of pension plans by including profit-sharing and stock bonus plans. Prentice-Hall estimates that about two thirds of all qualified plans are pension plans, and so arrives at approximately 23,000 qualified pension plans. Although there are probably some non-qualified pension plans also operating, the literature does not assign these a place of prominence.

10. "14,000,000 Belong to Pension Plans," New York *Times,* January 2, 1957, p. 89.

11. "Private Pension Plans," *Federal Reserve Bank of New York Monthly Review,* XXXV (1953), 187.

12. Figures through 1954 are found in U. S., Internal Revenue Service, *Statistics of Income—1954, Corporation Income Tax Returns,* p. 151. The 1955 figure comes from the later *Statistics—1955, Corporation Returns,* p. 9.

13. U. S., Securities and Exchange Commission, *Survey of Corporate Pension Funds, 1951–54,* p. 32.

14. Institute of Life Insurance, *Life Insurance Fact Book, 1956,* pp. 32–33.

15. U. S., Securities and Exchange Commission, *Survey, 1951–54,* p. 32.

16. Parish and Peacock feel it may never arrive because of increasing wages leading to increasing payments into the funds with a lag in increased pensions. See F. W. Paish and A. T. Peacock, "The Economics of Pension Funds," *Lloyds Bank Review* (new series), No. 34 (1954), p. 23.

17. T. D. 2090, December 14, 1914 (unpublished), quoted in Rainard B. Robbins, *Impact of Taxes on Industrial Pension Plans*, p. 71.

18. *Regulations 33*, art. 136.

19. *Revenue Act of 1921*, sec. 219(f); *Revenue Act of 1926*, sec. 219(f). (Italics added.) The former gave favorable treatment to profit-sharing and stock bonus plans for the benefit of some or all employees. Although this was held to apply to pension plans, too, the 1926 Act formalized the treatment.

20. *Revenue Act of 1942*, sec. 162(a). This became sec. 165(a) of the Internal Revenue Code of 1939 and sec. 401(a) of the Internal Revenue Code of 1954. See sec. 404(a) of the latter Code for other requirements for employer deductibility. For a list of general requirements see Appendix V.

21. *Internal Revenue Code of 1954*, sec. 404(a)(5). A nonforfeitable interest, like a vested interest, in a pension fund represents a legal claim by the employee. In general it appears that "nonforfeitable" means the employee will eventually receive the money spent on his behalf; vested pension rights are not so definite and may mean that the employee will receive the money spent on his behalf only if he lives to retire. Variations in vesting are numerous. For a discussion of the treatment of employer contributions under the 1954 Code, see Norman Block, "Deductibility of Employer Contributions to Qualified Pension and Profit-Sharing Plans," *New York University Thirteenth Annual Institute on Federal Taxation* (1955), pp. 409–27.

22. *Internal Revenue Code of 1954*, sec. 72(d).

23. *Ibid.*, sec. 402(b), 72(b).

24. 26 Code of Federal Regulations 1.402(b)–1.

25. *Internal Revenue Code of 1954*, secs. 402(a)(2), 403(a)(2).

26. *Ibid.*, sec. 101(b)(2)(A).

27. *Ibid.*, sec. 402(a)(2).

28. American Federation of Labor, *Pension Plans*, p. 2. (Italics in original.)

29. *Ibid.*

30. This provision is not peculiar to recipients of pension plan benefits but applies to all recipients of annuity benefits. The law also makes it possible for the annuitant to recover less than the amount paid for the annuity. However, the recipient under the pension plan fares better than his counterpart who privately purchases a similar annuity. The former will lose capital on which no personal income tax has been paid, while the latter loses both capital and income tax paid on that capital.

31. *Ibid.,* sec. 402(a)(2).

32. *Ibid.*

33. *Ibid.,* sec. 101(b). The balance, if paid within one taxable year of death, may be considered a long-term capital gain.

34. *Internal Revenue Code of 1954,* sec. 2039(c).

35. The American Federation of Labor points out that workers can secure larger benefits under a negotiated pension plan than they could if they individually sought to secure retirement insurance. See American Federation of Labor, *Pension Plans,* pp. 5–6. *Business Week* spells out the advantages of the qualified pension plan to executives. Using a numerical example, the writer shows how an executive can retain twice as much money by using a qualified pension plan rather than a similar, privately purchased plan. See "Personal Business," *Business Week,* June 15, 1957, pp. 165–66.

36. Blum, "The Effects of Special Provisions in the Income Tax on Taxpayer Morale," in U. S., Congress, Joint Committee on the Economic Report, *Federal Tax Policy,* p. 252.

37. Challis A. Hall, Jr., "Retirement Contributions, the Spending Stream, and Growth," in U. S., Congress, Joint Committee on the Economic Report, *Federal Tax Policy,* p. 788.

38. *Ibid.,* p. 796.

39. U. S., Congress, House of Representatives, Committee on Ways and Means, *Hearings, Individual Retirement* (1955), p. 13.

40. Prentice-Hall, *Pension and Profit Sharing Service,* XVII, 2.1.

41. Hall, "Retirement Contributions, the Spending Stream, and Growth," in U. S., Congress, Joint Committee on the Economic Report, *Federal Tax Policy,* p. 788.

42. *Ibid.,* p. 796. See also U. S., Congress, Joint Committee on the Economic Report, *Hearings, Federal Tax Policy for Economic Growth and Stability,* 84th Cong., 1st Sess., 1956, p. 642.

43. See Eleanor S. Daniel, "Retirement Funds, Capital Markets, and Growth," in U. S., Congress, Joint Committee on the Economic Report, *Federal Tax Policy*, pp. 772–85.

44. American Federation of Labor, *Pension Plans*, pp. 4–5.

45. See Brissenden, "Labor Mobility and Employee Benefits," *Labor Law Journal*, VI (1955), 762–68; Rowe and Paine, "Pension Plans under Collective Bargaining," *Monthly Labor Review*, LXXVI (1953), 241–45. It should be pointed out that, although reduced mobility of labor is considered to stem from non-vested pension plans, non-vesting provisions are not required for "qualification" for tax postponement. For the view that pension plans do not significantly restrict mobility of labor, see the statement by Leonard Lesser in U. S., Congress, Joint Committee on the Economic Report, *Hearings, Federal Tax Policy* (1956), pp. 643–47. His argument is that a prospective pension means very little to the younger workers who are the most mobile. While the pension may mean more to older workers, they are also for other reasons not given to change jobs. Ball, however, cites figures showing that, in 1948, 25 percent of all workers covered by OASI were employed in more than one industry. For workers in the 45 to 65 age group, 23.4 percent were employed by more than one employer during 1948. Ball, *Pensions*, p. 16. Figures for 1950 are given in U. S., Bureau of Old-Age and Survivors Insurance, *Handbook of Old-Age and Survivors Insurance Statistics, 1950*, p. 97.

46. See the comment by C. A. Vinson, a worker on strike at Woodward Iron in Bessemer, Alabama. The strike had lasted ten weeks and he had taken a job at Nashville, Tennessee, when he stated, "But anyone with any time with the company will be back when it's settled. They can't afford to throw away all that seniority and pension money." "Ten Week-Old Strike at Woodward Iron is Pinching Pocketbooks of Customers, Merchants, and Workers," *Wall Street Journal*, January 9, 1957, p. 24.

47. U. S., Congress, Joint Committee on the Economic Report, *Hearings, Federal Tax Policy* (1956), p. 647.

48. Harold M. Groves, *Financing Government*, p. 198.

49. James E. Walter, "Some Implications of Private Pension Funds," *Southern Economic Journal*, XXII (1955), 233. Cf. William L. Carey, "Pressure Groups and the Increasing Erosion of the Revenue Laws," in U. S., Congress, Joint Committee on the Economic Report, *Federal Tax Policy*, p. 269.

50. Robbins, *Impact*, pp. 30–44.

51. U. S., Congress, Joint Committee on Tax Evasion and Avoidance, *Hearings, Tax Evasion and Avoidance*, 75th Cong., 1st Sess., 1937, p. 5.

52. Vickrey, *Agenda*, pp. 172–97.

53. Simons, *Personal Income Taxation*, p. 154.

54. Vickrey, *Agenda*, pp. 64–67.

55. *Internal Revenue Code of 1954*, sec. 264.

56. *Ibid.*, sec. 72(a)–(c).

57. I. T. 2915, *Cum. Bul.* XIV–2 (1935), p. 98.

58. Testimony by Mrs. Eleanor S. Daniel quoting estimates made by an actuarial firm in U. S., Congress, Joint Committee on the Economic Report, *Hearings, Federal Tax Policy* (1956), pp. 650–51. The assumed vesting provisions call for full vesting after two years of service, no age requirement, a deferred annuity starting at normal retirement age, and no cash value or death benefit. See also the testimony of Leonard Lesser on the same subject, that vesting provisions in the contract between General Motors and the United Automobile Workers raised costs about 5 percent but other vesting provisions would have raised costs about 9 percent. (p. 651).

59. Workers who are covered by pension plans and who die before retirement would affect both non-refundable, vested, and non-vested plans the same way. Thus, there is no additional cost from this source if the vested, non-refundable pension plan is adopted.

60. For details of these plans see "Making SUP More Tangible," *Business Week*, September 17, 1955, p. 166.

61. See Rowe and Paine, "Pension Plans under Collective Bargaining," *Monthly Labor Review*, LXXVI (1953), 242. See also the statement by Lesser in U. S., Congress, Joint Committee on the Economic Report, *Hearings, Federal Tax Policy* (1956), p. 645.

62. Groves, *Trouble Spots*, p. 52.

63. Canada, *Income Tax Act*, 1954, secs. 11(1)(g)–(i) and 6(a).

64. Rev. Rul. 56–249, *Cum. Bul.* 1956–1, p. 488.

65. Bureau of Internal Revenue Letter of March 22, 1956, to Pittsburgh Plate Glass Co., reprinted in Prentice-Hall, *Pension and Profit Sharing Service*, par. 11,918.

66. See Joseph A. Pechman, "A Practical Averaging Proposal," *National Tax Journal*, VII (1954), 261–63. The sections in the 1954 Code corresponding to sec. 107 of the 1939 Code referred to in this article are secs. 1301–4. Those particularly applicable to

the problem above seem to be secs. 1301 and 1303. In fact, sec. 1303 states that retirement pay received in one year shall be allocated over the years earned and taxed as if earned in those years, but this treatment applies only under certain conditions that are likely to occur infrequently.

67. Hall estimates benefit payments at $538 million in 1954. See Hall, "Retirement Contributions, the Spending Stream, and Growth," in U. S., Congress, Joint Committee on the Economic Report, *Federal Tax Policy*, p. 788.

68. See the discussion of Herman Biegel, Leonard Lesser, and Eleanor Daniel on the cost of changing a non-vested pension plan into a vested one. The differences in their estimates seem to indicate a difference in concepts. U. S., Congress, Joint Committee on the Economic Report, *Hearings, Federal Tax Policy* (1956), pp. 650–51. See also U. S., Congress, House of Representatives, Committee on Ways and Means, *Hearings, Individual Retirement* (1955), pp. 38–42.

69. Knowlton, *Profit Sharing Patterns,* p. vi.

70. Prentice-Hall, *Pension and Profit Sharing Service,* par. 1012.

71. For the view that an important difference between the two is in the vesting provisions and the resulting effect on costs, see Hilary L. Seal, "Pensions, Profit-Sharing and Stock Options Under New Tax Law," *Commercial and Financial Chronicle,* CLXXX (September 23, 1954), 1171, 1192.

72. Knowlton, *Profit Sharing Patterns,* p. 12.

73. Edwin B. Flippo, *Profit Sharing in American Business,* pp. 10-11.

74. Knowlton, *Profit Sharing Patterns,* p. 13.

75. Flippo, *Profit Sharing,* pp. 10–11.

76. From a report of the eighth annual meeting of the Council of Profit-Sharing Industries as reported in "More Profits in Workers' Stockings," *Business Week,* December 24, 1955, p. 93.

77. See the two preceding notes.

78. "More Profits in Workers' Stockings," *Business Week,* December 24, 1955, p. 93.

79. See the results in Knowlton, *Profit Sharing Patterns,* pp. 12, 16–21.

80. Chamber of Commerce, *Fringe Benefits, 1953,* p. 10.

81. Calculated from figures given in U. S., Internal Revenue Service, *Statistics of Income—1954, Corporation,* p. 151.

82. Hall, "Retirement Contributions, the Spending Stream, and Growth," in U. S., Congress, Joint Committee on the Economic Report, *Federal Tax Policy*, p. 788.

83. U. S., Internal Revenue Service, *Commissioner of Internal Revenue Annual Report 1956*, pp. 47–48; also *Annual Report 1957*, 44–45; and *Annual Report 1958*, p. 49.

84. In a study of 182 deferred profit-sharing plans, 179 were found to contain some plan for vesting and the other three did not report on the subject. Knowlton, *Profit Sharing Patterns*, p. 48.

85. Hall, "Retirement Conrtibutions, the Spending Stream, and Growth," in U. S., Congress, Joint Committee on the Economic Report, *Federal Tax Policy*, p. 788.

86. Knowlton, *Profit Sharing Patterns*, pp. 47–54, particularly p. 49.

87. For a good example of employer reporting to employees, see the sample of the annual account card sent to each participant in the Sears, Roebuck and Company Savings and Profit-Sharing Pension Fund in Council of Profit-Sharing Industries, *Revised Profit-Sharing Manual* (1951), p. 242.

88. An unconscious appreciation of this tax favor may be the cause of the present trend in profit-sharing plans away from cash payment plans toward plans which are at least partially of the deferred payment type. This trend is cited by Joseph B. Meier, executive secretary of the Council of Profit-Sharing Industries. The main reason for this shift, he states, is that deferred profits grow. For example, in 1954 the Motorola Company put $2.9 million in its deferred payment profit-sharing plan, while the earnings of the profit-sharing fund in the same year were $2.4 million. "More Profits in Workers' Stockings," *Business Week*, December 24, 1955, p. 93. As of December 31, 1953, the company reported $17.6 million in the profit-sharing fund and over 9,000 employees. Moody's Investor Service, *Moody's Industrial Manual 1955*, p. 2365.

NOTES TO CHAPTER V. LIFE INSURANCE AND DEATH BENEFITS

1. *Internal Revenue Code of 1954*, sec. 101(a).
2. L. O. 1014, *Cum. Bul.* 2 (1920), pp. 88–90.
3. *Ibid.*, p. 89.
4. O. D. 627, *Cum. Bul.* 3 (1920), p. 104; G. C. M. 16069, *Cum.*

Bul. XV–1 (1936), p. 84; *Commissioner* v. *Bonwit,* 87 F 2d 764 (1937).

5. Mim. 6477, *Cum. Bul.* 1950–1, p. 16. However, if the group-permanent insurance is forfeitable on the part of the employee if he leaves the employment, it is not considered income. The distinction is similar to that between refundable and non-refundable pension plans discussed above.

6. *Internal Revenue Code of 1954,* sec. 3121(a)(2).

7. *Ibid.,* sec. 3306(b)(2).

8. Institute of Life Insurance, *Life Insurance Fact Book 1957,* p. 25.

9. Institute of Life Insurance, *Fact Book 1958,* p. 26.

10. "Insurance—New 'Fringe' on Executive Paychecks," *Personnel,* XXX (1953), 71.

11. Institute of Life Insurance, *Fact Book 1957,* p. 36. The *Fact Book 1958* shows payments of $829 million to 318,000 recipients for an average of about $2,600. However, the text points out that only 182,000 of these recipients were covered by group life insurance; the balance were covered by group credit life insurance, which is group insurance on the lives of borrowers. The 182,000 group life beneficiaries received $754 million for an average benefit of about $4,150. While this figure is more accurate, a similar breakdown for earlier figures is not available for comparision purposes (pp. 41–42).

12. Cf. Paul, "Erosion of the Tax Base and Rate Structure," in U. S., Congress, Joint Committee on the Economic Report, *Federal Tax Policy,* p. 301; U. S., Division of Tax Research, *The Income Tax Treatment of Pensions and Annuities,* pp. v–vi.

13. For a contrary view see Guttentag *et al.,* "Federal Income Taxation of Fringe Benefits: A Specific Proposal," *National Tax Journal,* VI (1953), 260–64.

14. Gordon, "Tax Effects of Union Welfare Plans," *Tax Law Review,* VI (1950–51), 48.

15. *Ibid.* This statement corresponds to the recommended treatment in the case of income insurance, which is what Gordon refers to; but in the case of insurance on property used in consumption the statement does not hold. Vickrey notes that such property insurance is part of the cost of guaranteed consumption of the good. See Vickrey, *Agenda,* pp. 60–62. In practice it would seem that if an employer were to grant a fringe benefit in the form of fire in-

surance on the employee's home, this would be considered as income at the time of premium payment.

16. Institute of Life Insurance, *Fact Book 1957*, p. 36.

17. *Internal Revenue Code of 1954*, sec. 164(b)(1)(A).

18. The tax is levied in secs. 1401–1403, *Internal Revenue Code of 1954*. This is part of the Subtitle dealing with income taxes, and as an income tax it is not deductible.

19. I. T. 3447, *Cum. Bul.* 1941–1, p. 191.

20. G. C. M. 17920, *Cum. Bul.* 1937–1, p. 68; I. T. 2960, *Cum. Bul.* XV–1 (1936), p. 98.

21. For a more complete discussion of the tax treatment of old-age and survivors insurance, see B. U. Ratchford, "The Tax Status of Social Security Benefits," *Southern Economic Journal*, XX (1953), 156–62.

22. U. S., Social Security Administration, *Social Security Bulletin*, Annual Statistical Supplement, 1957, pp. 20, 44.

23. *Ibid.*, p. 16.

24. *Ibid.*, p. 15. The contribution to the trust fund by self-employed workers was $486 million. This amount was included in taxable income of the self-employed.

25. *Ibid.*, p. 16.

26. In 1954, 5.3 million of the 14 million persons over 65 were receiving social security benefits; another 1.4 million were eligible but were working. Thus over half the population over 65 was ineligible for these benefits. However, it is estimated that by 1980 all retired aged persons in the United States will be eligible for social security. Statements by the U. S. Commissioner of Social Security, Charles I. Schottland. See "Aid to the Aging Termed Urgent," New York *Times*, October 28, 1955, p. 28.

27. Calculated from figures given in U. S., Social Security Administration, *Social Security Bulletin*, Annual Statistical Supplement, 1957, p. 20.

28. See this and other comments in "Minor Bills Make Few Headlines in Congress but Pack Potent Punch," *Wall Street Journal, April* 20, 1956, pp. 1, 13; "Tax Relief Is Opposed," New York *Times*, July 4, 1956, p. 14.

29. U. S., Division of Tax Research, *Tax Treatment of Pensions*, p. iv.

30. U. S., Social Security Administration, *Social Security Bulletin*, Annual Statistical Supplement, 1957, pp. 15, 16.

31. Since part of this benefit represents a return of previously taxed income, he may or may not find himself better off with this treatment. He will be better off if the product of the proportion of the benefit which is income rather than a return of capital times his marginal tax rate is greater than the 20 percent tax credit offered other recipients of income. In the case of an individual receiving old-age and survivors benefits which are calculated to be, say, 40 percent return of capital and 60 percent income, he would gain from receiving old-age and survivors benefits rather than other forms of retirement income only if his marginal tax rate were 33 percent or greater.

32. O. D. 1017, *Cum. Bul.* 5 (1921), p. 101.

33. *Regulations 111*, sec. 29.22(a)–2.

34. I. T. 3329, *Cum. Bul.* 1939–2, p. 153.

35. I. T. 4027, *Cum. Bul.* 1950–2, p .9.

36. *Revenue Act of 1951*, sec. 302(a)(1)(B); *Internal Revenue Code of 1954*, sec. 101(b).

37. Cf. the cases *Ruth Hahn,* 13 TCM 308 (1954); *Estate of Ralph W. Reardon,* 14 TCM 577 (1955); *Marie G. Haskell,* 14, TCM 788 (1955).

38. *Estate of Arthur W. Hellstrom,* 24 TC 916 at 919 (1955).

39. *Ibid.*

40. *Peters* v. *Smith,* 55–1 USTC par. 9346, 221 F 2d 721 (1955); later reversed, 51 AFTR 1238 (1956).

41. *Fisher* v. *U. S.,* 55–1 USTC par. 9326, 129 F Supp. 759 (1955).

42. The reasoning advanced for this treatment is that these payments are inducements to employment in these fields. Still, statutory payments by the U. S. government on the death of a member of the armed forces are considered gratuities and nontaxable. Widows of Congressmen also receive statutory payments which are considered nontaxable. See Rev. Rul. 55–609, *Cum. Bul.* 1955–2, pp. 34–35; Rev. Rul. 55–581, *Cum. Bul.* 1955–2, 381–82.

43. Harry Yohlin, "Employer Payments to the Widow of a Deceased Employee," *Taxes,* XXXIV (1956), 92–93. This is a good summary of the history and development of the tax laws relating to the widow's benefits.

44. "Interpretations," *Taxes,* XXXIII (1955), 707–8. Cases are cited to substantiate these conclusions. Reasons (1), (2), and (4) were cited in the Hellstrom case as reasons for nontaxability. In addition, the Court noted that payment was made to the widow and

and not to the employee's estate and cited this as a reason for non-taxability. *Estate of Arthur W. Hellstrom,* 24 TC 916 at 920 (1955).

45. Yohlin, "Employer Payments to the Widow of a Deceased Employee," *Taxes,* XXXIV (1956), 95–96.

46. Reinhold Groh, "Voluntary Payments to an Employee's Widow," *Taxes,* XXXVI (1958), 334, 338–39.

47. Guttentag *et al.,* "Federal Income Taxation of Fringe Benefits: A Specific Proposal," *National Tax Journal,* VI (1953), 260–63.

48. H. R. 10578 and H. R. 11764 introduced in the 84th Cong. 2nd Sess., 1956.

49. See "Now It's 'Fringe Benefits' for Big Executives," *U. S. News and World Report,* January 17, 1958, pp. 81–82.

50. Cf. Burton Crane, "A Stake for Executives, "New York *Times,* May 5, 1956, pp. 23, 29.

51. U. S., Congress, Joint Committee on the Economic Report, *Federal Revenue System,* p. 106.

52. *Internal Revenue Code of 1954,* sec. 421.

53. Burton Crane discusses some of the major variations in "Option Tax Held Unfair to Heirs," New York *Times,* February 12, 1956, p. 2F.

54. See New York Stock Exchange, *Stock Ownership Plans for Employees,* pp. 1, 117–207; also "Management Briefs," *Business Week,* July 9, 1955, p. 107, which tells of the distribution to 8,100 Sun Oil employees of stock valued at $11 million, which cost employees only $3.4 million.

NOTES TO CHAPTER VI.   UNEMPLOYMENT AND
HEALTH INSURANCE

1. G. C. M. 17920, *Cum. Bul.* 1937–1, p. 68; I. T. 2960, *Cum. Bul.* XV–1 (1936), p. 98.

2. Mim. 4595, *Cum. Bul.* 1937–1, p. 63.

3. I. T. 3111, *Cum. Bul.* 1937–2, p. 85; I. T. 3970, *Cum. Bul.* 1949–2, p. 28.

4. I. T. 3230, *Cum. Bul.* 1938–2, p. 136.

5. *Internal Revenue Code of 1954,* sec. 3306(a), (b)(1).

6. "In Labor," *Business Week,* October 29, 1955, p. 166.

7. U. S., Social Security Administration, *Social Security Bulletin,* Annual Statistical Supplement, 1957, pp. 9, 14, 15, 19. The number of beneficiaries and workers covered in 1940 was found in U. S.,

Department of Commerce, *Statistical Abstract of the United States, 1950,* p. 242.

8. See "Auto Workers Ask Severance Pay," *Business Week,* November 30, 1957, p. 127.

9. For a description and analysis of these plans, see "SUB for GAW," *First National City Bank Monthly Letter,* July, 1955, pp. 75–80; "Making SUP More Tangible," *Business Week,* September 17, 1955, p. 166; Philip W. Cartwright, "The Economics of the UAW-Ford Contract," *American Economic Review,* XLV (1955), 932–37.

10. Rev. Rul. 56–249, *Cum. Bul.* 1956–1, p. 488.

11. Bureau of Internal Revenue Letter of March 22, 1956 to Pittsburgh Plate Glass Co., reprinted in Prentice-Hall, *Pension and Profit Sharing Service,* par. 11,918.

12. "Unions Hint at Demands to Come," *Business Week,* September 3, 1955, pp. 89–90.

13. *Revenue Act of 1942,* sec. 127 to amend *Internal Revenue Code of 1939,* sec. 23.

14. *Regulations 111,* sec. 29.23(x)–1.

15. Letter ruling dated October 26, 1943, reported in full in Prentice-Hall, Inc., *Federal Tax Service* (1943), par. 66,326. Cited in Prentice-Hall, Inc. *Federal Tax Course* (1955), par. 1830(b).

16. *Internal Revenue Code of 1954,* sec. 104(a)(3).

17. *Ibid.,* sec. 105 (a),(b).

18. Let w be the worker's wage including any hospitalization insurance fringe benefit; let h be the amount of hospitalization insurance; let m be medical expenses other than hospitalization insurance. If, then, the worker buys his own hospitalization insurance, his deduction will equal $m + h - .03w$. If, on the other hand, his employer furnishes the insurance, his tax base will be reduced by a medical deduction of $m - .03 (w - h)$ and by h. This is equivalent to $m + h - .03 (w - h)$ if the medical expense is large enough to qualify as a deduction. It can be seen that, when the medical expense is sufficiently large, the deduction under the fringe benefit always exceeds the deduction without the benefit by $.03h$, which means the larger the value of h as a fringe benefit, the more benefit accrues to the recipient of the fringe benefit. This last observation is important because hospitalization is only one form of health insurance and this group of fringe benefits appears likely to grow.

19. In Chapter II, pp. 42–44, it has been pointed out that the

fringe benefit reduces the recipient's taxable income by 9/10 of the amount of the fringe benefit. The tax saving would be the marginal tax rate times this reduction in the tax base.

20. Those taxpayers who itemize their deductions but lack sufficient medical expenses to include them will profit more than the 3 percent of the fringe benefit and so reduce the tax base by a larger amount.

21. The Health Insurance Council, *Accident and Health Coverage, 1951,* p. 16. See also Evan Keith Rowe, "Health, Insurance, and Pension Plans in Union Contracts," *Monthly Labor Review,* LXXVIII (1955), 993–1000, for a description of increased coverage of unionized workers only.

22. See Prentice-Hall Editorial Staff, *Successful Employee Benefit Plans,* p. 43; U. S., Bureau of Labor Statistics, *Digest of Selected Plans, 1954,* Bulletin 1180 (1955), p. iii.

23. *Internal Revenue Code of 1954,* secs. 3121(a)(2), 3306(b)(2). Wages under the Fair Labor Standards Act are defined more generally in *United States Code* (1952 ed.), title 29, sec. 203(m). It is possible that here, too, premiums and benefits would not be counted as wages.

NOTES TO CHAPTER VII. FRINGE BENEFITS IN KIND

1. O. D. 265, *Cum. Bul.* 1 (1919), p. 71. See also note 19, Chapter II, above.

2. For a warning that the rate of increased use of fringe benefits is rather rapid and is likely to lead to increased taxation of these benefits, see "Tax Report," *Journal of Commerce,* February 23, 1956, p. 1.

3. There are several good treatments of the historical development of tax policy with regard to income in kind. Cf. Kletzing, "Tax Treatment of Compensation in Kind," *California Law Review,* XXXVII (1949), 632–33; Landman, "The Taxability of Fringe Benefits," *Taxes,* XXXIII (1955), 179–80; Gutkin and Beck, "Some Problems in 'Convenience of the Employer,'" *Taxes,* XXXVI (1958), 153–65; the opinion in *Robert H. Saunders* v. *Commissioner,* 215 F 2d 768 (1954). The latter three references cite O. D. 265, *Cum. Bul.* 1 (1919), p. 71, as the beginning of the "convenience of the employer" rule; Kletzing says it goes back to November, 1914, when the question arose over a case where rooms in excess of the number allowed by law were furnished to army officers. These

were held to be for the convenience of the government and were not considered as taxable income.

4. See rulings O. D. 814, O. D. 862, O. D. 914, O. D. 915, and O. D. 921 on pp. 84–86 and O. D. 874 on p. 348, all in *Cum. Bul.* 4 (1921).

5. *Clifford Jones* v. *U. S.,* 60 Ct. Cl. 567 (1925).

6. Mim. 6472, *Cum. Bul.* 1950–1, p. 15.

7. For example, in *Robert H. Saunders* v. *Commissioner,* 215 F 2d 768 (1954), the Court was concerned with whether or not $665 received by Saunders, a New Jersey state trooper, in lieu of rations, was income. The Court considered Mim. 6472 but held that it was not "evident" that this was compensation for his services, although a brochure describing the job to prospective employees stated that "the annual minimum salary of a trooper, which is $3,-480 plus maintenance" would be received.

8. See Landman, "The Taxability of Fringe Benefits," *Taxes,* XXXIII (1955), 186–87. Cases supporting his opinion are cited.

9. Employees of New York City hospitals were required in 1956 to begin paying a gradually increasing proportion of the cost of meals which had previously been furnished free. The cost of meals, which was to be charged to employees, was 40 cents for breakfast, 80 cents for lunch, and 80 cents for dinner. The City estimated that it would save about $2 million a year when the program was completed. Since 33,000 workers were receiving meals free prior to this ruling, it indicates an expenditure of about $60 per worker per year. In view of the above charge per meal, this figure appears rather low. A person working a five-day week with eight holidays during a year and a two-week vacation would work about 240 days during the year; if he ate all three meals at the hospital each day, the value of food consumed at the above prices would be $480 a year. If he ate only breakfast, the cheapest meal, the total charge would be $96 a year. See "City Hospital Fee for Food Upheld," New York *Times,* August 22, 1956, p. 13.

10. Break, "Effects of Taxation on Work Incentives," in U. S., Congress, Joint Committee on the Economic Report, *Federal Tax Policy,* p. 195. See also pp. 49–50 above.

11. Vickrey, *Agenda,* p. 37.

12. Mim. 5657, *Cum. Bul.* 1944, p. 550. An earlier interesting case regarding the taxability of meals under the Social Security Act may be found in the *Cum. Bul.* 1937–2, pp. 449–50 and *Cum. Bul.*

1938–1, pp. 456–58. In this case the M Company inquired whether meals furnished employees in one plant, while additional cash payments were given to employees in other plants where meals were not furnished, were wages under the Social Security Act. The Bureau of Internal Revenue cited art. 14, Regulations 91, and held that the fair value of the meals was wages. The M Company then amplified its position, pointing out that among other things these meals helped employees by keeping them from "losing time or impairing their efficiency due directly or indirectly to securing lunches which are improperly prepared or served elsewhere." The Bureau consequently ruled: "The M Company has now established that the free lunch privileges are afforded to promote its own interests . . . and benefit the company by promoting the health, good will and efficiency of its employees." Hence the lunches were not considered as wages.

13. Kletzing, "Tax Treatment of Compensation in Kind," *California Law Review*, XXXVII (1949), 630–31.

14. Guttentag *et al.*, "Federal Income Taxation of Fringe Benefits: A Specific Proposal," *National Tax Journal*, VI (1953), 260.

15. *Hyslope* v. *Commissioner*, 21 TC 131 (1953).

16. *Herman Martin*, 44 BTA 185 (1941).

17. See Havemann, "Exprense Account Aristocrats," *Life*, March 9, 1953, pp. 140–52.

18. Vickrey, *Agenda*, p. 41.

19. Guttentag *et al.*, "Federal Income Taxation of Fringe Benefits: A Specific Proposal," *National Tax Journal*, VI (1953), 260.

20. Kletzing, "Tax Treatment of Compensation in Kind," *California Law Review*, XXXVII (1949), 630–31.

21. Canada, *Income Tax Act*, 1954, sec. 5(a).

22. *Ibid.*, sec. 9(a).

23. O. D. 265, *Cum. Bul.* 1 (1919), p. 71.

24. Mim. 6472, *Cum. Bul.* 1950–1, p. 15.

25. *Internal Revenue Code of 1954*, sec. 119(2).

26. Cf. Vickrey, *Agenda*, p. 37; Kletzing, "Tax Treatment of Compensation in Kind," *California Law Review*, XXXVII (1949), 630–31; Guttentag *et al.*, "Federal Income Taxation of Fringe Benefits: A Specific Proposal," *National Tax Journal*, VI (1953), 257–60.

27. See Chapter III, p. 72, above.

28. Vickrey notes that the state of Iowa specifically excludes the value of quarters when the employee maintains another residence.

Iowa State Tax Commission, *Rules and Regulations Relating to the Personal Net Income Tax* (1941–42), art. 27. Cited in Vickrey, *Agenda,* footnote e, p. 40.

29. See "U. S. Big Business Setting New Pattern on Clyde, I. B. M. Plant Features Amenities for Workers," New York *Times,* December 10, 1955, p. 23; "How British Businessmen Keep Going," *Fortune,* May, 1950, p. 85; "It's the Same the World Over," *Life,* December 10, 1951, p. 36.

30. Vickrey, *Agenda,* p. 39; Guttentag *et al.,* "Federal Income Taxation of Fringe Benefits: A Specific Proposal," *National Tax Journal,* VI (1953), 257–59.

31. Mim. 6472, *Cum. Bul.* 1950–1, p. 15.

32. See Thompson, *Cooperative Medical Programs* (Studies in Personnel Policy, No. 134, 1953).

33. U. S. military personnel, for example, often have these more elaborate facilities available, although see "Morale and the Military," New York *Times,* January 8, 1955, p. 45, and "House Votes Care for Military Kin," New York *Times,* March 3, 1956, p. 21, for stories of shortages of facilities. A new development in this field is for the unions, rather than the employers, to furnish this service, although funds come primarily, or entirely, from employers. This aspect of fringe benefits is discussed on pp. 177–78 below.

34. See "Physical Checkup—In Style," *Business Week,* September 23, 1950, pp. 84–90. Increased interest followed President Eisenhower's heart attack. See "Spurt in Executive Health Plans," *Business Week,* October 15, 1955, p. 130.

35. George W. Bachman and Associates, *Health Resources in the United States,* p. 243.

36. "Longer Lives for Executives," *Business Week,* September 11, 1954, pp. 101–2. In 1953 this firm examined 35,000 people, although not all examinations were of the $300 quality. U. S. Rubber spent about $25,000 for these examinations, an average expenditure of $35 per employee. The growth of this service is indicated by the fact that in 1946 the service was used by 27 companies, while in 1953 over 300 companies purchased the service.

37. Vickrey says that a good case can be made for giving employees this service, even though concessions in income taxation might not be the best approach. Vickrey, *Agenda,* p. 43.

38. *Regulations 106,* sec. 402.227(a).

39. For other proposals for tax treatment see Vickrey, *Agenda,* p.

43; Gordon, "Tax Effects of Union Welfare Plans," *Tax Law Review*, VI (1950–51), 51.

40. Elmer W. Earl, Jr., *Employee Education* (Studies in Personnel Policy, No. 119, 1951), pp. 15, 20; "G. E. 'University' to Get a Campus," New York *Times*, August 28, 1955, p. 1–F; "Concern to Pay Staff's Tuition," New York *Times*, November 29, 1956, p. 59; "Employees Get Tuition," New York *Times*, January 2, 1957, p. 90; Doris M. Thompson, *Tuition Aid Plans for Employees* (Studies in Personnel Policy, No. 151, 1956), p. 29.

41. Earl, *Employee Education* (Studies in Personnel Policy, No. 119, 1951), pp. 6, 7.

42. *Ibid.,* p. 31.

43. See note 40 above.

44. Many of the advertisements in the mid-1950s by companies seeking to employ engineers have carried promises of further graduate study at company expense. One of the more explicit of these is the advertisement by the Westinghouse Corporation, New York *Times,* June 17, 1956, p. 13–F.

45. George V. Moser and Allison V. MacCullough, *Executive Development Courses in Universities* (Studies in Personnel Policy, No. 142, 1954), pp. 5–7.

46. "Company Towns, 1956," *Time,* April 16, 1956, pp. 100–1; "Personal Business," *Business Week,* July 9, 1955, pp. 139–40; "Tax Report," *Journal of Commerce,* February 2, 1956, p. 1.

47. Examples of these activities may be found in the following news stories and studies: "*Life* Goes to Houston's Paradise for Office Girls," *Life,* September 15, 1952, pp. 150–55; "Havana Jaunt for 132, All on the Boss," *Life,* December 16, 1957, pp. 125–26; "Hunters Get a Break; Safari Is Deductible," New York *Times,* December 21, 1955, p. 57; "Greenwich Sees the Ghost of 1656," New York *Times,* August 1, 1956, p. 25; "They Sail for Pfizer and for Pfun," New York *Times,* November 12, 1956, p. 47; "Jersey Company Builds Pool for Its Employees," New York *Times,* July 27, 1958, p. 1–F.

48. See pp. 74–75 above.

49. See "The Real Estate Side of Executive Changes," *Business Week,* April 16, 1955, pp. 122–26. Also see recent advertisements for engineers. One which might be cited is the advertisement of the RAND Corporation in New York *Times,* July 8, 1956, p. 17–F.

50. See Geneva Seybold, "Income Tax on Company Reimburse-

ment for Moving Expenses," *Management Record,* XX (1958), 422–23. Rev. Rul. 55–140, *Cum. Bul.* 1955–1, p. 317, covers the present tax treatment of moving expenses.

51. Due, *Government Finance,* p. 142; Guttentag *et al.,* "Federal Income Taxation of Fringe Benefits: A Specific Proposal," *National Tax Journal,* VI (1953), 264–65; Landman, "The Taxability of Fringe Benefits," *Taxes,* XXXIII (1955), 183; Vickrey, *Agenda,* p. 42.

52. In the case *Railroads* v. *Nonoperating Unions,* 22 LA 392 (1954), the carriers estimated that the cost of free transportation to employees was in excess of five cents per hour. For a normal work year this would amount to just over $100 per employee. Due describes incidental services and employee discounts as being "of considerable value." Due, *Government Finance,* p. 142.

53. "Prosperity Pains" (editorial), New York *Times,* August 23, 1955, p. 22; "U. S. Big Business Setting New Pattern on Clyde, I. B. M. Plant Features Amenities for Workers," New York *Times,* December 10, 1955, p. 23.

54. This opinion is advanced in Guttentag *et al.,* "Federal Income Taxation of Fringe Benefits: A Specific Proposal," *National Tax Journal,* VI (1953), 268–69.

55. See "Senate to Pay $965,000 for 285 Parking Spaces," New York *Times,* January 1, 1958, p. 5. Senator Paul A. Douglas is described as calculating the cost at over $3,000 a parking space, but this was the only protest voiced.

56. See Burton Crane, "A Stake for Executives," New York *Times,* May 5, 1956, pp. 23, 29. Here a loan is made at a nominal rate rather than at a zero rate, but the effect is the same. See Matthew F. Blake, "Fringe Benefit Programs," *Taxes,* XXXVI (1958), 860–61, for the application to insurance purchases. See also *Kiplinger Washington News Letter,* December 10, 1955, p. 3; "Interpretations," *Taxes,* XXXIII (1955), 243.

57. The writer has been reliably informed of a case where the company informally told certain employees to make freer use of company cars for personal use. Also the recorded instances of company approval of employees making personal use of company property such as cars, yachts, hunting preserves, seashore resorts, and the like indicate that companies, too, find these benefits preferable to wage expenditures; see the following note.

58. "New Price Tag on Policymakers," *Business Week,* July 16, 1955, p. 46.   For further examples of these fringe benefits see "The Private Life of a Self Made Millionaire," *Look,* May 3, 1955, p. 44; "Suit is Filed Against 5 Thermoid Officers Charging Manipulation," *Wall Street Journal,* June 17, 1955, p. 13.   For comments on the tax treatment of these benefits see Guttentag *et al.,* "Federal Income Taxation of Fringe Benefits: A Specific Proposal," *National Tax Journal,* VI (1953), 265–68; Hoffman, "Fringe Benefits for Employees," *Taxes,* XXXI (1953), 1006; Landman, "The Taxability of Fringe Benefits," *Taxes,* XXXIII (1955), 190; Charles D. Post, "The Quest for Indirect Compensation for Executives of Closely Held Corporations," *New York University Eleventh Annual Institute on Federal Taxation,* pp. 174–75.

59. Nicholas L. A. Martucci, "Executive 'Extras,'" *Management Record,* XX (1958), 433–34.

60. See "John Lewis's 250 Mile Chain of Hospitals," *U. S. News & World Report,* October 7, 1955, pp. 98–100.   For an evaluation of this procedure, an evaluation that can be held to support Blum's contention, see "The Miners' Fund—A Tribute to Good Management," *Reader's Digest,* September, 1956, pp. 173–80.   Here it is argued that the money going into the Welfare Fund is well spent and that consumers should not object to paying the increased price of coal.

61. Rev. Rul. 54–190, *Cum. Bul.* 1954–1, pp. 46–47.

62. *Regulations 118,* sec. 39.22(a)–2.

63. See "Union Service Keeps on Growing," *Business Week,* June 9, 1956, p. 59.   This story tells of the United Mine Workers hospitals and of a new $750,000 theater built by the International Ladies Garment Workers Union at Unity House, a resort area owned and operated near Bushkill in the Pocono Mountains in Pennsylvania for vacationing members.   See also "Union Dedicating Retirement Spot," New York *Times,* December 5, 1956, p. 42; "Anastasia Begins Medical Center," New York *Times,* June 24, 1956, p. 75.

NOTES TO CHAPTER VIII. SUMMARY AND CONCLUSIONS

1. Haig, *The Federal Income Tax,* p. 7.

2. Joseph A. Pechman, "Erosion of the Individual Income Tax," *National Tax Journal,* X (1957), 12–14, 24.

3. See Henry C. Simons, *Federal Tax Reform,* pp. 40–44; Vickrey, *Agenda,* pp. 164–97; Joseph A. Pechman, "A Practical Averaging Proposal," *National Tax Journal,* VII (1954), 261–63.

4. See Vickrey, *Agenda,* pp. 169–70, for a discussion of the experiences of Australia, Great Britain, and Wisconsin with various averaging proposals.

5. See "Deferred Pay: Still No Law," *Business Week,* July 23, 1955, pp. 41–44.

6. Pension plans and other retirement income plans can be important to employees in the lowest income tax bracket if, without these plans, they would have been left with sizable unused exemptions at the time benefits are received but not when contributions are made. And it should be remembered that a husband and wife over sixty-five have four exemptions.

Bibliography

OFFICIAL SOURCES

IN addition to the sources listed below, the reports of several courts have been used. The various revenue acts, laws, and internal revenue codes may be found in U.S. Statutes at large.

Canada. Income Tax Act. 1954.

U.S. Bureau of the Census. Statistical Abstract of the Unites States: 1958. 1958.

U.S. Bureau of Internal Revenue. Cumulative Bulletin, Volumes 1 to 1958-1.

U.S. Bureau of Labor Statistics. Pension Plans under Collective Bargaining. Bulletin No. 1147. 1953.

————. Digest of One Hundred Selected Health and Insurance Plans under Collective Bargaining. Bulletin No. 1180. 1955.

————. Problems in Measurement of Expenditures on Selected Items of Supplementary Employee Remuneration. Bulletin No. 1186. 1956.

U.S. Bureau of Old-Age and Survivors Insurance. Handbook of Old-Age and Survivors Insurance Statistics, 1950. 1953.

U.S. Code. 1952 edition.

U.S. Congress, Joint Committee on the Economic Report. Federal Tax Policy for Economic Growth and Stability. 84th Cong., 1st Sess., 1955.

————. The Federal Revenue System: Facts and Problems. 84th Cong., 1st Sess., 1955.

————. Hearings, Federal Tax Policy for Economic Growth and Stability. 84th Cong., 1st Sess., 1956.

U.S. Congress, Joint Committee on Tax Evasion and Avoidance. Hearings, Tax Evasion and Avoidance. 75th Cong., 1st Sess., 1937.

U.S. Congress, House of Representatives, Committee on Ways and Means. Hearings, Individual Retirement Act of 1955. H.R. 10, 84th Cong., 1st Sess., 1955.

U.S. Congress, Senate, Committee on Finance. Internal Revenue Code of 1954. Report No. 1622, 83rd Cong., 2nd Sess., 1954.

U.S. Department of Labor. The Termination Report of the National War Labor Board. Vol. III. 1947.

U.S. Division of Tax Research. The Income Tax Treatment of Pensions and Annuities. 1947. (Mimeographed.)

U.S. Internal Revenue (later Bureau of Internal Revenue; later Internal Revenue Service). Regulations.

U.S. Internal Revenue Service. Statistics of Income for 1951, Part I. 1955.

————. Statistics of Income—1954, Corporation Income Tax Returns. 1957.

————. Statistics of Income—1955, Corporation Income Tax Returns. 1958.

U.S. National War Labor Board. Wage Report to the President on the Wartime Relationship of Wages to the Cost of Living. 1945.

U.S. Office of Business Economics. National Income 1954. 1954.

————. Survey of Current Business.

U.S. Securities and Exchange Commission. Survey of Corporate Pension Funds 1951–54. 1956.

U.S. Social Security Administration. Social Security Bulletin.

U.S. Statutes at Large.

U.S. Steel Industry Board. Report to the President of the United States on the Labor Dispute in the Basic Steel Industry. 1949.

UNOFFICIAL SOURCES

In addition to the sources listed below, considerable use has been made of newspapers and magazines, particularly the New York Times, Wall Street Journal, and Business Week.

American Assembly, The. Economic Security for Americans. New York: Graduate School of Business, Columbia University, 1953.

American Federation of Labor. Pension Plans under Collective Bargaining. Washington: American Federation of Labor, 1952.

Associated Industries of Cleveland. "Employee Benefit Survey." Cleveland, February 17, 1954. (Mimeographed.)

Associated Industries of Massachusetts. Survey on Fringe Benefits in Massachusetts Industry. Boston: Associated Industries of Massachusetts, 1949.

Bachman, George W., and associates. Health Resources in the United States. Washington: The Brookings Institution, 1952.

Ball, Robert M. Pensions in the United States. (A study prepared for the Joint Committee on the Economic Report.) Washington: U.S. Government Printing Office, 1952.

Barkin, Solomon. "Financial Statements in Collective Bargaining," The New York Certified Public Accountant, XXIII (1953), 439–46.

Belfer, Nathan. "Hidden Costs in the Labor Agreement," Labor Law Journal, VI (1955), 402–14.

Bittker, Boris I. "The Individual as Wage Earner," New York University Eleventh Annual Institute on Federal Taxation. Albany: Matthew Bender & Co., Inc., 1953.

Blake, Matthew F. "Fringe Benefit Programs," Taxes, XXXVI (1958), 858–65.

Block, Norman. "Deductibility of Employer Contributions to Qualified Pension and Profit-Sharing Plans," New York University Thirteenth Annual Institute on Federal Taxation. Albany: Matthew Bender & Co., Inc., 1955.

Blum, Walter J. "The Effects of Special Provisions in the Income Tax on Taxpayer Morale," in U. S. Congress, Joint Committee on the Economic Report. Federal Tax Policy for Economic Growth and Stability. 84th Cong., 1st Sess., 1955.

Break, George F. "Effects of Taxation on Work Incentives," in U. S. Congress, Joint Committee on the Economic Report. Federal Tax Policy for Economic Growth and Stability. 84th Cong., 1st Sess., 1955.

Brissenden, Paul F. "Labor Mobility and Employee Benefits," Labor Law Journal, VI (1955), 762–68.

Brower, F. Beatrice. "Group Insurance for Employees and Their Dependents, 1945–53," Management Record, XVI (1954), 297–99.

———. Pension Plans and Their Administration (Studies in Personnel Policy, No. 149). New York: National Industrial Conference Board, 1955.

Butters, J. Keith, Lawrence E. Thompson, and Lynn L. Bollinger. Effects of Taxation: Investment by Individuals. Boston: Graduate School of Business Administration, Harvard University, 1953.

Carey, William L. "Pressure Groups and the Increasing Erosion of the Revenue Laws," in U. S. Congress, Joint Committee on the Economic Report. Federal Tax Policy for Economic Growth and Stability. 84th Cong., 1st Sess., 1955.

Cartwright, Philip W. "The Economics of the UAW-Ford Contract," *The American Economic Review*, XLV (1955), 932–37.

Chamber of Commerce of the United States of America. Fringe Benefits, 1953. Washington: Chamber of Commerce of the United States of America, 1954.

———. Fringe Benefits, 1957. Washington: Chamber of Commerce of the United States of America, 1958.

———. The Hidden Payroll. Washington: Chamber of Commerce of the United States of America, 1949.

Commerce Clearing House. Standard Federal Tax Reporter. Chicago: Commerce Clearing House, loose leaf, annual.

"'Costs' of Fringe Benefits," *AFL-CIO Collective Bargaining Report*, I (1956), 17–19.

Council of Profit-Sharing Industries. Revised Profit-Sharing Manual. Akron: Council of Profit-Sharing Industries, 1951.

Daniel, Eleanor S. "Retirement Funds, Capital Markets, and Growth," in U. S. Congress, Joint Committee on the Economic Report. Federal Tax Policy for Economic Growth and Stability. 84th Cong., 1st Sess., 1955.

Dearing, Charles L. Industrial Pensions. Washington: The Brookings Institution, 1954.

Due, John F. Government Finance, an Economic Analysis. Homewood, Illinois: Richard D. Irwin, Inc., 1954.

Earl, Elmer W., Jr. Employee Education (Studies in Personnel Policy, No. 119). New York: National Industrial Conference Board, 1951.

Fisher, Austin M., and John F. Chapman. "Big Costs of Little Fringes," *Harvard Business Review*, XXXII (1954), 35–40.

Fisher, Irving. Constructive Income Taxation. New York: Harper & Brothers, 1942.

Flippo, Edwin B. Profit Sharing in American Business. Columbus, Ohio: Bureau of Business Research, College of Commerce and Administration, The Ohio State University, 1954.

Goldberg, Arthur J. "Compensation Other Than Cash." (Paper presented before the Taxation Section of the American Bar Association, New York, N. Y., September 18, 1951. (Mimeographed.)

Gordon, Emanuel L. "Tax Effects of Union Welfare Plans," *Tax Law Review*, VI (1950–51), 1–51.

Groh, Reinhold. "Voluntary Payments to an Employee's Widow," *Taxes*, XXXVI (1958), 333–42.

Groves, Harold M. Financing Government. 4th ed. New York: Henry Holt and Company, 1954.

————. Trouble Spots in Taxation. Princeton: Princeton University Press, 1948.

Gutkin, Sydney A., and David Beck. "Some Problems in 'Convenience of the Employer,'" *Taxes*, XXXVI (1958), 153–65.

Guttentag, Joseph H., E. Deane Leonard, and William Y. Rodewald. "Federal Income Taxation of Fringe Benefits: A Specific Proposal," *National Tax Journal*, VI (1953), 250–72.

Haig, Robert Murray. "The Concept of Income," in Robert Murray Haig, ed., The Federal Income Tax. New York: Columbia University Press, 1921.

Hall, Challis A., Jr. "Retirement Contributions, the Spending Stream, and Growth," in U. S. Congress, Joint Committee on the Economic Report. Federal Tax Policy for Economic Growth and Stability. 84th Cong., 1st Sess., 1955.

Health Insurance Council, The. Acident and Health Coverage in the United States as of December 31, 1951. New York: The Health Insurance Council, 1952.

————. The Extent of Voluntary Health Insurance Coverage in the United States as of December 31, 1955. New York: The Health Insurance Council, 1956.

Heller, Walter W. "Appraisal of the Administration's Tax Policy," *National Tax Journal*, VIII (1955), 12–28.

Hewett, William Wallace. The Definition of Income and Its Application in Federal Taxation. Philadelphia: By the author, 1925.

Hill, James C. "Stabilization of Fringe Benefits," *Industrial and Labor Relations Review*, VII (1954), 221–34.

Hoffman, Raymond A. "Fringe Benefits for Employees," *Taxes*, XXXI (1953), 999–1006.

Holland, Daniel M. Suggestions for Research in the Economics of Pensions. New York: National Bureau of Economic Research, Inc., 1957.

Institute of Life Insurance. Life Insurance Fact Book 1956. New York: Institute of Life Insurance, 1956.

————. Life Insurance Fact Book 1957. New York: Institute of Life Insurance, 1957.

"Insurance—New 'Fringe' on Executive Payrolls," *Personnel,* XXX (1953), 71–72.

"Interpretations," *Taxes,* XXXIII (1955), 706–8.

Kletzing, Russell R. "Tax Treatment of Compensation in Kind," *California Law Review,* XXXVII (1949), 629–39.

Knowlton, Philip Arnold. Profit Sharing Patterns. Evanston, Illinois: Profit Sharing Research Foundation, 1954.

Landman, J. Henry. "The Taxability of Fringe Benefits," *Taxes,* XXXIII (1955), 173–90.

Lasser, J. K., and Henry V. Rothschild. "Deferred Compensation for Executives," *Harvard Business Review,* XXXIII (1955), 89–102.

Latimer, Murray Webb. Industrial Pension Systems in the United States and Canada. 2 vols. New York: Industrial Relations Counselors, Inc., 1932.

Latimer, Murray Webb, and Karl Tufel. Trends in Industrial Pensions. New York: Industrial Counselors, Inc., 1940.

Martucci, Nicholas L. A. "Executive 'Extras,'" *Management Record,* XX (1958), 406–9, 432–35.

McGill, Dan M., ed. Pensions: Problems and Trends. Homewood, Illinois: Published for The S. S. Huebner Foundation for Insurance Education, University of Pennsylvania, by Richard D. Irwin, Inc., 1955.

Mann, Everett J. "Deferred Compensation and Stock Option Plans May Be Legal, but Are They Ethical?" *The Journal of Accountancy,* XCIII (1952), 324–29.

Marsh, Donald B. "The Taxation of Imputed Income," *Political Science Quarterly,* LVIII (1943), 514–36.

Marshall, Howard D. "Unions and Labor Mobility," *Labor Law Journal,* VII (1956), 83–97.

Mendelsohn, Allan I. "Fringe Benefits and Our Industrial Society," *Labor Law Journal,* VII (1956), 325–28, 379–84.

Moser, George V., and Allison V. MacCullough. Executive Development Courses in Universities (Studies in Personnel Policy, No. 142). New York: National Industrial Conference Board, 1954.

National Industrial Conference Board. Industrial Pensions in the United States. New York: National Industrial Conference Board, 1925.

New York Stock Exchange. Stock Ownership Plans for Employees. New York: New York Stock Exchange, 1956.

Paish, F. W., and A. T. Peacock. "The Economics of Pension Funds," *Lloyds Bank Review,* New Series, No. 34 (1954), 14–28.

Paul, Randolph E. "Erosion of the Tax Base and Rate Structure," in U. S. Congress, Joint Committee on the Economic Report. Federal Tax Policy for Economic Growth and Stability. 84th Cong., 1st Sess., 1955.

———. Taxation in the United States. Boston: Little, Brown and Company, 1954.

Pechman, Joseph A. "A Practical Averaging Proposal," *National Tax Journal,* VII (1954), 261–63.

———. "Erosion of the Individual Income Tax," *National Tax Journal,* X (1957), 1–25.

Pigou, A. C. A Study in Public Finance. 3rd (revised) ed. London: Macmillan & Co., Ltd., 1951.

Post, Charles D. "The Quest for Indirect Compensation for Executives of Closely Held Corporations," New York University Eleventh Annual Institute on Federal Taxation. Albany: Matthew Bender & Co., Inc., 1953.

Prentice-Hall Editorial Staff. Successful Employee Benefit Plans. New York: Prentice-Hall, Inc., 1952.

Prentice-Hall, Inc. Federal Tax Course, 1955. New York: Prentice-Hall, Inc., 1954.

———. Prentice-Hall Pension and Profit Sharing Service. New York: Prentice-Hall, Inc., loose leaf.

"Private Pension Plans," *Federal Reserve Bank of New York Monthly Review,* XXXV (1953), 185–88.

Ratchford, B. U. "Practical Limitations to the Net Income Tax— General," *Journal of Finance,* VII (1952), 203–13.

———. "The Tax Status of Social Security Benefits," *Southern Economic Journal,* XX (1953), 156–62.

Reynolds, Lloyd G. The Structure of the Labor Market. New York: Harper & Brothers, 1951.

Robbins, Rainard B. Impact of Taxes on Industrial Pension Plans (Industrial Relations Monograph, No. 14). New York: Industrial Relations Counselors, Inc., 1949.

———. Pension Planning in the United States. New York: Teachers Insurance & Annuity Association of America, 1952.

Ross, Arthur M. "Fringe Benefits Today and Tomorrow," *Labor Law Journal,* VII (1956), 476–82.

Rowe, Evan Keith. "Health, Insurance, and Pension Plans in Union Contracts," *Monthly Labor Review*, LXXVIII (1955), 993–1000.

———, and Thomas H. Paine. "Pension Plans under Collective Bargaining," *Monthly Labor Review*, LXXVI (1953), 237–45.

Sargent, C. W. "Fringe" Benefits: Do We Know Enough About Them? Hanover, New Hampshire: Amos Tuck School of Business Administration, 1953.

Schroeder, Gertrude G. "The 'Stabilization' of Fringe Benefits under the 1951–53 Wage Controls Program," *Southern Economic Journal*, XXI (1955), 319–29.

Seal, Hilary L. "Pensions, Profit-Sharing and Stock Options under New Tax Law," *Commercial and Financial Chronicle*, CLXXX, September 23, 1954, 1171, 1192.

Seybold, Geneva. Employee Recreation Activities (Studies in Personnel Policy, No. 102). New York: National Industrial Conference Board, 1949.

———. "Income Tax on Company Reimbursement for Moving Expenses," *Management Record*, XX (1958), 422–23.

Sigafoos, Robert A. "The Municipal Income Tax—A Janus in Disguise," *National Tax Journal*, VI (1953), 188–93.

Simons, Henry C. Federal Tax Reform. Chicago: The University of Chicago Press, 1950.

———. Personal Income Taxation. Chicago: The University of Chicago Press, 1938.

Smith, Adam. The Wealth of Nations. New York: The Modern Library, 1937.

Smith, Dan Throop. "Two Years of Republican Tax Policy: an Economic Appraisal," *National Tax Journal*, VIII (1955), 2–11.

Stieglitz, Harold. Computing the Cost of Fringe Benefits (Studies in Personnel Policy, No. 128). New York: National Industrial Conference Board, 1952.

Strayer, Paul. "The Individual Income Tax and Income Distribution," *American Economic Review*, XLV (1955), 430–40.

Surrey, Stanley S. "Policy Issues in Federal Taxation," in Crucial Decisions in Government Finance (Current Business Studies, No. 10). New York: Trade and Industry Law Institute, Inc., 1951.

Thompson, Doris M. Cooperative Medical Programs (Studies in Personnel Policy, No. 134). New York: National Industrial Conference Board, 1953.

————. Tuition Aid Plans for Employees (Studies in Personnel Policy, No. 151). New York: National Industrial Conference Board, 1956.

United Automobile, Aircraft and Agricultural Implement Workers. UAW-CIO Collective Bargaining Handbook for Workers Security Programs. Detroit: UAW-CIO Social Security Department, 1949.

Vickrey, William S. Agenda for Progressive Taxation. New York: The Ronald Press Co., 1947.

————. Theoretical Economics (preliminary edition). New York, 1949. (Mimeographed.)

Walter, James E. "Some Implications of Private Pension Funds," *Southern Economic Journal,* XXII (1955), 230–42.

Wueller, Paul H. "Concepts of Taxable Income," *Political Science Quarterly,* LIII (1938). Part I on "The German Contribution" is found on pp. 83–110. Part II on "The American Contribution" is found on pp. 557–83.

Yane, Boris S. "Wages in Japanese Mining and Manufacturing," *Monthly Labor Review,* LXXXVIII (1955), 547–52.

Yohlin, Harry. "Employer Payments to the Widow of a Deceased Employee," *Taxes,* XXXIV (1956), 87–96.

Index

Administration of tax: difficulties discussed by Haig, 20; effect of several taxing bodies, 53; life insurance, 130–31; profit sharing, 120; sources of difficulty, 34–36; when fringe benefits are fully taxed, 67

Allocation of resources, 54 ff.; increased administration, 66; improved with fringe benefits, 69–72; meals, 163–64; pension plans, 115

American Federation of Labor: inflexibility of pensions, 100; pensions vs. wages, 65, 95

Annuities: non-refundable, 105–7; re-fundable, 104, 105

Associated Industries of Cleveland, 5, 187–88

Associated Industries of Massachusetts, 62

Averaging, 183–84; pension plans, 102–3

Avoidance, tax, 47

Barkin, Solomon, 44–45

Barter, fringe benefits as, 72

Blum, Walter J.: on use of tax favor, 98; on use of tax pleaders, 66

Break, George, 49

Brissenden, Paul F., 77–78

Bureau of Labor Statistics: health, insurance, and pension plans, 11; pension plans and mobility, 77

Butters, J. Keith, 46

Canada, pension plan taxation, 112–13; taxation of meals, 165

Capital gains: form of tax preference, 26; pension payments, 108, 114

Catastrophe medical insurance, see Major medical insurance

Chamber of Commerce of the United States: consumption fringe benefits, 79–80; measures of fringe benefits, 9–11, 189–90; profit sharing figures, 119

Civil service retirement, 143

Columbus, Ohio, 51

Commuting facilities, 175–76; housing as, 169–70

Conditions of work: change in concept, 7; development of the term, 24; Goldberg's definition, 31; guide for tax policy, 31–32, 72, 181; relation to wages, 7–8, 28–29, 33

Consumption, pension plans effect on, 100

Consumption of fringe benefits: when gain goes to employee, 57–59; when gain goes to employer, 60

Convenience of the employer: history, meals, 160–61; housing, 167; social security, 163; Treasury restrictions on use, 24

Cyclical stability, 78 ff., pension plans, 100–1

Dearing, Charles L.: on causes of fringe benefit growth, 15; on pension plans as fringe benefits, 42; on pensions vs. wages 64–65

Deductions and fringe benefits, 42–44

Deferred compensation, 144

Discounts on goods, 175

Drucker, Peter, 78

Due, John F., 65

Education, 174; vertical mobility, 75–76

Equity, 39; effect on collections, 45; hospitalization insurance, 152–53; municipal income tax, 83–84; old-age and survivors insurance, 137; pen-

Equity (*Continued*)
sion plans, 114–15; under changing tax rates, 47
Estate tax, 97
Executive fringe benefits, 27, 205; argument for fringe benefits, 45; deferred compensation, 144; health care, 30–31; pensions before 1942, 101; stock options, 144; widow's benefit, 140–41

Fair Labor Standards Act: compared to income tax, 50–51; effect of fringe benefits on, 52; exemption of supplemental unemployment benefits, 21
Federal Reserve Bank of New York, growth of pensions, 91
Fiscal policy, *see* Tax rates
Fisher, Austin M.: on fringe benefit growth, 1948–52, 11; survey in 1953, 26
Fisher, Irving, 19
Flugeladjutant, 30, 36, 65, 200–1
Foreign countries, 52
Fringe benefits: definitions, 4–7, 31, 33, 177; growth: national income figures, 8–9, Chamber of Commerce, 9–11; new, 15; to offset unpleasantness, 69–72; value to employee, 64–65

Gifts, widow's benefit, 140–42
Gladstone, William E., 45
Goldberg, Arthur, 31
Gordon, Emanuel L., 128
Groh, Reinhold, 140–41
Groves, Harold M.: on accounting and taxation, 112; on treatment of pensions, 102
Guttentag, Joseph H.: on cost and value, 66; on meals, 163–65; on Goldberg, 31; on tax preference for fringe benefits, 25

Haig, Robert M.: approval of concept of income, 3; definition of income, 19, 32, 67, 181; difficulties with departure from his definition, 21; on equity, 45
Hall, Challis A., Jr.: pension plan figures, 99; on pensions and saving, 100
Health Insurance: Blue Cross coverage, 11; effect on equity, 43; effect on saving, 80
Heller, Walter W., 42

Hewett, William W., 67
Hospitalization insurance: growth, 153–54; proposed treatment and effects, 155–57; tax treatment, 151–53
Housing, 167–70; different tax treatments, 51; to offset unpleasantness, 71; 1954 Code treatment, 25
Hyslope v. *Comm.*, 163

Incentive to work: effect of fringe benefits on, 48–50; profit sharing, 121–22
Income, definitions: courts, 22, 23, 66; Fisher, 19; Haig, 19, 67; Hewett, 67; Income Tax Act of 1913, 20; Simons, 19
Income tax: cause of fringe benefit growth, 14
Income Tax Act of 1913: definition of income, 20, 158
Individual Retirement Act of 1955: coverage, 17; tax favor, 99; vesting provisions, 98
Inflation and fringe benefits, *see* Cyclical stability
Institute of Life Insurance: pension contributions, 92
Insurance, income: pensions, 110; tax treatment, 104–5
Insurance, life, 125–31; growth, 127; proposed treatment and effects, 130–31; tax effects, 127–28; tax history, 125–26
Insurance, medical: coverage, 16; dependents coverage, 17
Interest-free loans, 176
International Ladies Garment Workers Union: pensions, 112

Japan: decline in fringe benefits, 73; tax treatment of fringe benefits, 52
Jones v. *U.S.*, 23, 66

Kletzing, Russell R., 163, 165
Knowlton, Philip A., 118

Landman, J. Henry: definition of fringe benefits, 4; definition of income, 23
Latimer, Murray W., 91
Leisure: component of income, 3; part of fringe benefits, 10, 27, 36
Life Extension Examiners, 172

Major medical insurance: growth, 58
Martin, Herman, 163

Meals, 159–67, 226; different tax treatments, 51; past tax treatment, 160–61, 227; present treatment and effects, 161–64; proposed treatment and effects, 166–67; to offset unpleasantness, 71, 160, 164; 1954 Code treatment, 25

Medical care: 171–73; forms, 30, by United Mine Workers, 177–78; due to job, 71; effect on equity, 43

Mobility of labor: effect of moving allowance, 74; fringe benefits ineffective, 59–60, 216; general, 73 ff.; life insurance, 128; pension plans, 101, 109–10; vertical, education, 75–76

Moving allowance, 175, 209; encourages mobility, 74–76

Municipal income tax, 83–84

National income: tax preferred fringe benefits, 28; wages and supplements, 8–9, 10–11

National Industrial Conference Board: attracting power of fringe benefits, 59; company education, 76; definitions of fringe benefits, 4–5; lists of fringe benefits, 5–7; value of fringe benefits to workers, 76

Net utility tax, 69–70; moving allowance, 74–75

New York Stock Exchange, 27

Old-age and survivors insurance, 131–38; growth, 132–33; present tax effects, 133–36; present taxation, 132; proposed taxation and effects, 136–38; tax compared to income tax, 50–51; tax on life insurance, 126; treatment of "small" fringe benefits, 35

Optional standard deduction, 153

Output of fringe benefits, 57, 60

Pension plans, 90 ff.; annual contribution, 18, 91–92, 99; benefits, 92; coverage, 17; effect on mobility, 77–78; effects from proposed treatment, 113–16; forms, 90; growth, 10, 90–92; non-qualified, 94; overtime contribution to, 61; similarity to profit sharing, 117; tax preference, 95–97; tax treatment, 92–95, 111–12; vesting provisions, 103–7, 109–11

Pension trusts: earnings, 103; size, 91; taxation, 93–94, 96

Pigou, A. C.: on administration, 29; on equity, 39

Policemen's subsistence allowance, 59

Prentice-Hall, Inc.: large pensions, 100; number of qualified plans, 191; requirements for qualification, 192

Price flexibility, 81–83

Profit sharing, 117 ff.; growth, 118–19, 219; present tax effects, 120–23; proposed tax treatment, 123–24; similarity to pension plans, 117

Profits, 60

Property and services, company, 176–77

Quality changes in consumption, 58–59

Railroad retirement system, 135–36, 143–44

Ratchford, B. U., 73

Recreation, 174–75

Retirement income credit, 134–35

Revenue Acts: 1921, 24; 1926, 24; 1942, 24, 93, 151; 1951, 139

Reynolds, Lloyd G., 59

Robbins, Rainard B., 102

Sargent, C. W., 5, 185–86

Saving, 79–81; hospitalization insurance, 154; pension plans, 100; profit sharing, 121; vesting, 103

Simons, Henry C.: on averaging, 103; definition of income, 19, 32; on wages and conditions of work, 30

Securities and Exchange Commission, growth of pensions, 91–92

Shoup, Carl S., vii, 49

Smith, Adam, 44

Smith, Dan Throop, 22

Social goals, 37–38

Social security, see Old-age and survivors insurance; Unemployment insurance

Social surplus, net, 48

Steel Industry Board, 12

Stock option, 144–45

Supplemental unemployment benefits: similarity to pensions, 112–13; tax treatment, 150–51; treatment by different tax units, 51

Surgical insurance, see Hospitalization insurance

Taft-Hartley Act, 15

Tax base: effect of fringe benefits on,

Tax base (*Continued*)
45; old-age and survivors insurance, 137; pension plans, 113–14

Tax brackets, effect on value of fringe benefits, 40–41, 100

Tax preference: amount, Chamber of Commerce, 26–28; amount, Fisher and Chapman, 26; amount, National Income, 28; forms, 26, 94–97; relation to tax bracket, 40–41, 55

Tax rates: and avoidance, 48; and fiscal policy, 82–83; effect due to fringe benefits, 46

Tennant v. Smith, 66

Toledo Area Pension Plan, 112

Unemployment insurance, 146–51; effects, 148–49; growth, 147; proposed treatment and effects, 149–51; tax compared to income tax, 50; tax on life insurance, 126; tax treatment, 146–47; treatment of "small" fringe benefits, 35

Union furnished fringe benefits, 177–78

United Automobile Workers: plans to expand supplemental unemployment benefits, 18; tax saving in fringe benefits, 14; vesting provisions in contracts, 16; Workers Security Programs incidence, 12, 65

United Mine Workers, 177–78

Unpleasant work, 69–72

Utility: gain due to fringe benefits, 63; loss due to fringe benefits, 61, 63–64

Van Rosen v. Comm., 23

Vesting: cost, 109–10, 217; forms of, 98; mobility of labor and capital, 101; pensions, 103–7, 109–11; saving, 103

Vickrey, William S.: on averaging, 103; on goods given employees, 163, 164–65; on gross vs. net utility, 69; on insurance, 104; on lack of free choice, 65; on net social surplus, 203–4; on wages and working conditions, 29–30

Wage continuation plans, 146

Wage controls, cause of fringe benefit growth, 12–13

Wages, definition, 32–33

Wages vs. fringe benefits, 65, 68, 162, 168–69

Walter, James E., 102

War and fringe benefits, 80–81

Widow's benefit, 138–43; proposed treatment and effects, 142–43; tax history, 138–40, Treasury change in policy, 25

Work, unpleasant, 69–72

Workmen's compensation, 146, 151

Yane, Boris S., 73

Yohlin, Harry, 139–40

DATE DUE
